America in the Cold War

AMERICA IN THE COLD WAR

A REFERENCE GUIDE

William T. Walker

Guides to Historic Events in America
Randall M. Miller, Series Editor

Santa Barbara, California • Denver, Colorado • Oxford, England

Library of Congress Cataloging-in-Publication Data

Walker, William T. (William Thomas), 1942–
    America in the cold war : a reference guide / William T. Walker.
pages cm. — (Guides to historic events in America)
    Includes bibliographical references and index.
    ISBN 978–1–61069–206–9 (hardcopy : acid-free paper) — ISBN 978–1–61069–207–6
(ebook) 1. United States—Politics and government—1945–1989. 2. Cold War.
3. United States—Foreign relations—1945– 4. Cold War—Biography. 5. World
politics—1945–1989. I. Title.
E743.W354   2014
909.82′5—dc23   2013029138

ISBN: 978–1–61069–206–9
EISBN: 978–1–61069–207–6

18 17 16 15 14   1 2 3 4 5

This book is also available on the World Wide Web as an eBook.
Visit www.abc-clio.com for details.

ABC-CLIO, LLC
130 Cremona Drive, P.O. Box 1911
Santa Barbara, California 93116-1911

This book is printed on acid-free paper ∞

Manufactured in the United States of America

For
Our Grandchildren
Joseph, Alexis, Matthew, Nicholas, and Noah

CONTENTS

LIST OF ILLUSTRATIONS

SERIES FOREWORD

Perhaps no people have been more difficult to comprehend than the Americans. As J. Hector St. Jean de Crèvecoeur asked during the American Revolution, countless others have echoed ever after—"What then is this American, this new man?" What, indeed? Americans then and after have been, and remain, a people in the process of becoming. They have been, and are, a people in motion, whether coming from a distant shore, crossing the mighty Mississippi, or packing off to the suburbs, and all the while following the promise of an American dream of realizing life, liberty, and happiness. The directions of such movement have changed, and sometimes the trajectory has taken a downward arc in terms of civil war and economic depression, but always the process has continued.

Making sense of that American experience demands attention to critical moments—events—that reflected and affected American ideas and identities. Although Americans have constructed an almost linear narrative of progress from the days of George Washington to today in relating their common history, they also have marked that history by recognizing particular events as pivotal in explaining who and why they believed and acted as they did at particular times and over time. Such events have forced Americans to consider closely their true interests. They also have challenged their commitment to professed beliefs of freedom and liberty, equality and opportunity, tolerance and generosity. Whether fighting for independence or empire, drafting and implementing a frame of government, reconstructing a nation divided by civil war, struggling for basic rights and the franchise, creating a mass-mediated culture, standing up for capitalism and democracy and against communism, to name several critical developments, Americans have understood that historic events are more than just moments. They are processes of change made clear through particular events but not bound to a single moment or instance. Such thinking about the character and consequence of American history informs this new series of Guides to Historic Events in America.

Drawing on the latest and best literature, and bringing together narrative overviews and critical chapters of important historic events, the books in the series function as both reference guides and informed analyses to critical events that have shaped American life, culture, society, economy, and politics and fixed America's place in the world. The books do not promise a comprehensive reading and rendering of American history. Such is not yet, if ever, possible for any single work or series. Nor do they chart a single interpretive line, though they share common concerns and methods of inquiry. Each book stands alone, resting on the expertise of the author and the strength of the evidence. At the same time, taken together the books in this new series will provide a dynamic portrait of that on-going work-in-progress, America itself.

Each book follows a common format, with a chronology, historical overview, topical chapters on aspects of the historical event under examination, a set of biographies of key figures, selected essential primary documents, and an annotated bibliography. As such, each book holds many uses for students, teachers, and the general public wanting and needing to know the principal issues and the pertinent arguments and evidence on significant events in American history. The combination of historical description and analysis, biographies, and primary documents also moves readers to approach each historic event from multiple perspectives and with a critical eye. Each book in its structure and content invites students and teachers, in and out of the classroom, to consider and debate the character and consequence(s) of the historic event in question. Such debate invariably will bring readers back to that most critical and never-ending question of what was/is "the American" and what does, and must, "America" mean.

Randall M. Miller
Saint Joseph's University, Philadelphia

PREFACE

O n Christmas night, December 25, 1991, President George H. W. Bush addressed the American people to report that the Soviet Union had ceased to exist and that a new Commonwealth of Independent States and several new countries, including Russia, had been recognized immediately by the United States. On January 28, 1992, in his State of the Union Address to a joint session of the Congress, Bush proclaimed that the United States had won the Cold War. In retrospect, most historians agree with Bush's claim, but they do not fully concur that the "war" ended with the demise of the Soviet Union in 1991. The Cold War lingered on as the United States worked out new relationships with the new Russian state and the People's Republic of China, continued to try to isolate Castro's Cuba, kept a watch on North Korea, and negotiated new understandings with Vietnam.

The struggle that had dominated and absorbed world politics since the close of World War II in 1945 was over, and—seemingly—an era of genuine peace was about to begin. The collapse of the Soviet Union was rapid and has led historians and pundits to consider a wide range of questions on that topic. Among them are: Who was responsible for the collapse? Was the leadership of the Soviet Union no longer committed to its Marxist ideology? Did American wealth and power overwhelm Soviet hopes for the future? and Was the Soviet Union an artificial state that succumbed to the nationalist identities and ambitions of its own people? These were, and are, not the only questions, but they were ones that generated much discussion in assessing the costs, character, and consequences of the Cold War. With access to previously unavailable Soviet archives and newly declassified American documents, scholars realized new opportunities to consider those concerns as well as those related to all aspects of the history of the Cold War.

This book is a reference guide designed to assist students and others in gaining a foundation of knowledge on the Cold War with a principal focus on American perspectives and interests. It also seeks to provide key research tools for additional research and study. The chronology begins with the Bolshevik Revolution on November 7, 1917, and includes events related to the first Red Scare in the United States after World War I, American investigations related to Soviet espionage during the 1930s and 1940s, the alliance with the Soviets during World War II, the collapse of the relationship immediately after the victory in 1945, and the Cold War. The final entry in the chronology is the May 9, 2010, participation of American troops in the Moscow Victory Day Parade commemorating the end of World War II. In addition to political, diplomatic, and military events, significant Cold War–related cultural developments have been included.

Chapter 1 provides an historical overview of America in the Cold War. Arranged chronologically, it considers the background and origins of the Cold War, its progress from 1945 to 1991, and its conclusion. The next chapter, "Origins and Early Development of the Cold War," covers the relationship between the United States and the Soviet Union prior to World War II, the collapse of the U.S.-Soviet wartime relationship in 1945, the emergence of the containment policy, the continuing impact of the Cold War on American politics, the Truman Doctrine, the Marshall Plan, and the establishment of the North Atlantic Treaty Organization (NATO). Chapter 3 examines the key developments of the 1950s and early 1960s until the 1962 Cuban missile crisis—McCarthyism, massive retaliation, flashpoints in the U.S.-Soviet relationship, and the impact of the Cold War on American life and culture. Chapter 4, on the Cuban missile crisis, examines the most dangerous episode of the Cold War in considerable detail and focuses on the quality of leadership in both the United States and the Soviet Union. It is followed by a chapter on Vietnam to détente that addresses the Vietnam war and the antiwar movement, Nixon's foreign policy of détente with the Soviet Union, the triangular diplomacy resulting from the opening with China, the Watergate scandal, and the decline of American prestige. The final chapter considers the impact of the end of the cold war and provides information on Carter's foreign policy based on human rights, his shift in policy during the last 18 months of his presidency, the two phases of Reagan's foreign policy, the unraveling of Soviet power and influence as well as the collapse of the Soviet Union itself, and finally, the new U.S.-Russian relationship to the presidency of Barack Obama.

Following the text are 19 brief biographies of noteworthy individuals involved with America during the Cold War. The book also provides 20 key primary documents, each with a brief introductory note, and an annotated bibliography of valuable print and online primary and secondary sources. Both the primary documents and the annotated bibliography will be useful for those conducting research on topics related to America and the Cold War.

ACKNOWLEDGMENTS

The researching and writing of this book have absorbed considerable time during the past year and would not have been possible without the assistance of several people. As with my previous books, Sister Mary Josephine Larkin, SSJ, Dean of the Library; Carol Consorto, Interlibrary Loan Coordinator; and Gail Cathey, Catalog Librarian at the Logue Library at Chestnut Hill College were most helpful in locating and obtaining important resources. I thank them for their support, labors, and many kindnesses. Our series editor, Dr. Randall M. Miller (St. Joseph's University), has offered valuable suggestions that have made this a better book, and I thank him for his encouragement and sage wisdom. Michael Millman, ABC-CLIO Senior Editor, facilitated the process from contract to production. I am grateful for his understanding and support.

Most of all, I thank my wife, Mildred Pacek Walker, for her encouragement, understanding, and love. Her comments on many relevant topics have been very helpful and greatly appreciated.

WTW
Bucks County, Pennsylvania
June 6, 2013

CHRONOLOGY

1917   November 7, Bolshevik Revolution in Russia

1918   March 3, Bolsheviks sign the Treaty of Brest-Litovsk, a separate
        peace with Germany

        April, Allied (British, French, American, and Japanese) forces
        begin arriving in Russia to support the "Whites" against the
        Bolsheviks

1919   May 1, May Day riots, Cleveland, Ohio

        June 2, Bombing of homes and offices of U.S. government
        leaders

        August 30, Communist Party of the United States is estab-
        lished

1920   September 16, Bombing on Wall Street, New York, 38 people
        killed

        November 7–January 2, 1920, U.S. attorney general A.
        Mitchell Palmer conducts "Red Raids"

        November, withdrawal of Allied forces from Russia (some
        Japanese forces remained as late as 1925)

1927   August 23, Execution of Nicola Sacco and Bartolomeo
        Vanzetti

1933   November 17, United States recognizes the Soviet Union and
        opens diplomatic relations

1936   July 18, Spanish Civil War begins

1938   May 26, House Un-American Activities Committee (HUAC) established

1939   August 24, Soviet-German Non-Aggression Pact is signed

            September 1, World War II begins with German invasion of Poland

            September 17, Soviet Union joins Germany in invasion of Poland, seizes eastern sector of country

            November 30–March 12, 1940, "Winter War" between Finland and Soviet Union, ends in Soviet victory and seizure of territory

1940   June 22, Germany invades Soviet Union

            Voice of America established within the U.S. Department of State

1941   December 7, Japanese attack Pearl Harbor

            December 8, United States declares war on Japan and enters World War II

1943   August 11–24, Quebec Conference

            November 28–January 12, 1944, Tehran Conference

1945   February 4–12, Yalta Conference

            May 8, End of World War II in Europe

            June 26, San Francisco Conference formally establishes the United Nations

            July 17–August 2, Potsdam Conference

            August 14, End of World War II in the Pacific

            August 17, United States and Soviet Union agree on the 38th parallel as a temporary line dividing their occupation zones in Korea

            September 2, Democratic Republic of Vietnam proclaimed by Ho Chi Minh

            November 27, American general George C. Marshall begins mission to China to resolve conflict between the Communists and Nationalists

1946   January 31, Reorganization of Chinese government announced

February 9, Stalin announces that capitalism and communism are "incompatible"

February 22, George Kennan issues "The Long Telegram"

February 28, Secretary of State James Byrnes presents speech that reflects a developing anti-Soviet policy

March 5, Winston Churchill delivers his "Iron Curtain" speech at Westminster College in Fulton, Missouri

April 18, Communist and Nationalist forces resume armed conflict in Manchuria

August, Communist and Nationalist leaders in China abandon all agreements with one another

September 10, Greek communists launch civil war

September 20, Henry Wallace was asked to resign as U.S. secretary of commerce because of his criticism of American government's anti-Soviet policy

November, HUAC is directed to investigate communist subversion in the United States

December 2, United States and Great Britain agree to merge their occupation zones in Germany

December 19, Indochinese War begins between French and Vietnamese Communist/Nationalist forces

1947   February 21, Britain announces that it can no longer aid Greece and Turkey

March 12, President Truman announces the Truman Doctrine to defend Greece and Turkey from aggression

March 21, Truman issues Executive Order 9835, investigating the loyalty of federal employees

June 5, Secretary of State George Marshall calls for a European Economic and Recovery Program for Europe (the Marshall Plan)

July, "Sources of Soviet Conduct" by "X" (George Kennan) is published in *Foreign Affairs*

September 2, Treaty of Rio signed to unify Western Hemisphere against aggression

October 18, House Committee on Un-American Activities begins investigating the film industry

December, Chinese civil war resumes

1948   February 25, Communist takeover of Czechoslovakia

April 1, Soviet Union obstructs traffic from Western German Zones to Berlin

April 2, Congress approves the Marshall Plan by setting up the Economic Cooperation Administration

April 30, Organization of American States established

June 24, Berlin blockade begins

June 26, Berlin airlift begins

August 3, Whittaker Chambers testifies that Alger Hiss was a communist

November 2, Truman defeats Republican Thomas E. Dewey in the presidential election

1949   January 22, Communist forces seize Peking (Beijing)

April 4, The North Atlantic Treaty Organization (NATO) is established

April 22, Chinese Nationalist forces abandon Nanking (Nanjing)

May 12, Soviet Union ends Berlin blockade

May 23, West Germany is established

August 5, U.S. State Department releases white paper on the pending victory of the communists in China

August 29, Soviet Union detonates first atomic bomb

October 1, People's Republic of China is proclaimed

October 7, East Germany is established

1950   January 21, Alger Hiss is convicted of perjury

February 9, Senator Joseph McCarthy gives speech in Wheeling, West Virginia, stating that he possesses the names of communists employed at the State Department

February 14, Sino-Soviet Treaty announced

April 7, U.S. National Security Council calls for extensive expansion of the American military (NSC-68)

April 25, Truman approves recommended expansion (NSC-68)

June 1, Senator Margaret Chase Smith (R-ME) delivers "Declaration of Conscience" speech

June 25, North Korean troops invade South Korea (beginning of the Korean War)

June 27, UN Security Council supports American resolution to defend South Korea

June 30, Truman approves use of American troops in Korea

October 28, Chinese communist forces enter the Korean War against the United Nations

December 31, Chinese communist forces invade South Korea

1951   March 29, conviction of Julius and Ethel Rosenberg as atomic spies

1952   November 1, United States detonates first hydrogen bomb

1953   January 22, Arthur Miller's *The Crucible* opens in New York

March 5, Stalin dies

June 17, Riots begin in East Germany and are suppressed by Soviet troops within weeks

June 19, Julius and Ethel Rosenberg are executed

July 27, Armistice is signed that ends combat in Korea

August 1, establishment of the U.S. Information Agency (USIA)

August 19, Iranian leader Mohammed Mossadegh is overthrown by CIA-supported coup

December 4–8, Bermuda Summit Conference; leaders of the United States, Great Britain, and France meet to discuss post-Stalin approaches to the Soviet Union

1954   January 15, Secretary of State John Foster Dulles announces that the United States is willing to use "massive retaliation" to confront threats

January 21, United States launches the *Nautilus*, world's first atomic submarine

March 1, Soviet Union detonates hydrogen bomb

March 9, Edward R. Morrow (CBS News) broadcasts first of two programs about McCarthy on *See It Now*

April 22, Army-McCarthy hearings begin

May 7, Viet Minh defeats French at Dien Bien Phu

June 27, Government of President Jacobo Arbenz of Guatemala is overthrown in CIA-sponsored coup

August 24, Communist Party of the United States is outlawed

September 8, Southeast Asia Treaty Organization (SEATO) is established; also known as the Manila Pact, it was a defensive treaty that included the United States, Great Britain, France, Australia, New Zealand, Pakistan, the Philippines, and Thailand

October 3, NATO approves rearmament of West Germany

December 2, U.S. Senate votes to censure Senator Joseph R. McCarthy

December 2, United States and Republic of China (Taiwan) agree to mutual defense treaty

1955   February 8, Nikita Khrushchev emerges as leader of Soviet Union

May 14, Warsaw Pact established

May 15, Soviet occupation of Austria ends

June 18, Geneva Summit Meeting (Eisenhower, Khrushchev, Eden, and Faure)

August 4, United States starts U-2 flights over the Soviet Union

1956   February 25, Khrushchev gives speech and begins de-Stalinization policy

March, Beginning of jazz diplomacy with tour of Dizzy Gillespie's band in southern Europe and the Middle East

June 28, Riots in Poznan, Poland, by workers protesting economic conditions

July 26, President Gamal Abdel Nasser of Egypt nationalizes the Suez Canal

October 23, Hungarian Revolution begins

October 29, Britain, France, and Israel attack Egypt over the Suez Crisis

November 4, Soviet forces enter Budapest to suppress the Hungarian Revolution

December 2, Fidel Castro and supporters return to Cuba to lead revolution against Fulgencio Battista

1957   January 5, Eisenhower announces American policy to provide military aid to nations that are victims of aggression in the Middle East (the Eisenhower Doctrine)

October 4, Soviet Union launches first satellite, Sputnik I

1958   May, Communist Chinese leader Mao Zedong begins Great Leap Forward

July–October, American troops sent to Lebanon to support its government

December 9, Robert H. Welch, Jr. and others meet in Indianapolis,

Indiana, to establish the John Birch Society

1959   January 1, Castro comes to power in Cuba

April 4, NATO confirms its commitment to West Berlin

July 29, The "Kitchen Debate" between Vice President Richard Nixon and Khrushchev in Moscow

1960   March 17, Eisenhower approves CIA plan for Cuban exiles to overthrow Castro

May 5, Khrushchev announces that an American U-2 spy plane was shot down on May 1 and the pilot, Francis Gary Powers, was captured

May 7, American government acknowledges the loss of the U-2 plane and pilot

May 16, Collapse of the Paris Summit Meeting between Eisenhower and Khrushchev

October 19, United States restricts most trade with Cuba

December 20, Vietnamese communists establish the National Liberation Front in South Vietnam

1961   January 1, United States ends diplomatic relations with Cuba

April 12, Soviet Union succeeds in placing first person (Yuri Gagarin) in orbit

April 17, Cuban exiles invade Cuba at the Bay of Pigs and are defeated by Castro's forces

May 5, United States succeeds in placing Alan Shepard in lower space

May 15, President John F. Kennedy announces that the United States will place a man on the moon before the end of the decade

June 4–5, Kennedy and Khrushchev hold a summit meeting in Vienna

August 13, East Germany closes the border with the West and begins construction of the Berlin Wall

1962   February 7, American embargo on all trade with Cuba

February 20, John Glenn is the first American to orbit the earth

July 23, Laos is recognized as a neutral state

October 14–28, The Cuban missile crisis

1963   June 20, Hotline established between Washington and Moscow

June 26, Kennedy visits Berlin

August 5, Limited nuclear test ban treaty signed by the United States, Great Britain, and the Soviet Union

1964   July 2, Civil Rights Act of 1964 becomes law

August 7, Congress passes the Gulf of Tonkin Resolution

October 1, Free speech movement begins, University of California, Berkeley

October 15, Leonid Brezhnev replaces Khrushchev

October 16, Communist China detonates its first atomic bomb

1965   February 7, Communist forces in South Vietnam attack American base at Pleiku

March 8–9, Arrival of U.S. marines in Vietnam

May 24–25, First major "teach-in" on Vietnam, University of Michigan, Ann Arbor

September 30–October 1, Communist coup fails in Indonesia

1967   June 6, Six Days War begins in Near East in which Israel confronts Egyptian, Syrian, and Jordanian forces

October 21, Thousands of Americans march on the Pentagon to protest war in Vietnam

1968   January 30, Tet Offensive in South Vietnam

March, Prague Spring in Czechoslovakia begins

March 16, My Lai Massacre, South Vietnam

May 10, United States and North Vietnam open peace talks in Paris

July 1, Nuclear Non-Proliferation Treaty signed by United States, Great Britain, and the Soviet Union

August 20–21, Warsaw Pact forces invade Czechoslovakia and end the Prague Spring

August 26–29, Democratic National Convention, Chicago, Illinois

November 12, Brezhnev Doctrine proclaimed; obligates all socialist states to aid one another when faced with threats from nonsocialist states

1969   March 2, Soviet forces in conflict with Communist Chinese troops on the Ussuri River

July 25, Nixon Doctrine (also known as the Guam Doctrine) announced; affirms U.S. treaty obligations, provides nuclear shield to allies and to others that are deemed essential to American national security, and states U.S. will provide military and economic support but not assume primary responsibility to states that are victims of aggression

July, United States lands men on the moon and returns them safely to Earth

November 17, United States and Soviet Union begin Strategic Arms Limitation Talks (SALT)

1970   April 30, "Cambodian Incursion" by American and South Vietnamese forces

May 4, Kent State incident

June 20, Angela Davis fired by the University of California for being a communist

1971   April 10, U.S. table tennis team visits Beijing; beginning of "ping-pong diplomacy"

June 13, The *New York Times* begins publishing the Pentagon Papers

July 15, President Richard Nixon announces that he will visit the Peoples Republic of China (Communist China)

1972   February 21, Nixon arrives in the Peoples Republic of China

May 26, U.S.-Soviet agreement on the SALT I treaty and the Anti-Ballistic Missile (ABM) Treaty

1973   January 27, Vietnam peace agreement

	January 27, End of the military draft in the United States
	October 6, Yom Kippur (or Ramadan) War with Egypt and Syria fighting Israel begins
	November 7, War Powers Act becomes law
1974	November 23–24, President Gerald Ford and Brezhnev concur on draft of SALT II Treaty
1975	April 17, Khmer Rouge take over Cambodia
	April 30, Fall of South Vietnam
1976	July 2, North and South Vietnam unified into one state
1977	March 17, President Jimmy Carter announces that human rights will be a priority in American foreign policy
1978	Vietnam invades Cambodia
1979	January 1, United States and the People's Republic of China open full diplomatic relations
	June 18, Carter and Brezhnev sign SALT II treaty
	July 17, Communist Sandinistas gain control in Nicaragua
	November 4, Iranian students seize the American embassy in Tehran; beginning of Iranian hostage crisis
	December 12, NATO agrees to deploy Pershing II and Cruise missiles in Western Europe
	December 27, Soviet Union invades Afghanistan
1980	January 3, Carter withdraws SALT II from Senate because of Soviet action in Afghanistan
	January 20, Carter declares that the United States will not participate in the Summer Olympics in Moscow unless the Soviet Union withdraws from Afghanistan
	January 23, Carter Doctrine proclaimed—any Soviet aggression in the area of the Persian Gulf would be viewed and responded to as a direct threat to the national interests of the United States
	April 7, United States breaks diplomatic relations with Iran

August 31, Polish dissident group Solidarity gains approval from the Polish government for a trade union movement

1981   January 20, American hostages in Iran are liberated

April 1, United States ends aid to Sandinista government in Nicaragua

December 13, Polish government clamps down on Solidarity and arrests its leaders

1983   March 8, President Ronald Reagan labels the Soviet Union, the "evil empire" in speech to the National Association of Evangelicals, Orlando, Florida

March 23, Reagan announces support for the Strategic Defense Initiative (SDI), sometimes referred to as "Star Wars"

October 5, Lech Walesa, the Solidarity leader, wins the Nobel Peace Prize

October 23, Arab terrorists kill 241 U.S. marines in a bomb attack on barracks in Lebanon

October 25, American invasion of Grenada

November 23, Soviet Union suspends negotiations with the United States on limiting intermediate-range nuclear weapons

1984   May 24, Congress prohibits additional aid to Contra forces in struggle with Sandinistas

1985   February 6, Reagan Doctrine proclaimed—announcing American support for all anticommunist rebels

March 11, Mikhail Gorbachev becomes the leader of the Soviet Union

May 20, John Anthony Walker, Jr. arrested by the FBI as a Soviet spy

November 19–21, Geneva Summit between Reagan and Gorbachev

1986   October 11–12, Reykjavik, Iceland, meeting between Reagan and Gorbachev

1987   May 5, Congressional hearings investigating the Iran-Contra Affair begin

December 8–10, Washington meeting between Reagan and Gorbachev where they agree to prohibit all intermediate-range nuclear missiles in Europe

1988   May 29–June 2, Moscow meeting between Reagan and Gorbachev

December 7, Gorbachev announces Soviets' unilateral reduction of conventional forces in Europe

1989   January 11, Hungary announces political reforms

February 15, Soviet Union withdraws forces from Afghanistan

May 2, Hungary starts to dismantle its fence along the border with Austria

June 3–4, China suppresses a liberal movement by attacking thousands in Tiananmen Square, Beijing

June 4–18, Solidarity wins free elections in Poland

October 9, Protests begin in Leipzig against the East German government

October 18, Erich Honecker is removed as the head of the East German Communist Party

November 9, East Germany opens the Berlin Wall

November 20, Demonstrators in Prague march against the Czechoslovak communist government

November 24, Czechoslovak communist government resigns

December 2–3, Malta Summit between President George H. W. Bush and Gorbachev

December 25, Romanian dictator Nicolae Ceaus¸escu and his wife, Elena, are tried and executed by military tribunal

December 29, Václav Havel becomes president of Czechoslovakia

1990   March 11, Lithuania declares independence from the Soviet Union

May 30–June 3, Washington meeting between Bush and Gorbachev

October 3, German unification

October 15, Gorbachev is awarded the Nobel Peace Prize

November 21, Charter of Paris signed to end the Cold War

1991   June 12, Boris Yeltsin elected president of Russia

July 1, Warsaw Pact abolished

July 21, Moscow Summit between Bush and Gorbachev, where they sign the Strategic Arms Reduction Treaty (START I)

August 19–21, Failed coup by Soviet Communist Party against Gorbachev

December 25, Gorbachev resigns as leader of Soviet Union

December 30, Soviet Union is dissolved

1993   January 3, United States and Russia sign START II agreement limiting the number of offensive nuclear weapons

1995   November 1–21, Dayton Agreement ends Bosnian War; ratified in Paris on December 14, 1995

1999   March 24–June 10, Kosovo War

2000   March 26, Vladimir Putin elected president of Russia

2001   September 11, terrorist attacks on the United States

October 7, United States, Great Britain, Australia, and the Afghan United Front (Northern Alliance) attack the Taliban-led government of Afghanistan

2003   March 19, United States leads coalition forces in attack on Iraq

2008   April 8, New START agreement between the United States and Russia to limit the number of nuclear warheads

2010   May 9, American troops participate in the Moscow Victory Day Parade commemorating the sixty-fifth anniversary of the end of World War II in Europe

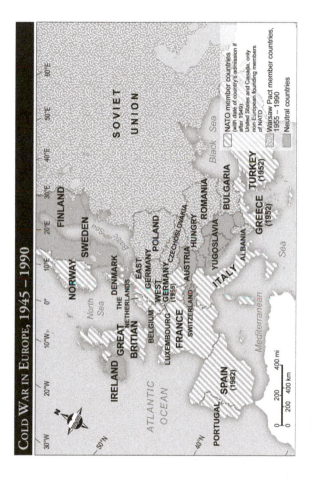

Cold War map.

CHAPTER 1

HISTORICAL OVERVIEW

I n his State of the Union address to a joint session of the Congress on January 28, 1992 (Document 20), President George H. W. Bush announced that the Cold War was over and that it had been won by the United States. A few weeks earlier on December 25, 1991, Bush had announced that America's mighty enemy for almost a half-century, the Soviet Union, had collapsed and was replaced by new nationality-oriented states. The reaction to these dramatic and historically defining developments was stunning yet simplistic—the United States was the only surviving superpower, capitalism had been victorious over communism, military budgets could be reduced significantly, and an era of goodwill with the new Russia was about to begin. The Cold War was indeed a struggle between two opposing views of the world and humankind—capitalism and freedom versus communism and totalitarianism—but it was also a geopolitical struggle between the two predominant nation-states of the era. Other than superficial reviews of the history of the Cold War by the world's media, only scholars began the intensive process of appraising the origins, history, and meaning of the Cold War—the commanding historical theme of world history during the second half of the twentieth century. Limited access to Soviet archives during the 1990s provided valuable resources for a reassessment of the Cold War. From the American historical perspective, questions related to the Cold War were manifold: How did the Cold War begin? What was at the core of the struggle? What sustained the Cold War to make it endure for almost a half-century? What impact did the Cold War have on American diplomacy, politics and culture? And, perhaps most intriguing in 1992 and thereafter, what would be the role of the United States in world affairs after the Cold War?[1]

THE BEGINNING: ALLIES BECOME ANTAGONISTS

Even before the Japanese attack on Pearl Harbor on December 7, 1941, and the German and Italian declarations of war on the United States on December 11, 1941, the United States extended Lend-Lease aid to the Soviet Union, which was reeling under the German offensive that had begun on June 21, 1941. During the war the United States continued to provide military and financial aid to the Soviets. President Franklin D. Roosevelt and Soviet premier Josef V. Stalin, along with Prime Minister Winston S. Churchill of Great Britain, met at Teheran (1943) and Yalta (1945) to discuss the progress of the war and the postwar world. While specific differences were clear, these allies appeared to be working to shape a postwar settlement within the context of international cooperation that would be sustained by the United Nations. Unlike Churchill, who reflected nineteenth-century geopolitical imperial values, Roosevelt and Stalin were, at least in theory, anti-imperialists who envisioned a new world order that was not dominated by the old European empires. Roosevelt died on April 12, 1945, and was replaced by President Harry Truman, who had no experience in international affairs and little, if any, knowledge of Roosevelt's vision for postwar Europe or his views on the Soviet Union. After the cessation of hostilities Truman, Stalin, and Churchill (who would be replaced on July 28 by a new British prime minister, Clement Atlee, after the British general election) met at Potsdam on July 17, 1945, to reestablish peace in Europe and to reach agreement on the general themes that would be reflected in a final peace treaties with Germany and its allies.

Even before the Potsdam Conference convened, the relationship between the United States and the Soviet Union began to fray. In August the United States used two atomic bombs against Japan; the American technological edge accelerated Soviet efforts to design its own nuclear weapon and to enhance its espionage activities in the United States to secure atomic technology. During the last months of the war, the Soviets pressed their advantage and violated some of their agreements with the allies related to Poland and Eastern Europe. Before the end of 1945 a visible strain in U.S.-Soviet relations was evident. As John Lukacs noted in *The Legacy of the Second World War*: "In late 1945 slowly, gradually, American popular sentiment, and even some segments of American public opinion, were turning against Communism and the Soviet Union, mostly consequent to the news of what Communists and Russians were doing and how they were behaving in Eastern Europe."[2]

The leadership of the American government had three options: attempt to roll back Soviet advances and risk a likely war, contain Soviet aggression diplomatically with sustained military strength, or, as advocated by Secretary of Commerce Henry Wallace, accommodate to Soviet policy. During the next two years the United States adopted policies that were intended to contain the Soviet Union. George F. Kennan's "Long Telegram" (Document 2), an analysis of the Soviet view of history, Stalin's leadership of the Soviet Union, and the pillars of its international policies, contributed to the Truman Doctrine (Document 3) that aimed to sustain the noncommunist governments in Greece and Turkey threatened by communist-led insurgencies, and the Marshall Plan (Document 5) that accelerated the economic recovery of Europe. Both of these measures were viewed as confrontational and hostile by the Soviet Union and strained the relationship with the United States. The Soviet Union pushed for the United States, Great Britain, and France to leave occupation zones in Berlin; on June 24, 1948, the Soviet Union and the East German regime[3] instituted the Berlin blockade that restricted Allied access by land and water to the city; the United States responded with a successful air relief effort that lasted through May 12, 1949, when the Soviet Union abandoned restricting access to Berlin. Tensions increased after August 29, 1949, when the Soviet Union detonated its first atomic bomb—America's military edge seemingly had vanished.

Anxiety with Soviet successes in Eastern Europe was aggravated by developments in Asia, specifically in China and Indo-China. During the war against Japan, China had been an ally of the United States; the American government had recognized the Nationalists under General Chang Kai-shek as the legal government of China. Prior to the Japanese attack on China in 1937, China had been engaged in a civil war between the Nationalists and the communists led by Mao Zedong. After a brief period of recovery at the end of the war, the Chinese civil war resumed and it was apparent to all astute observers that the Nationalist regime was riddled with corruption and that a majority of the Chinese people supported Mao Zedong. In 1949 the U.S. Department of State released a white paper in which it concluded that the communists would prevail in China. On October 1, 1949, Mao Zedong proclaimed the People's

Republic of China as the government of China; the Nationalists had withdrawn to the island of Formosa, which was later renamed Taiwan. Farther to the south, another anti-imperialist revolutionary, Ho Chi Minh, announced in 1946 the establishment of an independent Vietnamese state within French Indo-China. The French declared that Ho Chi Minh was an enemy, and a prolonged war began that led to a French defeat in 1954. It appeared to many American leaders and citizens that communism was advancing around the globe. The colonial order, which had dominated world affairs for centuries, was disappearing and, in many instances, being replaced by forces that were not friendly to the United States. The mounting fear of communism led the United States to take the lead in organizing the North Atlantic Treaty Organization (NATO) in 1949. This was a defensive alliance with the United States and Canada joining 10 Western European nations to hold the line of Soviet aggression in Europe.

Fear of communist infiltration of the American government and society was widespread and resulted in enhanced surveillance of American communists by the FBI, and investigations by the House Un-American Activities Committee (HUAC). The Truman administration enacted a Loyalty Oath (Document 4) on March 21, 1947, that empowered agencies throughout the federal government to investigate American citizens who were suspected of being involved in activities or associated with organizations that were considered disloyal to the United States. In 1947 HUAC began hearings on allegations that many actors, directors, writers, and producers of films were or had been affiliated with the Communist Party USA or sympathetic to the communist cause. These hearings resulted in the establishment of a blacklist that originated with the "Hollywood Ten"— a list of 10 directors, producers, writers, and actors who refused to provide information to the Committee. The blacklist grew during the 1950s and included many prominent individuals whose careers were ruined or restricted because of accusations, their refusal to cooperate with HUAC, or past support for communist causes. In 1950 leaders of the film industry issued the "Waldorf Statement" endorsing the actions of HUAC. On August 3, 1948, former communist Whittaker Chambers testified before a government committee that Alger Hiss, president of the Carnegie Endowment for International Peace who had served as an advisor at the Yalta Conference, held high positions within the U.S. State and

Agricultural Departments, and was involved in the establishment of the United Nations, was a communist and had provided secret information to the Soviet Union. The Hiss-Chambers case gripped the nation's attention for two years, and on January 21, 1950, Hiss was convicted of perjury and sentenced to prison. Chambers also testified that Harry Dexter White, the current U.S. director of the International Monetary Fund, was a Soviet agent whom Chambers had known during the 1930s when he was a courier for the Soviet Union. White testified that he was never a communist, and he died three days after his appearance before HUAC (evidence has validated Chambers's accusations).

POLITICIZATION OF THE COLD WAR IN THE UNITED STATES

Anxiety over communist expansion overseas and its infiltration of American government and society provided highly visible litmus tests for political officeholders and candidates for offices at all levels—national, state, and local. In many elections the issue was the intensity of the candidates' anticommunism. During the late 1940s Congressman Richard M. Nixon (R-CA) utilized his involvement in the Hiss-Chambers case to gain a national reputation as a leading anticommunist, a perception that propelled him as he sought to gain a Senate seat in 1950 and be nominated in 1952 as the Republican candidate for vice president. While the careers of Nixon and many others were aided by their stands against communism, Senator Joseph R. McCarthy (R-WI) manipulated the anticommunist issue with such vigor and, indeed, recklessness, that "McCarthyism" itself became a threat to American values. Until February 9, 1950, McCarthy was a little-known senator who had been elected in 1946 and was facing a potentially difficult race for reelection in 1952. On that day, McCarthy addressed the Republican Women's Club in Wheeling, West Virginia (Document 6) and announced that there were more than 200 communists working in the State Department.

During the next four years McCarthy's dishonest and unsubstantiated accusations produced a theatre of the absurd in Washington—in an already turbulent political environment that included the outbreak of the Korean War, the atomic spy case against Julius and Ethel Rosenberg, and the death of Stalin. During the next four years McCarthy conducted

hearings and issued statements that labeled many as communists, suspected communists, or dupes who supported communists. He violated
due process as well as the rights of most of those accused. If he encountered
opposition, as in the case of Senator Millard Tydings of Maryland, he
sought revenge. Among the institutions that he attacked were the Department of State, the U.S. Information Agency, and the U.S. Army. During
the televised Army-McCarthy hearings in the spring of 1954, McCarthy's
bullying behavior offended many who viewed the proceedings and
transformed many previous supporters into opponents. McCarthy's
political theatrics were compounded by his problem with alcohol abuse.
McCarthyism engendered fear within American politics that would not
be abated until courageous leaders such as Edward R. Murrow and Senators
William Benton, Ralph Flanders, and Margaret Chase Smith denounced
McCarthy and his tactics. The Senate censured McCarthy in December 1954, but the remnants of his legacy would continue to be evident in
American society for some time. Democratic and Republican candidates
for public office were expected to adhere to and support a unified nonpartisan anticommunist Cold War policy against the Soviet Union and other
communist states—straying far from the center on this issue was a political
liability that could lead to political defeat. During the presidential elections of 1952, 1956, and 1960, candidates identified themselves as anticommunists to pass the required litmus test of the day. The Cold War
permeated American culture and expressed itself in the elevated stress
and fear that came with the prospect of nuclear war; civil defense became
a national priority, and countless Americans built air-raid shelters for protection. The communist menace was evident in American films, literature,
and education; religious leaders railed against atheistic communism that
was bent on destroying the American way of life. At the same time, musicians and athletes participated in tours that were intended to improve the
world's perception of the United States and its values.

ARMS RACE

Another factor that both resulted from and sustained the Cold War
was the arms race between the Soviet Union and the United States. The
American monopoly on the atomic bomb was short lived; the Soviets
detonated a bomb in 1949. Likewise, both powers attained hydrogen

bombs during the early 1950s. Nuclear weapons were also attained by Great Britain (1952), the People's Republic of China (1964), and France (1960). Both the United States and the Soviet Union were interested in limiting the number of nations with nuclear weapons and also in eliminating nuclear tests in the atmosphere. This led to negotiations and a series of agreements beginning with the Limited Test Ban Treaty of October 10, 1963, between the United States, the Soviet Union, and Great Britain. While these weapons underwent continuous refinements to maximize destructive capacity, the focus for most of the Cold War was on improved delivery methods that were rapid and accurate. During the 1950s the United States relied on the new B-52 bombers and the Strategic Air Command, but both the Soviets and Americans were developing unmanned missiles (ICBMs, intercontinental ballistic missiles) as the primary delivery vehicles for nuclear weapons. The Soviet success in putting into orbit the first satellite (Sputnik) on October 4, 1957, accelerated the arms race—it would take the United States more than two years (until October 31, 1959) to launch its first satellite. In the American presidential election of 1960, an alleged "missile gap" became an issue, though no such gap actually existed at that time. With both Soviets and Americans proceeding to develop substantial arsenals of nuclear warheads and launchers, it was recognized that even the edge of a "first strike" would be meaningless because the attacked state would have enough nuclear weapons to destroy the aggressor. This Mutual Assured Destruction (MAD) was a reality that could be altered, even temporarily, only by a new class of nuclear weapons or through deployment of a reliable antimissile defense system. During the era of détente both sides were interested in stabilizing this nuclear arms race that was having a negative impact on their economies, and that mutual interest led to arms control agreements.

KOREA, BERLIN, CUBA, AND VIETNAM

On June 25, 1950, the Cold War heated up when North Korean troops invaded South Korea in an attempt to unify the peninsula. In 1945 the Soviet Union and the United States agreed to divide Korea at the 38th parallel into two separate states for a five-year period, after which Korea was to be unified. The Soviets installed a nationalist-communist regime in North Korea under Kim Il-Sung and proceeded to provide extensive military aid and training. South Korea experienced extensive civil discord, and the Americans accepted the conservative anticommunist nationalist Syngman Rhee as the political leader. By 1949 both the Soviet Union and the United States had removed their troops from Korea. Discussions on unification did not progress, and, on June 25, 1950, North Korea, with approval from the Soviet Union, invaded South Korea. The American response was immediate. On June 27, 1950, the UN Security Council agreed to support the American resolution to defend South Korea. For the next three years American troops, which comprised 88 percent of the UN forces, fought the North Koreans and, after December 31, 1950, Communist Chinese units in a bloody struggle that claimed the lives of 36,510 Americans.[4] Back home, McCarthy and his supporters denounced Truman and Secretary of State Dean Acheson for failing to be prepared for the North Korean invasion, for Truman's dismissal of General Douglas MacArthur (who wanted to threaten the Communist Chinese with nuclear weapons), and for the ineffective prosecution of the war. The war ended with an armistice during the first year of Dwight D. Eisenhower's presidency, on July 27, 1953, with no resolution on unification but with a general perception by Americans that the United States was involved in a long-term global struggle with communism.

Some of the most intense moments of the Cold War between the United States and the Soviet Union involved Berlin and Cuba. Different visions of the future of Berlin were evident at the Yalta meeting, and they continued to plague East-West relations for decades. Berlin, surrounded by Soviet-controlled East Germany, was divided into four sectors (American, Soviet, British, and French) that quickly became two—East Berlin (Soviet) and West Berlin (United States, Great Britain, and France). Determined to unify Berlin under their control, the Soviets and East Germans began the Berlin blockade on June 24, 1948, denying land and water access to the Americans, British, and French. Within two days the United States initiated the Berlin Airlift to sustain West Berlin during the blockade. The Soviets ended the blockade on May 12, 1949. The episode contributed to the further polarization between the West and the East and rallied the people of the West in support of the citizens of West Berlin.

Later, Berlin again served as the focus of East-West tensions when East Germans (with Soviet approval) began the construction of the Berlin Wall on August 13, 1961. Its purpose was to prevent Berlin from serving

Against a backdrop of war ruins, Berlin citizens gathered around a mobile loudspeaker of the American Radio Station Berlin to cheer the announcement that the 11-month Soviet blockade of the city would be lifted on May 12, 1949. (Bettmann/Corbis)

as an access path to the West for Germans and others who wanted to flee communist control. The United States immediately condemned the construction of the wall, and on June 26, 1963, President John F. Kennedy visited Berlin and committed himself and the United States to the freedom of West Berlin in his "*Ich bin ein Berliner*" speech (Document 12). Twenty-four years later, on June 12, 1987, President Ronald Reagan demanded that the wall be dismantled (Document 18). With the unraveling of the Soviet Union and communist control in Eastern Europe, on November 9, 1989, the Berlin Wall was demolished and access to West Berlin was open.

From the outset of the twentieth century, the United States was deeply involved in the domestic politics of Cuba, a former Spanish colony that had been liberated as a result of the American victory over Spain in the Spanish-American War (1898). By the 1950s Cuba was being ruled by the pro-American and corrupt dictator Fulgencio Batista. Cuban revolutionaries led by Fidel Castro drove out Batista and came to power on January 1, 1959. They immediately began to institute political, economic, and social reforms, and relations between Cuba and the United States quickly declined after American-owned assets were nationalized. By 1960 Castro was moving toward communism and a relationship with the Soviet Union that was viewed by President Dwight D. Eisenhower as unacceptable.

Eisenhower was determined to regain American hegemony in the Western Hemisphere. He authorized the Central Intelligence Agency (CIA) to develop a plan to train dissident Cubans and others for an invasion of Cuba that would overthrow the Castro regime. This authorization was based on the unfounded assumption that the Cuban people, upon learning of an invasion, would rise up in a general rebellion against Castro. Preparations continued into the early months of the Kennedy administration. Kennedy approved the operation that began on April 17, 1961. This Bay of Pigs invasion failed, with the anti-Castro invaders suffering a significant number of causalities and troops captured. It also expanded the relationship between Moscow and Havana. This failure, along with Kennedy's unimpressive performance at the Vienna summit with Primier Nikita Khrushchev on June 4, 1961, also contributed to the Soviet notion that they could penetrate the Caribbean further by placing nuclear-capable missiles in Cuba. They began that process in 1962 with Castro's approval, and American surveillance revealed the presence of missile sites in the fall. The Cuban missile crisis followed (October 14–28, 1962) and resulted in perhaps the most tense and dangerous moments of the Cold War—nuclear war appeared to be in sight. On October 22, 1962, Kennedy addressed the American people (Document 11) to inform them of the crisis. Nikita Khrushchev, the Soviet leader, backed down and agreed to remove the missiles. In turn, Kennedy authorized the removal of some American missiles from Turkey after confirmation that the Soviets had completed the withdrawal of their missiles from Cuba. Even after the end of the Cold War, American relations with Cuba have not been normalized—in spite of a lessening of tensions between the two states, the United States and Cuba still do not have formal diplomatic relations.

Kennedy also extended the commitment of American military advisors to South Vietnam to assist in suppressing a communist takeover. After the French were defeated at Dien Bien Phu in 1954, the future of French Indo-China was discussed in Geneva. While the United States desired that Vietnam remain unified—and that the independence of Laos and Cambodia be fully recognized—the Geneva Accords provided for a political division of Vietnam at the 17th parallel. The result was that North Vietnam, under Ho Chi Minh, was supported by the Soviet Union and the People's Republic of China, and South Vietnam, under first Bao Dai (1954–1955) and then Ngo Dinh Diem (1955–1963), came under the influence of the United States, Great Britain, and France. A reluctant Eisenhower found himself forced into defending his own Domino theory on the need to take a stand against expanding communism. American military advisors arrived in 1956 to train South Vietnamese forces, and during the following year a communist insurrection (with North Vietnamese support) broke out within South Vietnam. During his years as president, Kennedy increased the number of military advisors and the financial support for the Diem regime, which was plagued with corruption and the accompanying inefficiencies. In November 1963, weeks before the assassination of President Kennedy, Diem and his brother Nhu were assassinated in a coup d'état that had American support. Under President Lyndon Johnson the American commitment to South Vietnam expanded dramatically by 1968 to 549,000 American troops and $77 billion in funds. Nonetheless, the communists—both South and North Vietnamese—continued to prevail.

A vocal and effective antiwar movement emerged in the United States, and Johnson removed himself from campaigning for another term. The new American president, Richard M. Nixon, sought to end American involvement in Vietnam under the most favorable terms possible. His policy of "Vietnamization" of the war was accompanied by secret bombing of Cambodia and, eventually, by a reduction in the number of American troops. By 1972 serious negotiations on ending the war began, and a cease-fire became effective on January 28, 1973. American combat troops were removed from South Vietnam that year. After a brief period of peace, North Vietnam renewed its war against the South in 1974. By April 30, 1975, the North Vietnamese took Saigon and the South Vietnamese surrendered. American policy in Southeast Asia was in a shambles.

DÉTENTE

Twice during the Cold War it appeared that a condition of détente could be attained between the United States and the Soviet Union. In the first instance it was more of an aspiration held by some Americans rather than a realistic geopolitical assessment. The post-Stalin Soviet leadership under Nikita Khrushchev appeared to many Americans as an opportunity to move toward normalization in relations with the Soviet Union. Khrushchev condemned Stalin, initiated some modest reforms, and visited the United States. The crisis of the collapse of the Paris Summit in 1960, related to the shooting down of an American U-2 spy plane conducting surveillance over the Soviet Union, along with the developing Cuban-Soviet relationship, cooled any thaw in the Cold War.

A much more realistic opportunity for a workable détente between the powers emerged in the late 1960s when the geopolitical and economic situations changed for both powers. American strategists formulated a plan for détente in 1968 (Document 14), but it would not be until President Richard Nixon and National Security Advisor Henry Kissinger—in the wake of Sino-Soviet border disputes and the continuation of the Vietnam War—developed a policy of "triangulation" to sustain a strategic balance between the United States and the Soviet Union that détente became a realistic goal. In 1972 Nixon visited the People's Republic of China (Document 15) and expanded the wedge between China and the Soviet Union. In the same year the United States and the Soviet Union signed the SALT I arms limitation agreement. After Nixon's resignation (1974), President Gerald Ford's gaffes denying Soviet dominance in Eastern Europe and not appreciating the depth of the crisis on Jewish emigration from the Soviet Union, and the triumph of the communists in Vietnam (1975), undermined détente. However, it did survive, as was evident in the Helsinki agreements of 1975, which covered a wide range of issues, such as human rights, international travel, and workers' rights.

ENHANCED TENSIONS

Building on the sentiments and values expressed in the Helsinki Accords, President Jimmy Carter envisioned a lessening of tensions between the Soviet Union and the United States, a worldwide improvement in human rights, and a new agreement limiting nuclear weapons. Although Carter did succeed in bringing Israel and Egypt together for peace talks that culminated in the Camp David Accords in 1979 (Document 16), his hoped for expansion of détente with the Soviet Union did not happen.

President Jimmy Carter with Egyptian president Anwar Sadat and Israeli prime minister Menachem Begin during the signing of the Israel-Egypt peace treaty at the White House in Washington on March 26, 1979. (Associated Press)

Soviet-sponsored Cuba became enmeshed in Angola, and leftists made gains in Yemen, Nicaragua, and Cambodia. The Soviet Union enjoyed multiple successes as the United States was recovering from its failure in Vietnam and the Watergate scandal. Further, the Middle East became more unsettled with the overthrow of the pro-American shah of Iran by the Islamic fundamentalist Ayatollah Ruhollah Khomeini in 1979, and the subsequent attack on the American embassy in Teheran with the capture of Americans there. Carter's attempt to rescue those being held hostage failed and resulted in the additional loss of American lives. Strained U.S.-Soviet relations became more acute with the Soviet invasion of Afghanistan on December 25, 1979. Claiming that they were "invited," the Soviets seized Kabul and installed a puppet government. Although this would in the end prove disastrous for the Soviet Union, at the time the Soviets appeared to have gained a dominant hand in the Cold War. Carter responded by recalling the American ambassador, withdrawing American athletes from the Moscow Olympics, suspending planned SALT talks, imposing economic sanctions on the Soviet Union, ordering a buildup of

American nuclear and military capacity, and extending offers of aid to Pakistan and China. Clearly the Soviet actions had increased Cold War tensions. Carter was defeated in his bid to be reelected in 1980; Ronald Reagan was elected President. Cold War tensions and a difficult domestic economy in the United States contributed to Carter's defeat.

COLLAPSE OF THE SOVIET UNION AND THE END OF THE COLD WAR

In 1981 Ronald Reagan was inaugurated American president. He continued the hard anti-Soviet rhetoric that had characterized the last 18 months of the Carter administration. Reagan also directed an immediate expansion of the American military to establish clear superiority over the Soviets. Within the Soviet Union the long Brezhnev era was coming to an end. Leonid Brezhnev, who came to power in 1964, died on November 10, 1982, and was replaced by the head of the Committee for State Security (KGB), Yuri Andropov, whose brief tenure ended with his death on February 9, 1984. The frail Konstantin Chernenko succeeded Andropov on February 13, 1984. He served only 13 months as Soviet leader, dying on March 10, 1985. The following day, Mikhail Gorbachev was named first secretary of the Soviet Union. Little did he or others realize that he would be the last leader of the Soviet Union. Not only did the Soviet Union suffer a leadership crisis during the first half of the 1980s, but it also experienced an extremely difficult economic downturn with the decline of oil exports and the collapse in the price of oil, along with a mounting foreign policy and military debacle in Afghanistan. These problems were aggravated by Reagan's military buildup, the labeling of the Soviet Union as "the Evil Empire" (Document 17), and the utilization of the Helsinki Accords in Poland, where labor unrest blossomed into the Solidarity movement.

Gorbachev responded with a new direction for the Soviet Union that was embodied in *glasnost* (openness) and *perestroika* (restructuring). This policy was welcomed by most Soviet citizens and by the Western powers; however, these reforms resulted in widespread debate and criticism and, indeed, exacerbated the endemic problems of the Soviet system. Within a few years the Eastern European and Baltic states that had been under Soviet control for almost a half-century were breaking away, and identity

East German entering West Berlin in November 1989. The Berlin Wall was dismantled beginning on November 9, 1989. (David Turnley/Corbis)

based on communism was replaced by a more genuine and historically rooted allegiance to nationalities.

The so-called Revolutions of 1989 effectively ended Soviet dominance in Eastern Europe. The Berlin Wall was dismantled and within a year, Germany was reunited. Even within the Soviet Union, national identity prevailed; by 1990 Russian nationalists were operating freely within the Soviet Union. Some Soviet hardliners were determined to use force to reestablish the status quo, but most, like Gorbachev, were not. After a failed coup d'etat in August 1991, the momentum supporting fundamental changes increased. On December 25, 1991, Gorbachev announced the end of the Soviet Union, the emergence of independent states, and a loose Confederation of Independent States. That evening, President George H. W. Bush announced these changes to the American people—the Cold War had ended.

NOTES

1. Scholarly literature on the Cold War is extensive and continues to grow. Among the most notable sources are *The Cold War: A New History* by John Lewis Gaddis (New York: Penguin, 2005); *Origins of The Cold War: An International History* edited by Melvyn P. Leffler and David S. Painter, 2nd ed. (New York: Routledge, 2005); *From World War to Cold War: Churchill, Roosevelt, and the International History of the 1940s* by David Reynolds (New York: Oxford University Press, 2006); *The Legacy of the Second World War* by John Lukacs (New Haven, CT: Yale University Press, 2010); and *The Culture of the Cold War* by Stephen J. Whitfield (Baltimore: Johns Hopkins University Press, 1991). See the annotated bibliography for particular works on America and the Cold War.

Another indication of the continuing scholarly interest in America and the Cold War was the spring 2013 lecture series titled "The United States in World Affairs: The Cold War and Beyond" at the University of North Carolina, Chapel Hill. Lectures were presented by William Leuchtenburg ("U.S. Presidents and Foreign Policy: From Harry Truman to Barack Obama"), Frank Costigliola ("The Processes of Thought in George Kennan's Imaging of Russia"), Melvyn Leffler ("George W. Bush and Saddam Hussein: Why Did the United States Go to War against Iraq?"), Warren Kimball ("Nuclear Weapons, Roosevelt, Churchill, and the Transition to the Cold War"), Alfred McCoy (Epistemology of Empire: Asian Wars, Information Regimes, and the Future of U.S. Global Power"), and Dianne Kirby ("Religion and the Cold War").

2. Lukacs, 184.

3. East Germany was not established until October 7, 1949.

4. The U.S. Department of Defense has reported that 36,510 Americans died in the Korean War, which includes both combat and noncombat deaths. North Korean and People's Republic of China reports claim that more than 300,000 Americans were killed during the war.

CHAPTER 2

ORIGINS AND EARLY YEARS OF THE COLD WAR

T he late spring and early summer of 1945 was a joyous time for Americans. The wars in Europe and the Pacific were ending with victory, and the sacrifices experienced by most families appeared to be worth the cost—peace was at hand. Unlike 1918–1919, there would be no national debate or rejection on the joining of the new international peacekeeping organization, the United Nations. While some protested America's new expanded role in the world, most Americans recognized that the isolationism of the past would not provide adequate protection for American national interests nor secure a general peace. However, by the end of the year most Americans were aware that a new challenge had emerged from their former ally, the Soviet Union. Most Americans were not aware of how tense and difficult the wartime alliance with the Soviets had been—with frequent conflicts over military strategy, demands for additional financial aid from the West, and disputes at summit meetings over the future of Germany as well as Poland and Eastern Europe. However, Americans—especially those of east European heritage—were aware and outraged by Soviet actions in Eastern Europe. The U.S. government viewed these political machinations as violations of the agreements signed recently at Yalta and Potsdam. The American government should not have been surprised by Soviet movements in the Eastern Europe after the close of the war; Soviet conduct prior to Hitler's invasion had been unpredictable and centered more on traditional national, rather than ideological, considerations. Prior to the war Stalin signed the Nazi-Soviet Non-Aggression Pact on August 23, 1939, which paved the way for the German attack on Poland on September 1, 1939. During the next several

German officers discuss their discovery of slaughtered Polish officers at Katyn Wood, Poland, where 4,150 Polish officers were murdered by Soviet secret police. In April 1943 Germans announced that they had discovered the bodies in graves near Smolensk. (Corbis)

months the Soviet Union invaded eastern Poland; the Baltic states of Estonia, Latvia, and Lithuania; and Finland, and it pressured Romania to allow its occupation of three northeastern provinces. In 1940 Germany and the Soviet Union entered negotiations for the possible entrance of the Russians into the Axis alliance. While those talks did not result an agreement, they demonstrated the apparent willingness of the Soviet Union to consider such an option. In April and May 1940 the Soviets executed more than 22,000 captured Polish officers in the Katyn massacre—an atrocity that was not acknowledged until 1991.

Even after the German invasion of the Soviet Union on June 22, 1941, the Soviet approach to an alliance with Great Britain (and, after the attack on Pearl Harbor, the United States) rendered it a precarious partner in the war. Soviet losses were staggering and would approach 20 million combat and noncombat deaths by the end of the war. Stalin's demands for a second front in the west were justified. By 1944 American and British intelligence had become aware of Soviet intentions in Poland and Eastern

Europe; Churchill was alarmed at the prospect of a Soviet-dominated Poland but failed to convince Roosevelt that a very firm stand had to be taken with the Soviets to avoid their seizure of all of Eastern Europe. The Second World War ended in 1945, but a new struggle—the Cold War—began and would dominate world affairs until 1991 when the Soviet Union collapsed. Unlike previous conflicts in American history, the Cold War was more than a geopolitical struggle—it was a cultural conflict in which fundamental values and beliefs were at risk.

With American entrance into the First World War on April 7, 1917, President Woodrow Wilson's domestic progressive agenda gave way to the war effort. At first, the March 8–12, 1917, revolution in Russia was welcomed by the American government and people—another autocratic ruler had fallen, and the forces of liberalism appeared to have been victorious. The moderate revolutionaries established a provisional government that proceeded to enact a liberal agenda centered on a representative democracy, equality, and civil rights for all. Also, it committed Russia to remaining in the war against Germany. However, on November 6, 1917, the Bolsheviks overthrew the provisional government that had been established by the moderates. The United States did not recognize the Bolshevik seizure of power or their government and denounced the Bolshevik interest in withdrawing from the war by making a separate peace with Germany. American leaders were also alarmed by the radical nature of the Bolshevik revolution, which replaced capitalism with communism that rejected private property, profit, competition, banks, and religion.

Wilson, with little opposition from Congress or the public, joined the British, French, and Japanese in sending troops to Russia to safeguard war materials that were at risk to German or Bolshevik seizure. Other factors that provided the rationale for this Allied military intervention included providing assistance to the 40,000 Czechs who were isolated along the Trans-Siberian railroad so that they could return and participate in the European conflict, and supporting counter-revolutionary and local insurgent forces that opposed the Bolsheviks. The American commitment consisted of two distinct forces: the Northern Russian Expedition and the American Expeditionary Force Siberia. The Northern Russian Expedition consisted of 5,000 U.S. troops that occupied areas around Archangel on the White Sea. This occupation lasted from September 1918 to July 1919 and resulted in the loss of almost 100 American lives. The American

Expeditionary Force Siberia involved 7,950 American troops occupying camps from August 1918 to April 1920 in and around Vladivostok in eastern Siberia on the Pacific coast. This force experienced 189 fatalities during the occupation. Both of these American contingents failed to achieve their stated goals, and they did not have any substantive impact on the Russian Civil War. The new Communist regime in Moscow condemned the United States and the other powers for intervening in the internal affairs of Russia. In spite of the ongoing civil war between the Bolsheviks and the Whites, who identified with the old order, the Bolsheviks succeeded in withdrawing Russia from World War I by signing a separate peace (the Treaty of Brest-Litovsk) on March 3, 1918. They prevailed in the civil war against the Whites that concluded in 1920.

With the end of hostilities in World War I on November 11, 1918, and the subsequent Peace of Versailles on June 28, 1919, Americans and others hoped for a prolonged peace and a return to "normalcy." However, the world had been changed forever and thrust into the uncharted dynamics of the twentieth century. The turbulence, chaos, and ideological fervor associated with the Russian revolution appeared to gain momentum. While the leftist Spartacus rebellion in Germany and the emergence of radical "1919ism" in Italy failed, they indicated that the world order was threatened by radicalism that was not confined to the Soviet Union. In 1919 the Communist Party of the United States was founded in Chicago and within months had more than 60,000 members. In April 1919, political radicals—anarchists and communists—attempted to assassinate more than a score of American political and financial leaders through bombs distributed by the U.S. Post Office. The plot was discovered and it failed, but it enhanced the anxiety of American leaders—the first "Red Scare" was underway. The radical leftists persisted and were more successful when eight of their bombs were detonated, killing one bomber and a security guard and causing extensive damage. The targets included U.S. attorney general A. Mitchell Palmer, Cleveland mayor Harry E. Davis, federal and state judges, a state representative, a manufacturer, and a Roman Catholic Church in Philadelphia. Parallel race riots in several American cities occurred during the summer 1919.

The American government connected all of these activities and concluded that America was the target of a communist plot to ferment a revolution in the United States. In August 1919 Palmer established the

General Intelligence Unit within the Justice Department and appointed a young lawyer, J. Edgar Hoover, to lead it. Using the data that Hoover's office provided, Palmer launched a series of raids (the Palmer Raids) between November 1919 and January 1920. The raids resulted in the arrest, detention, and deportation of hundreds of foreign-born radicals. States followed the lead of the federal government by curtailing the rights of many foreign-born American citizens. On September 16, 1920, radicals set off a bomb at Wall and Broad Streets in New York—outside the main offices of the J. P. Morgan bank and investment firm. Thirty-eight people were killed and hundreds wounded. Arrests and prosecutions followed. This Wall Street bombing was viewed as an attack on American society, and it left a permanent mark on the American memory showing that communism and anarchism were enemies that had to be suppressed.

Terrorist bombing on Wall Street—outside the offices of J. P. Morgan Company in New York—on September 16, 1920. Thirty-eight were killed and 143 seriously injured. (Corbis)

During the 1920s the Soviet Union, first under Vladimir Lenin and then Josef Stalin, advanced rhetoric calling for an international workers' revolution and the dismantling of capitalism. Its economy was in shambles, the 1920 war with Poland was costly and resulted in no gains, internal unrest was evident from the peasant uprisings and the naval mutiny at Kronstadt in 1921, and its support for the strikers during the British General Strike in 1926 resulted in London breaking diplomatic relations with the Soviet Union. In the United States the return to normalcy resulted in the drastically reduced funding for the military. Then the onset of the Great Depression crippled the American economy and caused Americans to look critically at capitalism.

In 1932 Governor Franklin D. Roosevelt of New York was elected president and took office on March 4, 1933. After lengthy negotiations with the Soviet government, the United States extended full recognition and diplomatic relations on November 17, 1933, and the Soviets pledged to abstain from conducting propaganda within the United States. That was a rather moot promise since the Communist Party of the United States served as a secret agent for the Soviets; however, the party was frequently paralyzed and rendered ineffective because of its factionalism. The impact of the Great Depression and the liberal policies of the Roosevelt administration moved the United States to the left but not toward the Soviet model. Nonetheless, some Americans were attracted to the Soviet experiment, entered the federal government, and provided secret information on American policies and interests to the Soviet Union. Both powers were consumed by internal problems and concerns during the 1930s. Roosevelt's America embarked on new initiatives directed primarily at economic recovery and reducing unemployment. It achieved limited success and encountered opposition from the Supreme Court, but Roosevelt's New Deal programs won wide support among Americans. Stalin's Soviet Union experienced a major famine during the early 1930s and endured Stalin's purges during the second half of the decade. Both leaders increasingly became alarmed at the startlingly economic recovery and rearmament of Germany under the fascist chancellor Adolph Hitler.

In summary, prior to 1945 the American experience with the Soviet Union and radical leftists was negative and predisposed the United States to suspect the Soviet Union's leadership and goals in general, particularly its motives and actions in Eastern Europe.

In 1945, with the end of the war in sight, the differences in American, Soviet, and British war aims became increasingly more evident. The United States was focused on the clear and decisive defeat of Germany and Japan; its emergence as the world's greatest economic power, replacing Great Britain and its empire; and the establishment of the United Nations to secure the general peace. The Soviets were concerned primarily in establishing hegemony in Eastern Europe and the permanent disabling of Germany as a threat, and America's monopoly in possessing the atomic bomb. In *The Atomic Bomb and the Origins of the Cold War*, Campbell Craig and Sergey Radchenko argue that American use of the atomic bomb in August 1945 was a major cause for the outbreak of the Cold War. Stalin feared American global domination and the isolation of the Soviet Union.[1] Martin J. Sherwin, in *A World Destroyed: The Atomic Bomb and the Grand Alliance*, concluded that the Manhattan Project that produced the atomic bomb was strategically intended to create a weapon to defeat America's enemies and end the war, and—diplomatically—to intimidate the Soviet Union if necessary. Britain was invited to participate in the Manhattan Project as a junior member. While the Soviet Union had spies within the Manhattan Project and was aware of its progress, it did not receive official notification until three weeks prior to the bomb's use against Japan.[2] Some historians, such as Gar Alperovitz in *The Decision to Use the Atomic Bomb*, have challenged the prevailing view that the United States used the atomic bomb to ensure the quick surrender of Japan and to eliminate the potential loss of a million American soldiers in an invasion of Japan. To Alperovitz, the use of the bomb shaped the postwar geopolitical world and was a major cause for the Cold War.[3]

Britain's (i.e., Churchill's) war aims were not as ambitious nor were they realistic—holding onto the British Empire, retaining a strong presence in the Mediterranean, and utilizing an Eastern Europe of independent states as a buffer between Western Europe and the Soviet Union. A key factor in attaining these war aims was continuity of leadership. Here the Soviets held the edge because of these world leaders, only Stalin remained in power after the war. Roosevelt, who conducted a very personal foreign policy during the war,[4] died on April 12, 1945, and was replaced by President Harry S. Truman, who had served as vice president only since January 20, 1945. Truman knew little about Roosevelt's plans or his conversations with Stalin and Churchill.[5] Churchill's Conservatives were devastated in the general elections of July 1945, and he was replaced as prime minister by the Labour leader Clement Atlee. Atlee and his Labour Party had no sympathy for imperialism, and they were committed to an extensive domestic agenda of recovery and reform.

Even before the war concluded, the Soviet Union was extending and deepening its control of the territories that it occupied in Eastern Europe. It established and controlled communist parties and suppressed all opposition organizations. One of Stalin's principal lieutenants, Lavrentiy Beria, was charged with politicalizing Eastern Europe. In addition to East Germany (which would be formally established later), the Soviets and their agents established the People's Republics of Poland, Bulgaria, Albania, Romania, Hungary, and, in 1948, the Czechoslovak Socialist Republic. Free multiparty elections were not held, and opposition parties and candidates were suppressed using a wide range of tactics that included occasional assassinations and court-ordered executions. The Soviets also annexed the pre-1941 occupied Latvia, Lithuania, and Estonia, and parts of Poland, Romania, and Finland, and the Soviets also seized part of Manchuria and the northern half of the Korean peninsula. Soviet control of these puppet or satellite regimes was direct and comprehensive. National leaders who accepted Soviet dominance and communism were provided with positions.

From the American and British perspectives, long-term Soviet power throughout Eastern Europe constituted a threat to Western Europe, and that concern was acerbated by the developing influence of communist parties in Italy and France. On February 22, 1946, in response to an inquiry from the U.S. Treasury Department related to the Soviet failure to be involved with the new World Bank and International Monetary Fund, George F. Kennan, deputy head of the American mission in Moscow, sent "The Long Telegram" (Document 2) to Secretary of State James F. Byrnes. This communiqué—which exceeded 5,000 words—advanced an analysis of Soviet policies and behavior that became a cornerstone in the formulation of American foreign policy. Kennan (1904–2005) began working at the State Department in 1925 and quickly focused on the Soviet Union. He served in Latvia, and in 1933 with the establishment of diplomatic relations with the Soviet Union, he was assigned to the new Moscow embassy. After a stint in Washington during the mid-1930s, Kennan was sent to the American embassy in Prague in September 1938 during the

Munich crisis. Between 1939 and the German invasion of the Soviet Union on June 22, 1941, Kennan argued against providing any Lend-Lease aid to the Soviets because of their unreliability. By the end of the war Kennan was back at the Moscow embassy.

In "The Long Telegram" Kennan advanced a five-part review and analysis of salient factors upon which Soviet policy was predicated and motivated, and he advanced recommendations for a proposed American strategy. Kennan, arguing that peaceful coexistence with capitalist states was anathema to Soviet leaders, identified the Soviet Union as an inherently aggressive state determined to destroy capitalism and its advocates, and install pro-Soviet socialist regimes throughout the world; however, subversion rather than a general conflict was always a preferred means. Loyalty to the Soviet Union was required for all Marxists/socialists if they were to work for world revolution, and nonaligned socialists were dangerous to Soviet interests. Soviet aggression mirrored traditional Russian policies and was based on a general paranoia of Western motives and values. The Soviet system was designed to disguise and distort truth and reality both internally and externally so that confusion and misinformation would abound. In the closing section of "The Long Telegram," Kennan assessed the geopolitical strengths and weaknesses of the Soviet Union and the West; he concluded that the Soviet Union was weak and vulnerable and that the United States possessed the resources necessary to project a positive self-image and attract the support of the world community.

A fortnight later (March 5, 1946) and a little more than nine months after his removal as British prime minister, Winston Churchill, who was leader of the Conservative opposition and who had accepted Truman's invitation to speak, made an address at Westminster College in Fulton, Missouri. Truman had accompanied Churchill on the journey from Washington to Fulton, and he succeeded in rekindling the special relationship with Churchill that Roosevelt enjoyed during the early years of the war. The American admiration for Churchill explained why 40,000 people came to hear him speak. Churchill, in this speech entitled "The Sinews of Peace," described the new geopolitical reality in Europe—an "Iron Curtain," erected by the Soviet Union and its minions, separated Western and Eastern Europe. Reception to Churchill's speech was mostly positive and helped to inform the public about the new reality and the new threat. In the same month the Soviets failed to meet the agreed deadline for the withdrawal of their troops from Iran. On September 27, 1946, Nikolai Vasilevich Novikov, the Soviet ambassador to the United States, sent a lengthy cable to Soviet foreign minister Viacheslav Molotov providing an assessment of American foreign policy. Novikov argued that the imperialist United States intended to establish supremacy throughout the world and dominate a monolithic capitalism world order. The impact of the Novikov communiqué on Soviet policy was significant, comparable to Kennan's "The Long Telegram" on American policy.[6]

Between July and September 1946 Clark Clifford, a Truman advisor and aide, was charged to assess the world situation and Kennan's "The Long Telegram," and to formulate a draft of policy statements. Assisted by Commander George M. Elsey, a White House naval advisor assigned to the Map Room, Clifford met with Kennan, Charles Bohlen, a State Department Russian expert, and other military and intelligence specialists. The result was a top secret report entitled *American Relations with the Soviet Union* that was presented to Truman on September 24, 1946. It provided a history of U.S.-Soviet relations, details on the ongoing Soviet violations of agreements, a call for the American public to be made aware of Soviet actions, and an explanation of the need to contain the Soviet Union.[7] While this report remained confidential, the American public became aware of the Truman administration's positions upon the publication of "The Sources of Soviet Conduct" in *Foreign Affairs* in July 1947. The author was listed as "X," but it was soon realized that it was George F. Kennan. Clearly stating that the United States should adopt a long-term policy of containing the Soviet Union—a statement that Kennan later would argue was misunderstood—it set the direction of American foreign policy for decades.[8]

On September 12, 1946, Secretary of Commerce Henry Wallace, who had preceded Truman as Roosevelt's vice president (1941–1945), gave a speech at Madison Square Garden in New York in which he argued that the current direction of American foreign policy could lead to World War III. Previously, Wallace had sent a letter to Truman stating that the only effective response to communism would be to raise standards of living throughout the world. Secretary of State Byrnes responded to Wallace's New York speech, denouncing it and urging Truman to take action against Wallace. On September 20, 1946, Truman removed Wallace from his administration.

In the spring of 1947 Britain informed the American government that it no longer possessed the necessary resources to sustain the defense of Greece and Turkey from takeovers by communist insurgencies that threatened to topple the pro-Western governments in both nations. A civil war had been raging in Greece for years, and since 1945 communists supported by the Yugoslav communist leader Josip Tito had been in armed conflict with the pro-Western government that had the backing of Great Britain. Paralleling the Greek crisis, conditions in Turkey were precarious. The Soviets demanded access to and joint control of the Dardanelles and Bosporus, the straits that connected the Black and Mediterranean Seas. Since the eighteenth century Britain's foreign policy in this region had been predicated on denying Russia access to the Mediterranean. Britain also had followed a difficult policy in supporting both Greece and Turkey, which viewed one another as enemies.[9]

At the same time that the crisis was unfolding in Greece and Turkey, Truman replaced James Byrnes as secretary of state on January 21, 1947, when George C. Marshall assumed that position. Truman was disappointed that Byrnes had failed to provide him with a thorough report on conversations with the Soviets as well as Byrnes's failure to advocate adequately for Soviet withdrawal from Iran. Truman's distrust of the Soviets continued to increase—he feared that communist victories in Greece and Turkey would result in not only jeopardizing access to oil in the Middle East, but also that it would demonstrate America's lack of resolve in addressing the communist threat. With the notion of containment in mind, Truman feared that if these nations succumbed to communism, others would follow (i.e., the domino theory).[10]

On March 21, 1947, Truman addressed Congress and requested aid for both Greece and Turkey. He used the containment argument and advanced the Truman Doctrine (Document 3). With the support of Republicans such as Senator Arthur H. Vandenburg, who was a new convert to internationalism, Truman was able to gain enough support to overcome the isolationist block led by Senator Robert A. Taft (R-OH), and his proposal was funded. With the Truman Doctrine and bipartisan support, the containment policy was implemented and became the centerpiece of American foreign policy for more than a generation.

While the end of World War II was welcomed by most, its impact on the infrastructure and industry of Europe had been devastating and caused widespread suffering and unemployment. The recovery that began in 1945 was slower than anticipated, and widespread food and housing shortages along with labor unrest, even in Great Britain (which had not suffered as much as the continental states), further hampered recovery efforts. One of the major factors that contributed to the meager economic situation was the impact that the war had had on the transportation system—many roads, bridges, railroads, harbor facilities, airports, and canals had been either destroyed or rendered useless. This extensive economic distress resulted in enhanced popularity for communist parties in Western Europe, and the American government believed that Italy and France could come under communist control. During the spring of 1947 George F. Kennan, then director of policy planning, and William L. Clayton, under secretary of state for economic affairs, developed a plan that called for direct American aid to assist the economic recovery of Europe. It was thought

George F. Kennan (1904–2005) served as an American diplomat and foreign policy adviser to many presidents during the Cold War. He was the author of "The Long Telegram" and is credited with the policy of containing the Soviet Union after World War II. (Bettmann/Corbis)

that a clear and sustained recovery would reduce the prospect of communist parties' success and diminish Soviet ambitions in Western Europe. Kennan was assisted by Paul Nitze, deputy director of the Office of International Trade Policy, who, while supportive of containment, was vocal in calling for a significant expansion of the American military.

An essential component in the formulation of this economic reconstruction plan was the recovery of Germany, which, in itself, mandated a change in American policy. At the Quebec meeting between Roosevelt and Churchill on September 16, 1944, the American and British leaders agreed to the Morgenthau Plan that had been developed and proposed by the American secretary of the treasury Henry Morgenthau, Jr. While some of its provisions were overridden by agreements at Yalta, the Morgenthau Plan envisioned an agrarian Germany that would be unable to prosecute wars in the future. This plan enjoyed support until 1946, when it was recognized that it was not feasible and that differences with the Soviet Union made it not desirable. Americans argued that the economic recovery of Germany was essential for the restoration of European economic vitality, and of course, the other European states would be assisted to rebuild their economies.

During the winter of 1947 American diplomats attempted to convert the Soviets to this view but to no avail. Kennan and Clayton developed the proposal that Marshall announced at Harvard University on June 5, 1947 (Document 5). The most significant—and perhaps the wisest—component of Marshall's plan was that Europeans were to create their own plans within the context of a general European recovery. Then the United States would finance the implementation of the plans. The United States extended the offer to most of the European states (excluding Spain and very small states such as Andorra), including the Soviet Union and Eastern European nations, and Great Britain and France quickly moved to accept the plan. Stalin was unsuccessful in his attempts to paralyze deliberations on the proposal by trying to force the United States to negotiate on Germany and European cooperation. These were non-negotiable. The Soviet Union feared that the implementation of the Marshall Plan would undermine its control of Eastern Europe, result in the reemergence of a strong Germany, and weaken the influence of communist parties in Western Europe. Consequently, the Soviet Union condemned the Marshall Plan as a violation of the founding charter of the United Nations and as an instrument of American "fascism."

It subsequently forced its Eastern European satellites to reject the invitation to participate.[11]

The participating states eventually met in Paris and, with the assistance of American representative William L. Clayton, began the long process of developing their plans and requests. By early 1948 the Europeans had requested $22 billion, which Truman reduced to $17 billion. The actual costs over four years came to $12.7 billion, and additional costs were incurred by special grants and loans.[12] The proposal to Congress encountered strong opposition from the isolationists led by Senator Robert Taft (R-OH), who argued that the United States needed to maintain a balanced budget rather than fund foreign recovery programs. However, after the Soviet-approved coup in Prague in February 1948 that overthrew an independent government and installed a pro-Soviet regime, Truman called a special joint session of Congress on March 17, 1948, and, in spite of continuing opposition to the plan, garnered sufficient votes to pass the Economic Cooperation Act (the Marshall Plan), which he signed on April 3, 1948. It became operational in July 1948 and lasted four years. The impact on the recipient nations was transformative. Their economies revived dramatically, and some of them moved to economic integration with the establishment of the European Coal and Steel Community in 1951, which was the first step toward the Common Market and then the European Union.[13] From the perspective of the Cold War, the Marshall Plan was an American triumph, and at the same time it clarified the polarization between East and West.

In response to American support for the re-establishment of a strong German economy, the Marshall Plan, and the Soviet priority of controlling a defeated Germany, the Soviets moved to drive the Allies from their sectors in Berlin. Stalin and other Soviet leaders believed that control of Berlin determined control of Germany and thus Central Europe. During the war they were committed to their exclusive seizure and occupation of Berlin. After the war the division of Berlin into four zones (Soviet [East Berlin] / American, British, and French [West Berlin]) resulted in the city serving as a gateway or escape route for hundreds of thousands Germans and Eastern Europeans. Once in West Berlin, refugees from the East sought sanctuary in many Western countries. In 1946 the Soviet Union began attempts to restrict Allied access to their sectors in Berlin, and the Allies responded by curtailing the movement of German industrial reparations to the Soviet Union. By late spring 1948 the Soviets concluded that they needed to isolate Berlin and force the Allies to abandon it. On June 24, 1948, the Soviets denied all canal, rail, and road access to Berlin, a maneuver that failed when the Western powers—mostly American, British, and Canadian air forces—airlifted supplies to sustain the city for almost a year. The Berlin Blockade concluded on May 12, 1949, though Berlin remained a flashpoint for U.S.-Soviet tensions for the next 40 years.

Soviet dominance in Eastern Europe, the use of communist parties in the Western European states to advance its interests, increasing belligerent rhetoric, and—most of all—concerns over national defense led to the Treaty of Brussels (March 17, 1948), a mutual defense alliance between Great Britain, France, Belgium, Netherlands, and Luxembourg. After the Soviet blockade of Berlin started, this alliance established the Western European Union's Defence Organization on September 28, 1948. The member states recognized that they did not possess adequate military resources to defend themselves against the overwhelming strength of the Soviet Union and its Eastern European allies. During the fall and winter (1948–1949) deliberations with the United States and other powers were conducted that resulted in the North Atlantic Treaty, which was signed on April 4, 1949. It established the North Atlantic Treaty Organization (NATO) and added the United States, Canada, Denmark, Iceland, Italy, and Norway to the alliance. NATO served as a major deterrent to Soviet aggression in Europe throughout the Cold War, and it continues to the present with an expanded membership and extended agenda.[14]

The Cold War was not confined to Europe during the late 1940s. In 1925, Sun Yat-sen, president of the Chinese Republic and leader of the Kuomintang (the Chinese National Party) died and was succeeded by General Chiang Kai-shek. From the outset, Chiang Kai-shek's control of China was precarious. He was challenged by regional Chinese warlords and the new Chinese Communist Party that was established during the 1920s under the leadership of Mao Zedong. The situation became more complex with the Japanese invasion and seizure of Manchuria in 1931, and their re-establishment of the Manchu Empire. Military conflicts between the Nationalists and the Communists steadily increased during the 1930s. In 1937 Japan invaded what remained of China, causing Chiang Kai-shek and Mao Zedong to use most of their resources against the Japanese. During the period from 1937 to the defeat of Japan in

1945, the civil war between the Nationalists and the Communists was suspended. As U.S.-Japanese relations deteriorated during the late 1930s and early 1940s, Americans sympathized with the Chinese. China specialists at the State Department and American missionaries in China provided a steady flow of information on Japanese atrocities in China. American volunteers served as the "Flying Tigers" under General Claire Lee Chennault and flew missions against the Japanese.

After the attack on Pearl Harbor, the United States provided large quantities of military supplies and financial assistance to Chiang Kai-shek's regime. American general Joseph Stilwell, who had served in China and East Asia during the 1920s and 1930s, was appointed commander of Allied forces in the Burma-Chinese theater of operations and as a military advisor to Chiang Kai-shek. Stillwell quickly determined that the Nationalist regime was corrupt. During the war, Nationalist forces had few successes against the Japanese, and military materials "disappeared." Stillwell was among the first Americans to recognize that while the Chinese people feared but detested the Nationalists, they respected and supported the communists because of their policies and practices. Stillwell submitted reports in which he articulated these views to Washington and confronted Chiang Kai-shek.

Stilwell was relieved of his command.[15] After the surrender of Japan in 1945, the Chinese civil war resumed. Truman dispatched General George C. Marshall to China to mediate a truce. An agreement was signed on January 10, 1946, but it was short-lived. To support the Nationalists and prevent a communist takeover in China, the United States expended more than $3 billion in military supplies and other aid to Chiang Kai-shek's regime. Corruption in the Nationalist government was open and was condemned by increasing numbers of Chinese. American experts—the so-called China Hands (John Paton Davies, John Carter Vincent, and John Stewart Service)—familiar with the increasing unpopularity of Chiang's government sent repeated warnings to Washington that American aid was being wasted, that the tide in China was moving against the Nationalists in favor of the communists, and that a major shift in American policy in Asia was necessary so that the United States would be in a position to deal with the new incoming leadership (i.e., Mao and his communist movement). For years these "shots across the bow" had no impact because of the strength of the "China Lobby," a group of private and public leaders who strongly supported Chiang and included Henry Luce (publisher of *Time, Fortune,* and *Life* magazines), industrialist Alfred Kohlberg, Claire Lee Chennault of the Flying Tigers, Senators William Knowland (R-CA) and Styles Bridges (R-NH), and Congressman Walter Judd (R-MN). By the fall of 1948 the situation for Chiang and his Nationalists had become desperate. The China Lobby blamed Truman, Marshall, and the State Department for the situation in China, and it endorsed Governor Thomas Dewey, the Republican candidate for president in the 1948 election. In addition to the Democratic (Truman) and Republican (Dewey) candidates, the Dixiecrat Party ran Governor Strom Thurmond of South Carolina, and the Progressive Party offered Henry Wallace, Truman's former secretary of commerce and Roosevelt's vice president during FDR's third term, who was sympathetic to the Soviet Union. Truman won the election and appointed Dean Acheson to replace Marshall as secretary of state in January 1949.

The situation in China moved toward a communist victory during 1949, and on June 26, 1949, Acheson presented the "China White Paper," which argued that the corruption and incompetence of Chiang's regime was responsible for his forthcoming defeat. Truman released the report to the public on August 4 and immediately was denounced for failing in China. A witch hunt ensued during which careers of many innocent professionals were either destroyed or severely interrupted.[16]

On October 1, 1949, Mao Zedong declared the establishment of the People's Republic of China, and in December 1949 the remaining Nationalist forces fled the mainland for the island of Taiwan and established a pro-West government there. Thus, the Cold War emerged as a two-front conflict for the United States and its allies as both Europe and Asia were areas of contention and potential conflict. The United States did not begin the process of recognizing the People's Republic of China until President Richard Nixon's initiative in 1972. President Jimmy Carter finally announced on December 15, 1978, that the United States would recognize the People's Republic of China as the government of the Chinese people. The diplomatic isolation of China and the "two-Chinas" policy of the 1970s were significant developments in the evolution of American Cold War strategy and policy in Asia.

In addition to direct conflicts with the Soviet Union and China, the American government became increasingly aware between 1945 and

1950 of the depth of Soviet spying and espionage within the United States.[17] Through recantations of former spies, including Elizabeth Bentley and Whittaker Chambers, the American government learned of the extent and dangers of the Soviet infiltration of the government and other institutions that shaped and influenced policy. On March 21, 1947, Truman issued regulations that required a loyalty oath from all new federal employees and a review process for current employees to ensure their loyalty to the United States (see Document 4). While the House Un-American Activities Committee (HUAC) can be credited with a few successes in pursuing Soviet agents, it must be held accountable for its reckless policies and actions that violated the freedom of speech of many Americans. HUAC was established in 1938 and was initially chaired by Martin Dies (D-TX). It has been referred to as the Dies Committee. Prior to the United States' entrance into World War II, HUAC centered its attention on alleged communist infiltration of the film industry in Los Angeles. The committee cleared all of those accused of being communists or supporting communism except one actor, Lionel Stander, a founding member of the Screen Actors Guild. After the war, Stander was backlisted and found employment difficult to attain for two decades. HUAC resumed its investigation of supposed communist influence in the film industry in 1947. Ronald Reagan (president of the Screen Actors Guild), Walt Disney, and others testified that communism was a real threat to America's film industry. Ten screenwriters and directors (Alyah Bessie; Herbert Biberman; Lester Cole; Edward Dmytryk; Ring Lardner, Jr.; John Howard Lawson; Albert Maltz; Samuel Ornitz; Adrian Scott; and Dalton Trumbo) refused to testify and were held in contempt. Each member of the infamous "Hollywood Ten" received a one-year prison term, which could be reduced if they testified. On December 3, 1947, the leaders of the American film industry met in the Waldorf-Astoria Hotel to develop a joint response to this crisis. They produced the "Waldorf Statement," which declared that those who refused to testify would be blacklisted from all film productions. Blacklisting continued for years and had a negative impact on First Amendment rights in the United States as well as on the careers of many, including Paul Robeson, Lillian Hellman, Dashiell Hammett, Leonard Bernstein, Aaron Copland, Peter Seeger, and Langston Hughes.[18] Clearly, a culture war had begun.

In 1945 Elizabeth Bentley, a native-born American, fearing that she would be killed, defected from the Communist Party and her service as

The Hollywood Ten, blacklisted writers and producers, arrived at the U.S. District Court in Washington, DC, on April 12, 1948, to plead not guilty to charges of contempt of Congress. Left to right, first and second rows, are director and producer Herbert Biberman; writer Dalton Trumbo; attorney Martin Popper; writer John Lawson; attorney Robert W. Kenny; and writers Alva Bessie, Albert Malz, Samuel Ornitz, and Lester Cole. In the rear, left to right, are writer Ring Lardner, Jr., director Edward Dmytryk, and producer Adrian Scott. (Bettmann/Corbis)

a Soviet spy (1938–1945) and confessed to the FBI. Her testimony provided grist for the Red Scare as she identified many pro-Soviet agents and supporters both in government as well as the private sector. Bentley was involved in the Silvermaster spy ring and served as a courier between Jacob Golos (a Soviet agent) and Nathan G. Silvermaster (leader of the spy group). Bentley testified in public during 1948 and substantiated earlier testimony by Whittaker Chambers that accused Harry Dexter White of the U. S. Treasury Department of being a Soviet agent. Her statements were challenged by some until the Soviet archives were opened during the 1990s and collaborated Bentley's remarks.[19]

Bentley's revelations paved the way for the most significant and dramatic accusations advanced by Whittaker Chambers. Chambers was an intelligent and eccentric thinker and writer who was attracted to Marxist-Leninist ideas during the 1920s, and between 1925 and 1938 he was a member of the Communist Party of the United States. In 1932 Chambers became a Soviet spy and was assigned to Washington, DC, where he became connected with the Ware spy group, which was named after its leader Harold Ware. Chambers served as a courier for the Soviet Union between 1932 and 1938, receiving important and secret American government information from federal employees, including Alger Hiss, his brother Donald Hiss, Lee Pressman, and Harry Dexter White. Disgusted with Stalin's purges and fearing for his life, Chambers fled the Ware spy ring and the Communist Party of the United States in 1938, and went into hiding. Chambers took with him a collection of documents and microfilm that he hoped would safeguard him and his family. In September 1939 Chambers met with Assistant Secretary of State Adolf Berle and described the extent of Soviet espionage within the American government. Berle informed the White House and the FBI of the meeting and Chambers's statements. The FBI did not follow up until 1943, when its agents interviewed Chambers. Meanwhile, Chambers had acquired a position with *Time* magazine. After Elizabeth Bentley testified before HUAC, Chambers was asked to testify. On August 3, 1948, Chambers provided a detailed account of his work as a Soviet agent and stated that Alger Hiss, the president of Carnegie Endowment for International Peace, and others had been members of the Ware spy ring. During the 1930s Hiss entered Roosevelt's New Deal administration in the Department of Agriculture but quickly moved to the Department of State, where his responsibilities and power steadily increased. Hiss played significant roles at the Yalta Conference and at the San Francisco Conference that first convened the United Nations. Hiss denied Chambers's accusations, sued Chambers for these allegations, and demanded that they be withdrawn. It was at that point that Chambers provided documents and microfilm. Hiss was indicted and tried. The first trial resulted in a hung jury, and the second found Hiss guilty (in January 1950) of perjury.[20] By 1950 the United States, only five years after the close of World War II, was being challenged by communist expansion in Europe and Asia and also, perhaps, threatened by internal subversion by American citizens who were serving the interests of the Soviet Union.

NOTES

1. See *The Atomic Bomb and the Origins of the Cold War* by Campbell Craig and Sergey Radchenko (New Haven, CT: Yale University Press, 2008).

2. See *A World Destroyed: The Atomic Bomb and the Grand Alliance* by Martin J. Sherwin (New York: Random House, 1975).

3. See *The Decision to Drop the Atomic Bomb* by Gar Alperovitz (New York: Vintage, 1996).

4. Roosevelt's highly personal style in conducting foreign policy in which he did not share significant details on intent or conversations with Stalin and Churchill has been addressed and criticized in *FDR and Stalin: A Not So Grand Alliance, 1943–1945* by Amos Perlmutter (Columbia: University of Missouri Press, 1993), and, more recently, in *Roosevelt's Lost Alliances: How Personal Politics Helped Start the Cold War* by Frank Costigliola (Princeton, NJ: Princeton University Press, 2011), and *Six Months in 1945: FDR, Stalin, Churchill, and Truman; From World War to Cold War* by Michael Dobbs (New York: Knopf Doubleday, 2012).

5. Recent studies have criticized Truman's handling of the American relationship with the Soviet Union and have blamed his inexperience and provincial worldview as partially responsible for the outbreak of the Cold War. See *Another Such Victory: President Truman and the Cold War, 1945–1953* by Arnold A. Offner (Stanford, CA: Stanford University Press, 2002), and *Roosevelt's Lost Alliances: How Personal Politics Helped Start the Cold War* by Frank Costigliola (Princeton, NJ: Princeton University Press, 2011).

6. Kenneth M. Jensen (ed.), *Origins of the Cold War: The Novikov, Kennan, and Roberts "Long Telegrams" of 1946* (Washington, DC: United States Institute of Peace, 1991), 3–16.

7. Clark Clifford (in collaboration with Richard Holbrooke), *Counsel to the President: A Memoir* (New York: Random House, 1991), 201–10; George McKee Elsey, *An Unplanned Life: A Memoir* (Columbia, MO: University of Missouri Press, 2005), 178ff.

8. X [George F. Kennan], "The Sources of Soviet Conduct," *Foreign Affairs*, 25, no. 4 (1947): 566–82.

9. Alan Bullock, *Ernest Bevin, Foreign Secretary: 1945–1951* (Oxford: Oxford University Press, 1985), 110ff.

10. Elizabeth E. Spalding, *The First Cold War Warrior: Harry Truman, Containment, and the Remaking of Liberal Internationalism* (Lexington: University Press of Kentucky, 2006), 64–65.

11. Gerhard Wettig, *Stalin and the Cold War in Europe: The Emergence and Development of the East-West Conflict, 1939–1953*, The Harvard Cold War Studies Book Series (Lanham, MD: Rowman and Littlefield, 2007), 137–39.

12. For financial data for each nation as well as numerous cumulative reports on the Marshall Plan, see *The Marshall Plan: Fifty Years After*, Europe in Transition: The New York University European Series by Martin A. Schain with a valuable introduction by Tony Judt (London: Palgrave Macmillan, 2001).

13. Nicolaus Mills, *Winning the Peace: The Marshall Plan and America's Coming of Age as a Superpower* (New York: Wiley, 2008), 195–97; Alan S. Milward, *The Reconstruction of Western Europe, 1945–1951* (Berkeley: University of California Press, 1984), 46–49; Martin Dedman, *The Origins and Development of the European Union*, 2nd ed. (Oxford: Routledge, 2008), 60–65.

14. David C. Isby and Charles Kamp, Jr., *Armies of NATO's Central Front* (London: Jane's, 1985), 13–15.

15. For a thorough assessment on Stilwell and Chiang Kai-shek, see *Stilwell and the American Experience in China, 1911–1945* by Barbara W. Tuchman (New York: Grove, 1971).

16. See the next chapter for specific information on this point.

17. The most important books on this topic include *The Haunted Wood: Soviet Espionage in America; the Stalin Era* by Allen Weinstein and Alexander Vassiliev (New York: Modern Library, 2000), *Venona: Decoding Soviet Espionage in America* by John Earl Haynes and Harvey Klehr (New Haven, CT: Yale University Press, 2000), and more recently, *Stalin's Secret Agents: The Subversion of Roosevelt's Government* by M. Stanton Evans and Herbert Romerstein (New York: Threshold, 2012) and "Rethinking Post–World War II Anticommunism," by Jennifer Delton in *Journal of the Historical Society*, 10, no. 1 (March 2010): 1–41.

18. William T. Walker, *McCarthyism and the Red Scare: A Reference Guide* (Santa Barbara, CA: ABC-CLIO, 2011), 22–24. In 1950 *Counterattack*, a right-wing journal, published *Red Channels: The Report of Communist Influence in Radio and Television* in which it accused 151 people of involvement in communist infiltration of the media.

19. Walker, *McCarthyism and the Red Scare*, 101–3.

20. Ibid., 103–6.

CHAPTER 3

MCCARTHYISM, EISENHOWER, KENNEDY, AND THE CULTURE OF THE COLD WAR

T he decade of the 1950s began with the emergence of Senator Joseph McCarthy as a strident and reckless anticommunist, the formalization of American Cold War policy in the top secret National Security Council (NSC) Report 68, the outbreak of the Korean War, and American society and culture continuing to adapt to a new reality—the ongoing Cold War with the Soviet Union and living in the nuclear age. The decade witnessed the conviction and execution of spies Julius and Ethel Rosenberg; two successful campaigns for the presidency by Dwight D. Eisenhower; the death of Stalin and the rise of Khrushchev; the rapid expansion of the American economy and the Soviet Union's slow recovery from the ravages of World War II; demands for civil rights for African Americans; demonstrations for political, economic, and civil liberties in Poland, Czechoslovakia, and Hungary; American supported coup d'états in Iran and Guatemala; a developing crisis in Southeast Asia (Indo-China/Vietnam); the development of ballistic missile technologies by the Soviet Union and the United States; and revolution in Cuba.

With the Soviet success in detonating an atomic bomb, the fall of China to communists, and the establishment of NATO, President Truman on January 31, 1950, directed that the National Security Council establish a study group consisting of State and Defense Department leaders along with others appointed by Truman to review the challenges that confronted the United States and to develop a comprehensive strategy. The study group was formed immediately and was headed by Paul Nitze. It submitted its report to the NSC (NSC-68; see Document 7) on April 7, and the NSC sent it to Truman on April 14. While it was based on George Kennan's policy of containment, NSC-68 focused more on American military capabilities than diplomacy. It argued that what was a stake in the Cold War was the survival of the United States and Western civilization, that it could become necessary to triple defense expenditures, and that initial outlays could require extensive funding. Fundamentally, NSC-68 recommended a strategy that would both defend the United States and its allies and defeat the Soviet Union in the event of war. Truman did not accept NSC-68 when it was presented—he wanted more specifics and feared the economic impact of financing it. Some of Truman's advisers thought that implementing NSC-68 would escalate the Cold War and aggravate the already poor relationship with the Soviet Union. The debate on NSC-68 evaporated with the outbreak of the Korean War in June 1950. Truman signed NCS-68 on September 30, 1950, but demanded additional budgetary reviews through 1951. NSC-68 remained a guiding document in American Cold War strategy for a generation.[1]

On February 3, 1950, FBI director J. Edgar Hoover revealed that the British MI6 had arrested and charged German scientist Klaus Fuchs as a Soviet spy. Fuchs was associated with Manhattan Project research on the atomic bomb and had worked at Los Alamos, New Mexico. Americans believed—in part, correctly—that technology used to make the Soviet atomic bomb had been stolen from the United States by the Soviet Union and its agents.[2] How else, they asked, could the communists have developed an atomic bomb so rapidly.

In the midst of the public fervor on that issue, on February 9, 1950, Senator Joseph R. McCarthy (R-WI) gave a Lincoln's birthday speech (Document 6) to the Republican Women's Club in Wheeling, West Virginia. McCarthy was a first-term senator who had not developed a record of achievement to use as a basis for his re-election campaign in 1952. McCarthy had moved from being a moderate Republican to the right; but unlike Democratic right-wingers such as Joseph P. Kennedy, who supported McCarthy, Republican conservatives such as Senator

Robert Taft had little regard for the Wisconsin senator. McCarthy used the opportunity in Wheeling to denounce the Truman administration, particularly Secretary of State Dean Acheson, for being soft on communism. He claimed to have the names of 205 State Department employees[3] who were communists.

McCarthy drew national attention as a result of these accusations. In subsequent speeches McCarthy continued his condemnation of the State Department. He was asked for documentation and when he did not provide it, he was condemned by leading newspapers. On February 20, McCarthy elaborated on his charges in a Senate speech, and a Senate subcommittee was established to investigate his charges and report back to the Senate. Headed by Senator Millard Tydings (D-MD), the subcommittee's hearings resulted in McCarthy accusing Owen Lattimore, an academic and popular writer, of being the leading Soviet spy in the United States. The Tydings Committee's hearing dragged on for months, and McCarthy persisted with his anticommunist rhetoric. Indeed, when McCarthy appeared to be in a hopeless position, he would lash out with new unfounded accusations. Democrats, academics, and some major newspapers condemned McCarthy for his recklessness and for destroying the reputations of many innocent people. On July 17, 1950, the Tydings Committee presented its majority report to the Senate. This report denounced McCarthy and his methods and argued that his charges were indeed baseless.[4] In spite of this report, McCarthy gained an extensive public following that not only provided political support, but also gave McCarthy financial assistance to continue his fight against the perceived internal communist threat. The Republican Party recognized the value of the communist threat as a political issue in the 1950 and 1952 elections; thus, it failed to rein McCarthy in, and he continued to extend his influence. However, a group of Republican senators led by Senator Margaret Chase Smith (R-ME) condemned McCarthy's tactics as an attack on free speech and on the Senate's tradition of shared respect for all members. In her "Declaration of Conscience" speech on June 1, 1950 (See Document 8), Smith stated:

> Those of us who shout the loudest about Americanism in making character assassinations are all too frequently those who, by our own words and acts, ignore some of the basic principles of Americanism—the right to criticize; the right to hold unpopular beliefs; the right to protest; [and] the right of

independent thought. . . . The exercise of these rights should not cost one single American citizen his reputation or his right to a livelihood nor should he
be in danger of losing his reputation or livelihood merely because he happens
to know someone who holds unpopular beliefs. Who of us doesn't? Otherwise
none of us could call our souls our own. Otherwise thought control would
have set in. . . . The American people are sick and tired of being afraid to
speak their minds lest they be politically smeared as "Communists" or
"Fascists" by their opponents. Freedom of speech is not what it used to be in
America. It has been so abused by some that it is not exercised by others . . . [5]

Smith's statement made no impact on McCarthy, except that she was now
on his list of potential targets.

In addition to Acheson, McCarthy denounced Truman, Secretary of
Defense George Marshall, the U.S. Information Agency, and the U.S.
Army. McCarthy was re-elected to the Senate in 1952 and, with a
Republican Senate majority, became the chair of an investigating commit-
tee. He was successful in his effort to unseat Tydings from his Senate seat.
McCarthyism did not require evidence and was not concerned with truth.
Moreover, his method was predicated on groundless accusations, innu-
endo, a disregard for individual rights, and political greed. During 1953
McCarthy was at the height of his influence, and he was invited to speak
at events throughout the country. In 1954 McCarthy investigated the
U.S. Army, as he wanted to know who had approved security clearances
for alleged procommunists.

On March 8 and 9, 1954, three individuals clearly indicated that they
had had enough of McCarthy and his investigations. On the evening of
March 8, President Eisenhower attended the White House Correspond-
ents' Association dinner and supported Secretary of the Army Robert
Stevens by standing and applauding Stevens when he was introduced
(Stevens was one of McCarthy's current targets). The next day, March 9,
Senator Ralph Flanders (R-VT), in a speech on the Senate floor,
denounced McCarthy and his outrageous methods that were endangering
the country and the Republican Party. Later that evening, Edward R.
Murrow of CBS News, using carefully edited excerpts from McCarthy's
own speeches, denounced McCarthy, arguing that Americans were
responsible for the atmosphere in Washington and for McCarthyism.
The reaction to Murrow's speech was overwhelmingly favorable to
Murrow. On March 12, 1954, the New York Times ran a front-page article

on an investigation by the army that implicated McCarthy in illegal acts to gain preferential treatment for a friend. McCarthy's world was beginning to unravel. Between April and June 1954 the Army-McCarthy hearings were televised, and the nation witnessed McCarthy's abuse of witnesses, his disregard for rules and legal decorum, and his personal incoherence and mean-spiritedness. McCarthy's excessive drinking and his lack of sleep may have contributed to his appearance and poor performance. Joseph Nye Welch served as special army counsel during the hearings, and it became evident to Welch that McCarthy had no evidence to support any of his allegations that the army had promoted officers, enlisted soldiers, and civilians who were sympathetic to communism. On June 9, 1954, McCarthy broke an agreement that he had made with Welch that he would not mention that Fred Fisher, a colleague in Welch's law firm, had

American broadcast journalist Edward R. Murrow (1908–1965), sitting in front of a CBS radio microphone during World War II. In 1954 Murrow emerged as a critic of Senator Joseph R. McCarthy and McCarthyism. (Photo by Hulton Archive/Getty Images)

been a member of a procommunist lawyer guild, in exchange for Welch
not revealing that McCarthy aide Roy Cohn was not admitted to West
Point because of a physical condition. In his response to McCarthy's
revelations about Fisher, Welch did not reveal anything about Cohn's
physical problem. In a dramatic moment Welch declared: "Let us not
assassinate this lad [Fisher] further, Senator. You have done enough. Have
you no sense of decency, sir, at long last? Have you left no sense of
decency?"[6]

The audience in the hearing room reacted by applauding Welch, as did
most of those who watched the televised broadcast. Many newspapers
that had previously supported McCarthy turned against him. The Army-
McCarthy hearings concluded on June 17, 1954, with the army's leadership vindicated. Within a month Senator Flanders called upon the Senate
to censure McCarthy for his failure to respond to questions and charges
from a Senate committee, his responsibility for attacks on the U.S.
Information Agency, and—perhaps most important of all—his disregard
of personal rights and the integrity of people. On December 2, 1954, the
Senate voted 67 to 22 to censure McCarthy for his contempt of Congress.
While McCarthy's personal influence evaporated almost immediately, the
distrust, anti-intellectualism, and extralegal aspects of McCarthyism survived and continued to manifest themselves in American society.[7] On
December 9, 1958, the John Birch Society was founded in Indianapolis,
Indiana, by Robert Welch, Jr. and other anticommunists. It was named
after an American Baptist missionary and army intelligence officer who
was killed by communists in China in 1945. During the 1950s a revival
of the Ku Klux Klan incorporated ardent anticommunism into its racist
program defending segregation.

The anxieties that many Americans had over the threat from the Soviet
Union and the spread of communism took on a more substantive and concrete reality with the North Korean attack on and invasion of South Korea
on June 25, 1950. After the defeat of Japan and the surrender of Japanese
forces in Korea in September 1945, Korea was divided in half—North
Korea was a Soviet zone, and South Korea was occupied and managed by
a small American force. Korean-wide free elections were to be held during
1948, but the elections were not held, and neither the United States nor
the Soviet Union wanted to risk their interests to an open election. Nonetheless, negotiations on reunification between the North and South

American politician Senator Joseph R. McCarthy (1908–1957) (left) examines an unseen witness as attorney and chief army legal counsel Joseph N. Welch (1890–1960) listens, hand on his head, during the televised Army-McCarthy hearings in Washington, DC during May 1954. (Photo by Robert Phillips/Time & Life Pictures/Getty Images)

Koreans continued through 1949 and into 1950. On January 12, 1950, Secretary of State Dean Acheson, in a speech at the National Press Club, defined the American "defensive perimeter," and he omitted Korea and any American military commitment to South Korea. However, when the North Koreans attacked, the United States led the United Nations in denouncing the invasion on June 25. Truman justified a military response to the invasion, saying it was the test of all the talk about collective security. And indeed it was. With the Soviet Union absent from the Security Council and unable to exercise its veto power in protest of the Nationalist Chinese continuing to hold the Chinese seat, the Security Council authorized military action in Korea on June 27, 1950. The United States provided the largest military commitment, and 14 other members of the United Nations—with the largest contingents coming from Australia, Turkey, and Thailand—committed troops and material to the defense of South Korea.

Militarily, the war had four phases: first, the early months were success-ful for North Korea; second, the UN counteroffensive led by General Douglas MacArthur pushed back the North Koreans by October 1950; third, the Communist Chinese intervention on October 25, 1950, forced the United Nations to withdraw to near the 38th parallel; and fourth was a stalemate—characterized by trench warfare—that existed until the armistice. Negotiations on the armistice dragged on for many months. American secretary of state John Foster Dulles intimated that the United States might resort to using nuclear weapons if an armistice were not final-ized. That sentiment provided adequate motivation, and the armistice became effective on July 27, 1953. The Korean War resulted in 36,516 Americans killed (combat and noncombat) and 8,176 missing in action.

Although Americans supported the war, they also questioned it. McCarthy and others blamed the war on Truman and Acheson, and many Americans agreed. It also affirmed the existence of a global struggle with communism and enhanced the perception that the United States and its values were at risk.[8] The war also proved frustrating for Americans, who never fully accepted the underlying principle of containment. To the American mind, victory rather than a constant state of readiness and restraint best fit American interests and culture. Thus, when MacArthur suggested that the Chinese involvement had made a whole "new war" to which Americans should respond with full force, even nuclear weapons, many Americans applauded the promise of victory in Asia. Truman refused, and his generals, especially Omar Bradley, argued that a war against China would be the "wrong war" with the "wrong enemy" at that time. The focus of U.S. energy and resources needed to be on the Soviets. When MacArthur refused to accept Truman's decision, the president relieved the general from command on April 11, 1951. It was an unpopu-lar but necessary action.

The frustrations in Korea magnified concerns about American resolve at home. New evidence of spying convinced many Americans that the Truman administration was lax, if not complicit, in guarding American secrets.

One of the most astounding and divisive events that Americans experi-enced during the Cold War was the espionage case involving Julius and Ethel Rosenberg. Both were born in New York; they met one another at a meeting of the Young Communist League, USA in New York in 1936, where both were members and Julius was a young leader; and they married in 1939. He was educated as an electrical engineer who was employed by the army in the Signal Corps Engineering Laboratories at Fort Monmouth, New Jersey, until he was fired when the army learned that he was a member of the Communist Party USA. She wanted a career in the theater but held a clerical position. On August 28, 1949, the Soviet Union detonated an atomic bomb. The speed at which they researched and developed the weapon shocked American leaders, who had suspected that American nuclear secrets had been compromised. Breaking Soviet codes; the January 21, 1950, conviction of Alger Hiss on perjury regarding the transfer of secret documents to Whittaker Chambers; the arrest of physicist Klaus Fuchs in Great Britain; and confessions by suspected former spies for the Soviet Union, such as Harry Gold, led to the arrests of Julius Rosenberg on July 17, 1950, and of Ethel Rosenberg on August 11, 1950.

The Rosenbergs were charged with spying for the Soviet Union and transferring secrets related to the atomic bomb. Much of the key testimony against them came from relatives—especially David and Ruth Greenglass —who were also involved in pro-Soviet activities. During his interrogation in Britain, Fuchs identified Harry Gold as a courier in the plot. Gold was arrested on May 23, 1950, and implicated David Greenglass, a U.S. Army sergeant and machinist. Greenglass confessed and stated that he had been recruited by Julius Rosenberg in 1944. Greenglass also revealed that Rosenberg and his wife, Ethel, passed on information that he had provided to Soviet agent Anatoli Yakovlev. A U.S. grand jury indicted the Rosenbergs, David Greenglass, and Anatoli Yakovlev on 11 charges of espionage and conspiracy to commit espionage. Martin Sobell was later indicted. The indictment of Ethel Rosenberg was intended to exert pressure on her husband to reveal the identities of others involved in anti-American activities, but that strategy backfired when she refused to play such a part, even in exchange for a lesser charge. Many American liberals denounced the charges and proceedings against the Rosenbergs, particularly Ethel Rosenberg. In particular, they criticized as prejudicial to the defendants the behavior of the prosecutor, U.S. attorney Irving Saypol; the obvious bias of Judge Irving Kaufman; and widespread anti-Semitism.

The trial convened on March 6, 1951; the Rosenbergs were found guilty on March 29, 1951; and they were sentenced to death on April 5, 1951. The Rosenbergs maintained their innocence until their executions on

Julius Rosenberg and his wife, Ethel, arrive at a federal courthouse for their
espionage trial in New York City on March 21, 1951. Both were convicted and
executed. (AP Photo)

June 19, 1953. Evidence acquired later from Soviet archives supports the
charge of treason and espionage against Julius Rosenberg. It also suggests
that Ethel Rosenberg, while not directly involved, was aware of the spying.
The conviction and execution of the Rosenbergs supported McCarthyism
and the anticommunist fervor of the early 1950s.[9]

In 1952 Truman was expected to seek reelection, but—increasingly
unpopular and fearing defeat—he decided not to run. The Democrats
nominated Illinois governor Adlai Stevenson for the presidency with
Senator John Sparkman (D-AL) as his running mate. The Republicans
nominated former general Dwight D. Eisenhower of Kansas as their presidential candidate with Senator Richard M. Nixon (R-CA) as the vice
presidential candidate. While Stevenson's campaign focused on attacking
McCarthyism, Eisenhower ran a campaign on "Korea, Communism, and
Corruption" and advanced a domestic agenda that promised to curb

inflation, advance education, and bring peace. Eisenhower won a landslide victory, gaining 442 electoral votes to Stevenson's 89; taking 39 states to his opponent's 9; and receiving 55.2 percent of the popular vote to Stevenson's 44.3 percent. Eisenhower's victory was the first Republican presidential victory since 1928.

During his first term as president, Eisenhower agreed to an armistice in Korea, and he condemned Soviet suppression of protests in Poland and East Germany against their Soviet-controlled regimes; however, he would not intervene in supporting the protesters. Again, Eisenhower denounced (but again provided no direct support to) the Soviet Union as it suppressed the Hungarian Revolution of 1956 with a major invasion of Soviet and Eastern Bloc troops. Eisenhower and his secretary of state John Foster Dulles announced a significant shift in American policy that was defined by the threat of massive retaliation (Document 9), and they intervened covertly in Iran and Latin America to secure American interests; condemned the British, French, and Israeli attack on Egypt during the Suez crisis; participated in the Geneva summit meeting in 1955; and assisted in mediating the withdrawal of the French from Indo-China after their defeat at Dien Bien Phu on May 7, 1954. Three of these developments—the new reliance on massive retaliation and the interventions in Iran and Guatemala—reflected Eisenhower's priority in sustaining American political and economic interests on American, not Soviet, terms. Both Eisenhower and his Foster Dulles sought a determinant position in the Cold War so that it would be fought on American terms and not simply be reactive to Soviet initiatives. They wanted to minimize the political and military impact of the Cold War on the American economy. In their eyes, that meant avoiding any large or several traditional military operations that were costly. On January 12, 1954, Dulles delivered a speech (Document 9) to the Council on Foreign Relations in New York and announced that the United States would avoid regional conflicts in its struggle with communism. Rather, the United States would respond with massive (nuclear) retaliation against its enemies if necessary. This threat continued through the end of the Eisenhower presidency in January 1961, though in practice the government continued to use covert operations, as in Iran and Guatemala, to gain its objectives.[10]

In 1951 the democratically elected government of Prime Minister Mohammad Mosaddegh nationalized Iran's oil fields and production facilities. Previously the vast Iranian oil industry was controlled by the British-owned Anglo-Iranian Oil Company. The nationalization process was a major loss to the British, who attempted and failed to negotiate a settlement that was more satisfactory. With the approval of British prime minister Winston Churchill and President Eisenhower, the Central Intelligence Agency (CIA) developed and executed a coup d'état on August 19, 1953. Mosaddegh was arrested and later tried and imprisoned. Many of his aides and supporters were executed. The new pro-British and pro-American government was led by Mohammad-Rezā Shāh Pahlavi, who had previously served as a constitutional monarch. He was now an authoritarian monarch with a government headed by the new prime minister Faziollah Zahedi. British and American interests in and access to Iranian oil was secured, and the Soviet Union was blocked from extending its reach into the region and its assets.

American interests were also viewed to be at risk in Guatemala, where Jacobo Árbenz Guzmán was elected president in 1950 on a platform calling for political, economic, and social reforms. On June 27, 1952, Guzmán announced Decree 900, a planned seizure of unused land held by Guatemalan and foreign corporations. This action targeted the monopoly of the U.S. United Fruit Company, which owned more than 42 percent of the nation's arable land. United Fruit requested the U.S. government intervene and overthrow Guzmán. At the same time, the CIA advised Eisenhower that Guzmán's government was a puppet regime controlled by the Soviet Union. In fact, there were communists in Guzmán's government, but they had no connection with the Soviet Union. The CIA conducted an extensive misinformation campaign against Guzmán in Guatemala and supported the arming of a right-wing force under Colonel Castillo Armas. Guzmán was forced to resign on June 27, 1954, and Armas came into power. Guzmán was assassinated in 1957. The interests of United Fruit were secured, and a "communist" victory in Latin America was thwarted.[11]

In the 1956 presidential race, Adlai Stevenson was challenged in the primaries by Senator Estes Kefauver (D-TN) and at the convention by Governor W. Averall Harriman of New York. Stevenson was nominated on the first ballot. In spite of concerns over Eisenhower's health, the Republicans nominated the president and Vice President Nixon for another term. During the campaign Stevenson proposed that the United

States enter into treaties with the Soviet Union to minimize the risk of nuclear war and downsize the American military so that funds would be available for social programs. Eisenhower denounced these proposals and gained strength from his leadership during the Hungarian revolution and the Suez crisis. Both candidates tended to ignore the civil rights issue. Eisenhower defeated Stevenson even more decisively than in 1952. Eisenhower's second term witnessed the acceleration of the civil rights movement in the United States and his deployment of troops to desegregate the high school in Little Rock, Arkansas; Soviet success in orbiting Sputnik on October 4, 1958; the 1957 announcement of the Eisenhower Doctrine to provide military aid to Middle Eastern nations that were victims of aggression and the subsequent use of American troops in Lebanon in 1958; extended American interest in South Vietnam; Castro's success in toppling the regime of Fulgencio Batista in Cuba and the erosion of U.S.-Cuban relations that led the United States to break diplomatic relations with Cuba on January 1, 1960; the July 29, 1959 "Kitchen Debate" between Khrushchev and Vice President Richard Nixon in Moscow; and a crisis in U.S.-Soviet relations in May 1960 with American acknowledgment of U-2 spy missions over the Soviet Union and the collapse of the Paris Peace Conference on May 16, 1960. The most significant of these developments were the challenges of the mounting civil rights crisis in the United States and the U-2 crisis of May 1960 that revealed that the United States had lied to the world community about its spying on the Soviet Union.

Civil rights in the United States became a Cold War issue when the Soviet Union and others pointed to the hypocrisy of American society, where millions of African Americans were denied the right to vote, were forced to attend inferior segregated schools, and had limited access to higher education, good jobs, and decent housing. African American activists W. E. B. DuBois, Paul Robeson, Claudia Jones, and others condemned racism in America during the early years of the Cold War. DuBois and Robeson supported a Soviet petition that was presented to the United Nations condemning American racism. African American lawyers, such as Charles Houston and Thurgood Marshall, led the challenge against segregation that found success in the U.S. Supreme Court decision *Brown vs. Board of Education, Topeka* in 1954 that reversed the *Plessy vs. Ferguson* decision of 1896 that rendered the "separate but equal" decision that supported segregation. Soviet propaganda exploited the struggle of African Americans for civil rights, and the black leadership of some of the new independent states in Africa criticized the American government for its "hypocritical" record on civil rights. Even before the *Brown* decision, Truman recognized the political and moral case for ending segregation. Eisenhower was also cognizant that the United States was vulnerable to legitimate criticism on the issue of civil rights and that it was a transformative political issue. Ever so gingerly, he enforced *Brown* when necessary. The case for civil rights for African Americans was largely advanced, and eventually won, by increased involvement by African Americans through demonstrations and marches, and the success of legal challenges brought by liberal lawyers. It remained a major topic for Soviet propaganda into the 1970s.[12]

During Eisenhower's second term, an uneasy balance of power appeared to exist between the United States and the Soviet Union. With Stalin's death in 1953 and the rise of Nikita Khrushchev as the new Soviet leader, some hoped that Khrushchev would institute reforms and reduce Cold War tensions. While Khrushchev did denounce Stalinism and improved limited freedom of expression within the Soviet Union, any aspirations for a major reorientation of Soviet policy were dashed by the Soviet Union's enhanced controls over the Eastern Bloc; its support of leftists in Latin America, Africa, and Asia; and Khrushchev's unpredictable behavior.

The United States helped aggravate the Cold War through its deceptive policies and practices associated with U-2 flights over the Soviet Union. In 1957 the United States persuaded Pakistan to allow it to establish a secret base for the U-2 spy plane to use for flights over the Soviet Union. The U-2 flew at altitudes that Soviet planes and missiles could not reach, and its mission was to gather photographic information on Soviet ICBM and defense facilities. On May 1, 1960, a U-2 departed from Pakistan to conduct photographic surveillance and land in Norway. The Soviets were aware of the U-2 and succeeded in bringing it down almost intact and with the pilot (Francis Gary Powers) alive. The United States knew of the loss of the plane and assumed that the pilot was killed. The American government released a statement that a weather research plane was missing and presumed lost. The release indicated that the pilot had radioed that he was having difficulty with his oxygen supply. The Soviets

Appearing before the Soviet Parliament on May 7, 1960, Soviet premier Nikita Khrushchev holds aloft photos that he identified as views of military and industrial targets taken by downed American pilot Francis Powers. Khrushchev claimed that Powers, whom the Russians say was shot down over Soviet territory, was still alive and in good health. (Bettmann/Corbis)

reported that an American plane had been recovered. A week later, on May 7, 1960, the Soviets announced that most of the U-2 was recovered, including its cameras, and that the pilot had been captured. The Soviets processed the film and released some copies that demonstrated that the U-2 was spying on the Soviet Union. The American cover story was revealed as a lie, and Eisenhower was not only embarrassed, but—more importantly—discredited. Eisenhower, Khrushchev, President Charles de Gaulle of France, and British prime minister Harold Macmillan gathered in Paris for a summit meeting on May 16, 1960, to discuss Berlin and a potential reduction in nuclear arms. Khrushchev demanded that Eisenhower apologize for the U-2 spy flights. Eisenhower refused, and Khrushchev bolted from the summit and returned to Moscow.

With Eisenhower retiring, the Democrats viewed the 1960 presidential election has their opportunity to regain the White House. Senator John F. Kennedy won the nomination on the first ballot and selected Senator

Lyndon Baines of Texas Johnson as his vice presidential running mate. The Republicans met in Chicago and nominated Vice President Richard Nixon for the presidency on the first ballot. He selected former senator and U.S. ambassador to the United Nations Henry Cabot Lodge, Jr. as his running mate. The presidential campaign was characterized by more political gaffes than differences on policies. When Martin Luther King, Jr. was arrested in Atlanta as a result of a civil rights demonstration, Kennedy contacted King and his family and expressed his support. King's father (Martin Luther King, Sr.) then endorsed Kennedy. Nixon avoided any involvement in the King case. Kennedy accused Eisenhower and Nixon of allowing the Soviet Union to gain an edge in missile development (a missile gap), when in fact no such gap existed. The election on November 8, 1960, was very close. While Kennedy acquired 303 electoral votes from 22 states to Nixon's 219 electoral votes from 26 states, the margin of victory in the popular vote was extremely close—49.7 percent for Kennedy and 49.6 percent for Nixon.

On January 17, 1961, a few days before the inauguration, Eisenhower made a farewell address (Document 10) to the American people. In this speech he referred to the Cold War and warned that American culture and values could be adversely affected by the new military-industrial complex that had become a permanent element in American society with the advent of the Cold War. Eisenhower stated:

> In the councils of government, we must guard against the acquisition of unwarranted influence, whether sought or unsought, by the military-industrial complex. The potential for the disastrous rise of misplaced power exists and will persist. . . . We must never let the weight of this combination endanger our liberties or democratic processes. We should take nothing for granted only an alert and knowledgeable citizenry can compel the proper meshing of huge industrial and military machinery of defense with our peaceful methods and goals, so that security and liberty may prosper together.[13]

Between his inauguration on January 20, 1961, and the outbreak of the Cuban missile crisis in October 1962,[14] President Kennedy had limited successes in advancing his domestic agenda and foreign policy. In his inaugural address he proclaimed that a new age was beginning in the United States—the New Frontier—in which equality of opportunity and freedom were paramount values. Within a few months, especially after the debacle of the failed Bay of Pigs invasion of Cuba, it was apparent that Kennedy was proceeding with caution and not about to rush into any additional quick decisions on problematic issues, whether foreign or domestic.

On the domestic front one of the most pressing issues was the civil rights movement for African Americans. Kennedy provided the appropriate rhetoric in major speeches but was less than enthusiastic in pushing the necessary legislation. Civil rights leaders were disappointed by Kennedy's lack of action. The issue of civil rights for African Americans was more than a domestic political-social concern—the Soviets were using the American civil rights crisis as an effective propaganda tool throughout the world, especially in the Third (underdeveloped) World. The old European empires were vanishing, and dozens of new countries led by people of color were emerging. America was portrayed as a racist and contradictory society that was more representative of the past than the present and future.

Kennedy's relationship with Khrushchev was strained from the outset. The Soviet leader did not see in Kennedy any significant mark of personal achievement and thought him weak. Kennedy and Khrushchev met on June 4, 1961, in Vienna, Austria, where Kennedy warned Khrushchev that any interference with American rights in Berlin would be viewed as an act of war. The Soviets and East Germans were determined to stop the westward flood of emigrants who used Berlin as their access point. American and allied forces were bolstered during July in anticipation of Soviet seizure of the entire city, but the Soviets adopted a different approach and started constructing the Berlin Wall on August 13, 1961. It separated the Soviet zone from the American, British, and French zones, and stopped the flow of those fleeing from the east. Tensions were heightened, but war was averted.

Kennedy's establishment of the Peace Corps and his approaches in the Middle East, South Asia, Africa, and Latin America reflected new thinking on American foreign policy and the Cold War. As early as 1951 Congressman Kennedy called for the establishment of a volunteer organization through which Americans would assist developing countries with the technology and knowledge to improve the lives of their people. During his presidential campaign Kennedy resurrected that idea and named it the Peace Corps. On March 1, 1961, Kennedy announced the formation of the Peace Corps, which was authorized by Congress on September 22, 1961. Still in existence today, the Peace Corps helped to change the global image of Americans and American foreign policy. Tens of thousands of talented and committed Americans volunteered as teachers, medical workers, agricultural experts, engineers, businesspeople, social workers, and other needed professions to assist the peoples of scores of nations improve their daily lives.

In the Middle East Kennedy affirmed American support for Israel, developed contacts with Nasser's Egypt, and sided with revolutionaries in the North Yemen civil war that jeopardized the tenuous peace between Egypt and Saudi Arabia. In South Asia Kennedy sought to improve relations with nonaligned India and its leader Prime Minister Jawaharlal Nehru. This approach constituted a sharp departure from the Eisenhower-Dulles policy of considering nonaligned nations as probable enemies. Kennedy expanded foreign aid to both old and new nations, and some of the brightest young State Department leaders were dispatched to American embassies and consulates to assist African leaders in the political and economic transformation of their societies. The United States provided major financial assistance in supporting UN peacekeeping forces in Africa. In Latin America Kennedy attempted to contain communism through the creation of the Alliance for Progress, which provided aid to nations under siege and connected that aid to human rights. And yet Kennedy sanctioned existing plans for the Bay of Pigs invasion in Cuba and for the assassination of dictator Rafael Trujillo of the Dominican Republic on May 30, 1961.

American culture was transformed by the Cold War.[15] Society responded to the perceived threats of nuclear war with the Soviet Union and of communism infiltrating American life and undermining American values. Religious leaders such as Fulton Sheen, Billy Graham, Carl McIntire, and Billy James Hargis condemned the "godless" Soviets and communism not only from their pulpits, but on nationally syndicated radio and television programs that attracted millions of listeners and viewers.[16] Religious leaders were not the only anticommunists to use radio and television, however. For many Americans the daily 15-minute evening radio broadcasts of Fulton Lewis, Jr. provided right-wing insights on the news.[17] As the Cold War continued and televisions became standard in homes, some dramatic and conversational programming was based in whole or in part on Cold War issues. From 1954 to 1957 millions of Americans viewed *I Led Three Lives*, a program about an American double agent who was dedicated to defeating Soviet spies and infiltration in the United States. Later, in 1966, conservative publisher (of the *National Review*) and commentator William F. Buckley, Jr. began his weekly program, *Firing Line*, which considered a wide range of topics, many related to the Cold War. This popular program survived to 1999, making it the longest running public affairs series in television history.[18]

Theater, films, books, and music also reflected the impact of the Cold War on American culture. In the theater, an important critique of the American government's procedures and conduct during the early Cold War era was produced by Arthur Miller. During 1952–1953 playwright Miller, who had gained renown for *The Death of a Salesman* in 1949 (written in 1948), wrote *The Crucible*. It was focused on the 1692 Salem witch trials but was an attack on McCarthyism and the HUAC. Miller had appeared before HUAC and revealed his involvement with communist-leaning groups but refused to identify anyone else who shared in his views. He was charged and convicted of contempt, but that ruling was overturned. Miller's talent, courage, and integrity were later recognized when he was awarded the National Medal of Arts.[19]

Dozens of films—such as *On the Beach* (1959; based on Nevil Shute's 1957 novel); *Dr. Strangelove or: How I Learned to Stop Worrying and Love the Bomb* (1964); *Fail Safe* (1964); and later *The Day After* (1983)—focused on nuclear war with the Soviet Union. Others—such as *Invasion U.S.A.* (1952); *The Manchurian Candidate* (1962; based on Richard Condon's 1959 novel); *Red Dawn* (1984); *Amerika* (1987); and Tom Clancy's *The Hunt for Red October* (1990)—presented more complicated plots that were based on particular incidents, on the weakness of the United States, or on its succumbing to Soviet brainwashing.[20] Examples of best-selling books with Cold War themes included Pat Frank's postapocalyptic novel, *Atlas, Babylon* (1959); the satirical *The Cat's Cradle: A Novel* by Kurt Vonnegut (1963); Tom Clancy's *The Hunt for Red October* (1984), *Red Storm Rising* (1986), and *The Cardinal of the Kremlin* (1988); and Ian Fleming's James Bond series. During the early 1960s musicians such as Bob Dylan, Joan Baez, Pete Seeger, Marty Robbins, the Golden Gate Quartet, and others gained popularity as voices in the antiwar movement.

The Central Intelligence Agency (CIA) was involved in the utilization of American artists as significant components of its Cold War propaganda program. With the assistance of Nelson Rockefeller, banker and president of the Museum of Modern Art in New York, and John Hay Whitney, William Burden, and Alfred Barr of the Congress for Cultural Freedom, the CIA supported the promotion of the American abstract expressionist movement to demonstrate the cultural supremacy of American culture. Abstract expressionism emerged during the 1940s and was a reaction to the violence and inhumanity of the war and, in particular, the atomic bomb. CIA support was intended to demonstrate American freedom of expression and superiority in the arts. The CIA provided significant financial support for the Congress for Cultural Freedom, which advanced the art of Jackson Pollock, Robert Motherwell, Willem de Kooning, and Mark Rothko through acquisitions, exhibitions at the Museum of Modern Art, and travelling exhibits, such the 1958 New American Painting exhibit that was sent to Paris.[21]

During the 1950s the fear of a nuclear attack informed public policy and private concerns. National and local civil defense organizations were established to prepare for such a war; in large urban areas, subway systems were used to store supplies and serve as shelters. In June 1954 the first national civil defense drill was held in 54 cities, Alaska, Hawaii, and Puerto Rico. Canada also participated. Throughout the United States weekly air raid drills were held during the 1950s. Schoolchildren learned to "duck and cover," that is, to get under their desks for protection if a bomb came. Along the East and West Coasts, antiaircraft units were deployed to protect cities, bridges, and important facilities. Home air-raid shelters were constructed in basements and in backyards. These measures and any expectations of their success were unrealistic, as the Soviet Union did not possess an air force capable of a major assault on the United States, nor did it have an adequate supply of nuclear warheads or missiles. When the Soviets achieved that capacity, these preparations were abandoned for the most part. Still, air-raid sirens continued to be tested weekly through most of the Cold War.[22]

In 1948 the Ford Foundation funded the establishment of the nonprofit RAND (Research ANd Development) corporation to assist in the development of U.S. policy and decision making through objective research and analysis. Originally created in 1946 as Project RAND by General

A kindergarten teacher coaches a group of crouched children to duck and cover in a national air raid drill in Chicago, Illinois, in 1954. (Photo by Underwood Archives/Getty Images)

Henry H. Arnold, its initial charge was to conduct long-range planning of weapons systems. RAND emerged as an important think tank that focused on systems analysis and expanded the scope and range of its interests to include a multitude of concerns that included education, energy, the environment, economic development, crisis management, science and technology, intelligence, and terrorism. One of the most important RAND futurists who had a significant impact on American Cold War planning was Herman Kahn, the author of the controversial *On Thermonuclear War* (1960).[23] Kahn contended that a nuclear war was "winnable," and his arguments influenced Secretary of Defense Robert McNamara, who was impressed with data and systems analysis.

Other think tanks emerged during the Cold War. Kahn, along with Max Singer and Oscar Ruebhausen, formed the Hudson Institute in 1961 to look into the future in nontraditional ways, considering all options. In 1984 the U.S. government established the United States Institute of Peace to formulate ideas and plans that could resolve problems that could disrupt peace throughout the world. Some "think tanks" were more informal and centered around a particular individual. One example of such a think tank was the circle of disciples influenced by Albert Wohlstetter, a professor at the University of Chicago. Among those attracted to Wohlstetter's views[24] were Richard Perle and Paul Wolfowitz. Considered by many to be the founder of American neoconservatism, Wohlstetter argued for the steady expansion of the American military during the Cold War to counter Soviet aggression throughout the world.[25]

In 1956 the State Department initiated the Jazz Ambassador program as part of its Cold War strategy. Jazz musicians were to be sent to countries behind the Iron Curtain and in the Third World to demonstrate the United States' commitment to freedom and creativity. The first jazz ambassador was John Birks "Dizzy" Gillespie, who was followed in 1958 by Dave Brubeck and later by Louis Armstrong, Duke Ellington, Thelonious Monk, Benny Goodman, and Miles Davis. This program was an unqualified success, with the musicians drawing large audiences that occasionally included heads of state.[26] In addition to the Jazz Ambassador program, the United States joined the Soviet Union in allowing other musicians, such as the pianist Van Cliburn (winner of the 1958 International Tchaikovsky Piano Competition in Moscow) and ballet companies and performers to visit one another's countries. As early as 1954 the Eisenhower administration permitted American ballet companies and performers to visit the Soviet Union through cultural exchanges.[27] At the same time the United States and the Soviet Union sanctioned sports competitions in which each nation would send a visiting team to a particular event, such as the U.S.-U.S.S.R. track meet in Philadelphia, Pennsylvania, in 1956, or a team, such as ice hockey, that would play multiple games and teams while touring the host country. In 1948, after a hiatus of 12 years, the Olympic games were resumed in London. The United States won the most medals and the most gold medals. East-West tensions were evident as these games witnessed the first political defection from the Eastern Bloc when Marie Provazniková, president of the Czechoslovak Olympic Committee, refused to return to Czechoslovakia because of the communist seizure of the government. Throughout the Cold War the Olympics became enmeshed in the U.S.-Soviet struggle. In 1980 the American team did not participate in the Moscow Olympics, and four years later, the Soviet team did not appear in the Los Angeles Olympics.

NOTES

1. Paul Nitze, "The Development of NSC-68," *International Security*, 4, no. 4 (Spring 1980): 170–76; Paul Nitze and S. Nelson Drew (eds.), *NSC-68: Forging the Strategy of Containment* (Washington, DC: National Defense University, 1994), 6–10.

2. The Soviet atomic bomb was based primarily on their research and technology; however, the Soviet Union did receive information on the American bomb that accelerated the schedule of their research.

3. The reported number varies with eyewitness accounts.

4. Thomas C. Reeves, *The Life and Times of Joe McCarthy* (New York: Stein and Day, 1982), 287–315.

5. U.S. Government, *Congressional Record*, Senate, 81st Congress, 2nd Session, 7894–95.

6. Reeves, *The Life and Times of Joe McCarthy*, 651–52.

7. See William T. Walker, *McCarthyism and the Red Scare: A Reference Guide* (Santa Barbara, CA: ABC-CLIO, 2011), 84–95.

8. For an excellent political and military study, see Max Hastings, *The Korean War* (New York: Simon and Schuster, 1988).

9. The literature on the Rosenberg case is vast. Two worthwhile books on it are Ronald Radosh and Joyce Milton, *The Rosenberg File: A Search for the Truth* (New York: Henry Holt, 1983) and Aleksandr Feklisov and Sergei Kostin, *The Man behind the Rosenbergs* (New York: Enigma Books, 2003).

10. John Foster Dulles, "The Evolution of Foreign Policy," *Department of State Bulletin*, 30, no. 761 (1954): 107–10.

11. See Richard H. Immerman, *John Foster Dulles, Piety, Pragmatism, and Power in U.S. Foreign Policy* (Lanham, MD: Rowman and Littlefield, 1998).

12. See Mary L. Dudziak, *Cold War Civil Rights: Race and the Image of American Democracy*, Politics and Society in the Twentieth-Century America series (Princeton, NJ: Princeton University Press, 2011) and Thomas Borstelmann,

The Cold War and the Color Line: American Race Relations in the Global Arena
(Cambridge, MA: Harvard University Press, 2003).

13. Dwight D. Eisenhower, *Public Papers of the Presidents of the United States:
Dwight D. Eisenhower, 1960–1961* (Washington, DC: U. S. Government Printing
Office, 1961), 1035–40.

14. Events related to the Cuban Missile Crisis—including the failed Bay of
Pigs invasion—are discussed in the next chapter. Kennedy's involvement in
South Vietnam is addressed in Chapter 5.

15. The best book on this topic is still Stephen J. Whitfield's *The Culture of
the Cold War* (Baltimore: The Johns Hopkins University Press, 1991).

16. Irwin Winsboro and Michael Epple, "Religion, Culture, and the Cold
War: Bishop Fulton J. Sheen and America's Anti-Communist Crusade of the
1950s," *Historian*, 71, no. 2 (Summer 2009): 209–33. Also see Patrick Farabaugh,
*Carl McIntire's Crusade against the Fairness Doctrine: Fundamentalist Preacher
and Radio Commentator Challenges Federal Communications and its Fairness Rules*
(Saarbrücken, Germany: VDM Velag Dr. Müller, 2010); David Aikman, *Billy
Graham: His Life and Influence* (New York: Thomas Nelson, 2010); John H.
Redekop, *The American Far Right: A Case Study of Billy James Hargis and Christian
Crusade* (Grand Rapids, MI: William B. Eerdmans, 1968).

17. See Dan D. Nimmo and Chevelle Newsome, *Political Commentators in
the United States in the Twentieth Century: A Bio-Critical Sourcebook* (Westport,
CT: Greenwood, 1997) and Heather Hendershot's *What's Fair on the Air? Cold
War Right Wing Broadcasting and the Public Interest* (Chicago: University of
Chicago Press, 2011).

18. The television series *I Led Three Lives* was based on Herbert A.
Philbrick's *I Led Three Lives* (New York: McGraw-Hill, 1952). For Buckley, see
Carl T. Bogus, *Buckley: William F. Buckley, Jr. and the Rise of American Conserva-
tism* (New York: Bloomsbury Press, 2011) and Carl T. Bogus, *William F. Buckley,
Jr.: The Maker of a Movement* (Wilmington, DE: ISI Books, 2010).

19. See *Arthur Miller: His Life and Work* (New York: Da Capo Press, 2004)
and Arthur Miller, "Why I Wrote 'The Crucible,'" *New Yorker*, 72 (October 21,
1996): 158ff.

20. See Margot E. Henriksen, *Dr. Strangelove's America: Society and Culture
in the Atomic Age* (Berkeley: University of California Press, 1997) and Tony Shaw
and Denise J. Youngblood, *Cinematic Cold War: The American and Soviet Struggle
for Heats and Minds* (Lawrence: University Press of Kansas, 2010).

21. See Frances Stonor Saunders's *The Cultural Cold War: The CIA and the
World of Arts and Letters* (New York: New Press, 2001), and *Who Paid the Piper?:
CIA and the Cultural Cold War* (London: Granta Books, 2000).

22. See Bo Jacobs, "Atomic Kids: 'Duck and Cover' and 'Atomic Alert' Teach ChildrenHow to Survive Atomic Attack," *Film and History: An Interdisciplinary Journal of Film and Television Studies*, 40, no. 1 (Spring 2010): 25–44.

23. See Herman Kahn, *On Thermonuclear War* (Princeton, NJ: Princeton University Press, 1958).

24. See Albert J. Wohlstetter, *A Delicate Balance of Terror* (Santa Monica, CA: Rand, 1958) and Robert Zarate and Henry D. Sokolski (eds.), *Nuclear Heuristics: Selected Writings of Albert and Roberta Wohlstetter* (London: Military Bookstore, 2009).

25. See Andrew Rich, *Think Tanks, Public Policy, and the Politics of Expertise* (New York: Cambridge University Press, 2005); Thomas Medvetz, *Think Tanks in America* (Chicago: University of Chicago Press, 2012); and Sharon Ghamari-Tabrizi, *The Worlds of Herman Kahn: The Intuitive Science of Thermonuclear War* (Cambridge, MA: Harvard University Press, 2005).

26. See Penny M. Von Eschen, *Satchmo Blows Up the World: Jazz Ambassadors Play the Cold War* (Cambridge, MA: Harvard University Press, 2004) and Russell H. Bartley, "The Piper Played to Us All: Orchestrating the Cultural Cold War in the USA, Europe, and Latin America," *International Journal of Politics, Culture, and Society*, 14, no. 3 (2001): 571–619.

27. See David Caute, *The Dancer Defects: The Struggle for Cultural Supremacy during the Cold War* (New York: Oxford University Press, 2005); Naima Prevots, *Dancer for Export: Cultural Diplomacy and the Cold War*, Studies in Dance History series (Indianapolis, IN: Wesleyan, 1999); and Yale Richmond, *Cultural Exchange and the Cold War: Raising the Iron Curtain* (University Park: Pennsylvania State University Press, 2003).

CHAPTER 4

CUBAN MISSILE CRISIS

I n 1962 the summer was hot and lingering, with an average temperature about four to five degrees higher than normal. This was followed by unexpectedly warm days in late September and early October. On October 11, American Catholics were absorbed by the opening of the Second Vatican Council, and on October 17 the New York Yankees defeated the San Francisco Giants for their twentieth world championship. For many Americans, the Cold War seemed far away.

But trouble was coming. Early in October, the United States and the Soviet Union conducted atmospheric nuclear tests. Then the already tense relationship between the Soviets and Americans threatened to explode into a major confrontation. But the crisis point was not in Europe or Asia. Rather, it was at America's doorstep in Cuba. On a Monday evening—October 22, 1962—President John F. Kennedy addressed the American people on television and radio to announce that the Soviets were placing nuclear missiles in Cuba and that the United States demanded their removal. Kennedy added that the United States was establishing a quarantine restricting the delivery of Soviet missiles and supplies to Cuba and warned that any violation of that quarantine or any attack launched from Cuba would be viewed as a Soviet act of war. Many Americans expected that the nightmare of nuclear war was about to become a reality, and a near panic ensued. An estimated 10 million Americans fled densely populated areas for what they thought would be safer locations, a large number of guns were purchased, people entered their air-raid shelters, and hoarding of foodstuffs occurred. Still, for the most part, Americans waited—most were stunned, many were depressed, and some were hopeful.[1]

American interest and involvement in Cuba preceded the Cold War. Prior to the Spanish-American War in 1898, Americans were increasingly engaged in the Cuban economy. Americans invested in sugar plantations and mills, and in the broader agriculture of the island. With the Cuban civil war and the Spanish-American War, Spanish control of Cuba ended.

President Kennedy presiding over a meeting with senior White House officials to discuss the Cuban missile crisis, October 23, 1962. (Corbis)

American forces occupied Cuba from 1898 to 1902, but the American influence that was exerted on Cubans endured for much longer. With the Platt Amendment of 1901, Cuban was transformed into an American protectorate. The United States gained Guantanamo Bay as a naval base and retained the right to approve Cuban government loans from foreign banks, to approve all treaties with other nations, and to use military force to protect American interests. U.S. marines occupied Cuba from 1917 to 1923. American investment expanded. Not only did Americans control more than 50 percent of Cuban sugar production, they were also involved in hotels, gambling casinos, racetracks, and other similar activities.

American financial and political interests also influenced the Cuban government—Cubans considered the regimes of both Geraldo Machado (1925–1933) and Fulgencio Batista (1934–1944 and 1952–1958) as American puppet regimes. The popular election of Grau San Martin in 1933 on a platform calling for land reform was viewed as a threat to American interests. The United States—in spite of President Franklin D. Roosevelt's Good Neighbor Policy and the abandonment of the rights advanced in the Platt Amendment—did not recognize Grau as the new president of Cuba. Grau was overthrown in 1934 in a revolution led by a military junta that included Fulgencio Batista.

During the early 1950s a Cuban lawyer named Fidel Castro denounced both the Batista regime for its corruption and brutality and the long history of American control over Cuba. With others, Castro attempted to seize the Moncada army barracks on July 26, 1953. This effort failed; Castro was captured, convicted of treason, and pardoned; and then he went into exile in Mexico. Castro used his Mexican exile to develop a plan to invade Cuba and overthrow the Batista government. On December 2, 1956, Castro—with less than 100 supporters—landed in Cuba. Batista loyalists killed all but 15 of the invaders. Castro and the remnants of his force made its way to the Sierra Maestra Mountains, where they recovered and built a large (10,000-man) army consisting mostly of peasants. This revolutionary movement—known as the 26th of July Movement—received financial support from the Cuban middle class. Castro and the movement succeeded in defeating Batista's forces. He entered Havana on January 1, 1959, as the new leader of Cuba, and Batista fled into exile in Spain.

As Castro unfolded one political, economic, and social reform after another during 1959 and 1960, including the nationalization of American assets, the American government came to recognize that Castro was a liability to its interests in the Western Hemisphere. Some American leaders believed that if Castro could not be managed, it would be in America's interest to replicate previous successes in Iran and Guatemala by over-throwing unfriendly, communist, or communist-leaning leaders and installing pro-American regimes.[2]

The situation in Cuba became more complex with the increasing visibility of the Soviet Union in Cuba with its agents and, in February 1960, with the visit of Anastas Mikoyan, first deputy chairman of the Council of Ministers of the Soviet Union. In March 1960 Cuba withdrew from the Rio Treaty of 1947, which had been an early component in America's Cold War containment policy. During the same month President Eisenhower directed that plans be made to remove Castro from power. The Soviet Union formally recognized Castro's government in May. In June the Cuban government nationalized properties and operations owned by American oil companies. In July all other American-owned properties were seized.

As Cuban-Soviet relations improved and expanded, Cuban-American relations continued to deteriorate. The United States broke diplomatic relations with Cuba on January 3, 1961, less than three weeks before the inauguration of President John F. Kennedy. Preparations for the implementation of Eisenhower's plan to remove Castro continued during the early months of the Kennedy administration. Kennedy proceeded with the planned invasion of Cuba that would use exiled Cubans who would be delivered to Cuba on American ships.

The CIA-trained Cuban exile force of about 1,500 men landed on April 17, 1961, at the "Bay of Pigs" and were easily defeated by units of the Cuban army who had remained loyal to Castro. About 120 of the invaders were killed, and the remainder were captured in this humiliating defeat for the United States. American involvement could not be disguised. Kennedy, who refused to commit U.S. air assets to assist the invaders when they encountered trouble, assumed responsibility for the disaster, which was caused by poor planning, disorganization, and poor execution. Kennedy's reputation among segments of the American population plummeted, but—more importantly—the Soviet leadership thought Kennedy's performance indicated that he was weak and therefore vulnerable. The U.S. policy to remove Castro continued with another unsuccessful effort known as Operation Mongoose, which consisted of another effort to assist anti-Castro Cubans to incite a rebellion and failed plots to assassinate Castro. Such moves failed and served to reinforce Castro's conviction that the United States was hellbent on overthrowing the revolution. He thus drew closer to the Soviets for protection.

At the same time the exodus of middle-class and other Cubans from the island to south Florida created a political bloc that wanted the United States to act more forthrightly in reclaiming Cuba for capitalism and returning them to their country and property. Concerns about communism coming so close to the United States magnified the sense of danger to Americans, which pressured the Kennedy administration to take a strong stand against Castro. This was to be more than containment. In February 1962 the United States imposed an embargo against Cuba and began planning for another major military action in September or October 1962 to overthrow what was now referred to as Castro's Communist Cuba.

The revolutionary court where the mercenaries who invaded Cuba in the U.S.-backed Bay of Pigs invasion were tried on April 20, 1962. From left to right, the commandants who tried the mercenaries were Guillermo Garcia, Juan Almeida, Augusto Martinez Sanchez, Presidenti Commandant Sergio Vel Dalle, and Manuel Pinerro. (Photo by Keystone/Getty Images)

Soviet leader Nikita Khrushchev continued to develop his country's relationship with Castro. A communist Cuba in the Soviet orbit would break the old Monroe Doctrine that Americans believed kept the Western Hemisphere free from European and other interference and entrusted security to American power. With Cuba moving under Soviet influence, the United States worried that Cuba could be used as a bargaining chip in negotiations over the more important issue of Berlin, where the East Germans erected the Berlin Wall in 1961. Cuba could also be useful to the Soviets in addressing concerns related to American missile bases in Turkey. Finally, Cuba could provide a strategic launching pad for the Soviet intermediate-range nuclear missiles.

Khrushchev and Kennedy met in Vienna on June 4, 1961, to discuss a range of issues, including Berlin and Southeast Asia. Kennedy left the meeting fearing that the Soviets were willing to risk war over Berlin, and Khrushchev—who viewed Kennedy as weak and malleable—thought that he could maneuver the United States into situations that would benefit the Soviet Union.[3]

Early in 1962 the Soviets and Cubans began secret negotiations on the placement of Soviet nuclear weapons in Cuba. After initial reluctance, the Cubans agreed, thinking that the existence of Soviet missiles in Cuba would deter an American invasion. The accord was reached, and construction was secretly started in July. However, American U2 surveillance flights and reports from informants arriving from Cuba led the CIA (Central Intelligence Agency) to suspect that missile sites were under construction. Kennedy was advised of that concern on August 10. The first Soviet nuclear-capable intermediate-range ballistic missiles arrived on September 8. The Soviets were building nine different missile sites with a total of 40 launchers with a potential striking range—if they were offensive missiles—of 1,200 to 2,800 miles, depending upon the missile type. American intelligence was based on local reports as well as satellite, naval air, and U2 reconnaissance. By October 14 Americans concluded that the Soviets were deploying offensive missiles in Cuba. Kennedy received confirmation on October 15 and convened the 14-member Executive Committee of the National Security Council (EXCOMM) to consider the American response. Options ranged from an invasion of Cuba and a potential war with the Soviet Union to ignoring the deployment since some argued that it would have no impact on the balance of power. Kennedy recognized that an American military action in Cuba would likely lead to a Soviet military action in Berlin. He was also sensitive to the reactions of NATO leaders who might not enthusiastically support an American effort in Cuba if it led to a European war. At the same time Kennedy needed to respond to American concerns. A battery of nuclear warheads 90 miles from the United States—that could fall into the hands of Castro—was unacceptable, as it would change the balance of power.[4]

Between October 15 and October 22, mounting evidence was gathered that confirmed the presence of the Soviet missiles and launchers. On October 18 Kennedy met with Andrei Gromyko, the Soviet foreign minister, who assured Kennedy that the missiles had only a defensive capability. Kennedy knew that Gromyko was lying, which heightened his level of urgency. Meanwhile, the American military leadership prepared for an invasion of Cuba and war with the Soviet Union. By October 21 Kennedy had ruled out an invasion unless absolutely necessary; he was leaning toward a naval blockade or bombing the missile sites. The bombing option receded when the less belligerent term "quarantine"—rather than a "blockade"—gained the support of Kennedy and EXCOMM. On Monday, October 22 American diplomats briefed allies and solicited support for the quarantine of all ships bringing missile-related materials to Cuba. The Soviet Union was advised that Kennedy would address the American people and inform them of the Soviet offensive missiles in Cuba, the quarantine policy, and the demand for the Soviets to dismantle and remove the missiles immediately. In a nationwide television and radio address (Document 11) that evening, Kennedy provided a summary of what had happened, evidence of the Soviet missiles in Cuba, and the measured American response to this crisis. The most chilling sentence in his address was:

> It shall be the policy of this nation to regard any nuclear missile launched from Cuba against any nation in the Western Hemisphere as an attack by the Soviet Union on the United States, requiring a full retaliatory response upon the Soviet Union.[5]

The American military was placed on DEFCON 3 by 8:00 p.m. on October 22.[6] The response to Kennedy's speech was predictable. Most Americans found the evidence compelling, and the strategy measured and reasonable. Internationally, America's allies endorsed the strategy. Argentina and Colombia even offered ships to assist in the quarantine, and those offers were accepted. The Soviet Union, the People's Republic of China, and the Eastern Bloc nations condemned Kennedy and the United States, arguing that America was violating Cuba's sovereignty and denying the existence of the Soviet missiles in Cuba. On October 24, Khrushchev sent a telegram to Kennedy that the blockade was an act of aggression and that Soviet ships had been directed to ignore it.

The next few days were dangerous for all parties. The Soviets were humiliated at a meeting of the UN Security Council on October 25 when the American ambassador Adlai Stevenson—displaying photographic evidence of the missile sites—demanded that the Soviet ambassador Valerian Zorin at least admit that the missiles existed. A mortified and out-maneuvered Zorin remained silent, which many interpreted as an indication of Soviet duplicity.

Fearing that the Soviets might resort to military action, Kennedy, on October 25, ordered the American military to proceed to DEFCON 2 status (the next step to nuclear war) on October 26. A nuclear war with the Soviet Union appeared probable. In addition to American nuclear missiles being placed at the ready, B-52 bombers with nuclear bombs were maintained in the air awaiting orders. Also on October 25, Kennedy responded to Khrushchev, stating that the Soviet Union had lied and could not be trusted. Thus, the American action was justified to re-establish a Cuba free of offensive nuclear capable missiles. American surveillance flights over Cuba on October 25 indicated that construction at the missile sites was continuing. However, it was noted that more than a dozen Soviet ships en route to Cuba had either been stopped or were turning away from Cuba. On October 26 Kennedy thought that the United States would have to invade Cuba to remove the missiles and the Castro government.

That afternoon a back-channel conversation was held at a restaurant in New York between Soviet embassy counselor and spy Alexandr Feklisov, who initiated the contact, and ABC News correspondent John A. Scali. Feklisov requested that Scali ask his contacts in the American government to determine if the United States would consider a diplomatic settlement of the crisis that was based on the withdrawal of the Soviet missiles and a Cuban pledge not to accept such weapons in the future in exchange for an American promise not invade Cuba.[7] Later that same day a personal message to Kennedy from Khrushchev was received and reiterated the same terms but in the Soviet leader's personal style. The "wild card" in the crisis was Castro, who believed that an American invasion was imminent and who was urging Khrushchev to adopt a hard line with the United States and even consider a pre-emptive attack.

On the morning of October 27, a message from Khrushchev was transmitted by radio calling for a quid pro quo, with the Soviets withdrawing their missiles from Cuba, and the United States withdrawing its missiles from Italy and Turkey. Later that morning an official dispatch arrived from Moscow that advanced the same proposal and called for verification by the UN Security Council.[8] While the Italian government approved the plan, Turkish leaders indicated that they would not be pleased with the prospect of losing the American Jupiter missiles.[9] At noon on October 27 an American U-2 spy plane was shot down and its pilot killed by a Soviet surface to air missile (SAM). That evening representatives of both governments met secretly at a restaurant in Washington, DC, to conduct further negotiations.

Kennedy decided to ignore the most recent messages from Moscow and to respond positively to Khrushchev's initial plan, with no mention of the missiles in Turkey and Italy. Kennedy recognized that this ploy could place Khrushchev in an extremely difficult position if he had not shared his earlier message with other Kremlin leaders. Kennedy was willing to remove the Jupiter missiles, but he did not want that to be written in the text of an agreement. Late on October 27, the American government released copies of Kennedy's new letter to Khrushchev and awaited a reply. Most members of EXCOMM thought that the Soviets would reject the proposal and that war would begin. Khrushchev received another letter on October 27—from Fidel Castro. Castro urged the Soviets to launch a nuclear attack on the United States in the event of an American invasion of Cuba. From the Soviet perspective this crisis needed to be defused, as Cuba was not worth a nuclear war. On the evening of October 28, Khrushchev announced that the Soviet Union would remove its missiles from Cuba. Kennedy, who had secretly formalized his pledge to withdraw American missiles from Turkey and Italy, responded positively, indicating that Cuba's sovereignty would be respected by the United States and that the United States would not assist any group or nation in an invasion of Cuba.

Soviet intermediate-range ballistic missiles were dismantled and shipped back to the Soviet Union, with the last ship departing on November 9, 1962. Fearing a reckless decision on the part of Cuba, the Soviets also later removed all Soviet tactical missiles. The American Jupiter missiles in Italy and Turkey were removed by April 24, 1963. Another significant development resulting from the crisis was the agreement to install a direct telephone line between the White House and the Kremlin. Both powers recognized the need for clear and prompt communications in order to avoid misunderstandings that could contribute to a nuclear war.

In the United States Kennedy was perceived to have prevailed in the crisis, and indeed the ways the Kennedy administration described its decision making made it seem as if Kennedy and his inner circle of advisors were in control of events—they were masterful Cold War warriors who remained "cool" to defuse a very hot crisis. Clearly, it was a setback for Khrushchev, who had miscalculated Kennedy's resolve and leadership abilities, and the outcome undermined his power in the Soviet Union.

In fact, both Kennedy and Khrushchev demonstrated that they were responsible leaders who could agree to a diplomatic settlement in lieu of a nuclear war. Khrushchev was removed from power on October 14, 1964, and most Soviet experts concur that his dismissal was due, at least in part, to his failure in the Cuban missile crisis. In spite of assurances that the United States would not invade Cuba or attempt to disrupt its internal affairs, Castro was distressed that the Americans were still at the naval base at Guantánamo Bay and that the Soviets had left them out of the negotiations. Cuban-Soviet relations were estranged for many years. As October came to an end, Americans returned to their routines, many with a renewed hope that nuclear arms could be contained.[10]

During the decades since the crisis in 1962, information has emerged that revealed how very close the United States and the Soviet Union came to nuclear war. Prior to the crisis the Soviets had delivered tactical nuclear weapons to Cuba that could have been deployed on bombers and artillery rockets. In 2002 it was revealed that a Soviet submarine with a nuclear warhead was trapped by American surface vessels, and Soviet naval and political officers on board considered utilizing their nuclear torpedo. However, they decided against that action and instead surfaced for air.[11] Another dangerous moment occurred on November 22, 1962, when Soviet statesman Anastas Mikoyan, without clearance from Moscow, informed Castro that a promised transfer of nuclear-armed missiles to Cuba would not proceed because it would constitute a violation of Soviet law. No such law existed, but Mikoyan was troubled by Castro's mental condition and determined that it was not in the interest of the Soviet Union to go ahead with the transfer.[12]

NOTES

1. Alice L. George, *Awaiting Armageddon: How Americans Faced the Cuban Missile Crisis* (Chapel Hill: University of North Carolina Press, 2006), 3–16; Alice L. George, *The Cuban Missile Crisis: The Threshold of Nuclear War* (New York: Routledge, 2013). Also see *The Cuban Missile Crisis in American Memory: Myths versus Reality* by Sheldon Stern (Stanford, CA: Stanford University Press, 2012) and Sheldon Stern *The Week the World Stood Still: Inside the Secret Cuban Missile Crisis* (Stanford: Stanford University Press, 2005).

2. On August 19, 1953, the United States, with the assistance of Great Britain, overthrew the democratically elected government of Iran and Prime

Minister Mohammad Mosaddegh. In 1951 Mosaddegh's government, with the clear support of the Iranian parliament, had nationalized all aspects of oil production. The coup d'état installed Mohammad-Rezā Shāh Pahlavi as absolute ruler. He reversed the nationalization laws and process.Between June 18 and June 27, 1954, the American Central Intelligence Agency supported the successful overthrow of the popularly elected president Jacobo Árbenz Guzmán. The Guzmán reform program threated the interests of the American-owned United Fruit Company.

3. Jonathan Haslam, *Russia's Cold War: From the October Revolution to the Fall of the Wall* (New Haven, CT: Yale University Press, 2011), 175–213.

4. An excellent resource on the crisis is *The Cuban Missile Crisis, 1962: A National Security Archive Documents Reader*, edited by Laurence Chang and Peter Kornbluh (New York: New Press, 1992). It provides an extensive range of American documents as well as a reliable chronology and a glossary.

5. John F. Kennedy, *Public Papers of the Presidents of the United States: John F. Kennedy, 1962* (Washington, DC: U. S. Government Printing Office, 1963), 806–9.

6. The American military developed the five-step Defense Readiness Condition (DEFCON) system to alert its armed forces of the readiness requirements for a nuclear war. These levels are DEFCON 5 (lowest state of readiness), DEFCON 4 (increased intelligence watch and strengthened security), DEFCON 3 (increase in force readiness above the required normal readiness), DEFCON 2 (next step to nuclear war), and DEFCON 1 (nuclear war is imminent).

7. Chang and Kornbluh *The Cuban Missile Crisis*, 184–85.

8. Andrew Christopher, *For the President's Eyes Only: Secret Intelligence and the American Presidency from Washington to Bush* (New York: Harper Perennial, 1996), 688.

9. The Jupiter missiles were scheduled for replacement because they were deemed obsolete.

10. A meaningful and useful statement on the crisis is Michael Dobbs, "Why We Should Still Study the Cuban Missile Crisis," in *Special Report 205* (Washington, DC: United States Institute of Peace, 2008), 1–12.

11. See Michael Dobbs, *One Minute to Midnight: Kennedy, Khrushchev, and Castro on the Brink of Nuclear War* (New York: Alfred A. Knopf, 2008).

12. Graham Allison, "The Cuban Missile Crisis at 50," *Foreign Affairs*, 91, no. 4 (July/August 2012): 11–16.

CHAPTER 5

VIETNAM, DÉTENTE, AND WATERGATE

T he period from the Cuban missile crisis in October 1962 to the final days of the Nixon administration in August 1974 was a difficult and turbulent era for Americans. The uncertainties associated with the continuing Cold War combined with a series of domestic crises and substantive cultural changes challenged traditional views of society and faith in historic institutions. The assassination of President John F. Kennedy on November 22, 1963—and the subsequent assassinations of Martin Luther King, Jr. and Senator Robert F. Kennedy in 1968—shocked the nation. So, too, the success of the civil rights movement for African Americans tore at the fabric of white southern society; urban riots appeared to be leading to anarchy; the emergence of feminism was construed by some as an assault on the family; and student protest movements focused on free speech, democratization, a nuclear-free world, and American involvement in the Vietnam War and the country's policies throughout the world. As Americans withdrew from the failure in Vietnam, the Watergate scandal broke, and the country was thrown into a constitutional crisis.

In the wake of the Cuban missile crisis, the United States and the Soviet Union assessed their policies in light of the perceived results. While Kennedy was viewed in the West as the victor, the balance of power did not change. In both the Soviet and American camps, some argued for accelerated nuclear disarmament, while others called for the additional expansion of such weapons.

During 1963 the Kennedy administration pursued a more aggressive Cold War policy and, at the same time, supported an agreement with the Soviet Union to prohibit the testing of nuclear weapons in the atmosphere. On February 8, 1963, the United States supported the overthrow of Abd al-Karim Qasim's regime in Iraq.[1] His government had threatened Anglo-American control of Iraq's oil and purportedly was conspiring with communists. Between 1,500 and 5,000 Iraqis were killed between February 8 and 10, 1963, and Abd al-Karim Qasim was captured, tried, and executed on February 8,1963.

Between June 23 and July 2, 1963, Kennedy went on a European tour with state visits in West Germany, Ireland, the United Kingdom, Italy, and the Vatican. The most significant element of the tour was his visit to West Germany and West Berlin, where German chancellor Konrad Adenauer, who had served as West German leader since 1949, was planning to retire.[2] On June 26, 1963, Kennedy affirmed American support for West Berlin and West Germany in his famous *"Ich bin ein Berliner"* (I am a Berliner) speech. (See Document 12.) He argued:

> Freedom has many difficulties and democracy is not perfect, but we have never had to put a wall up to keep our people in, to prevent them from leaving us. I want to say, on behalf of my countrymen, who live many miles away on the other side of the Atlantic, who are far distant from you, that they take the greatest pride that they have been able to share with you, even from a distance, the story of the last 18 years. . . . While the wall is the most obvious and vivid demonstration of the failures of the Communist system, for all the world to see, we take no satisfaction in it, for it is, as your Mayor has said, an offense not only against history but an offense against humanity, separating families, dividing husbands and wives and brothers and sisters, and dividing a people who wish to be joined together.
>
> What is true of this city is true of Germany—real, lasting peace in Europe can never be assured as long as one German out of four is denied the elementary right of free men, and that is to make a free choice. . . .
>
> Freedom is indivisible, and when one man is enslaved, all are not free. When all are free, then we can look forward to that day when this city will be joined as one and this country and this great Continent of Europe in a peaceful and hopeful globe. When that day finally comes, as it will, the people of West Berlin can take sober satisfaction in the fact that they were in the front lines for almost two decades.
>
> All free men, wherever they may live, are citizens of Berlin, and, therefore, as a free man, I take pride in the words *"Ich bin ein Berliner."*[3]

An estimated 450,000 Germans had gathered for the speech that, predictably, was applauded in the West and denounced in the East.

President John F. Kennedy delivers his famous "I am a Berliner" ("Ich bin ein Berliner") speech in front of the city hall in West Berlin concerning the Berlin Wall, June 26, 1963. At far right is the mayor of West Berlin, Willy Brandt. (Associated Press)

Since 1961 Kennedy had been interested in reaching an agreement with the Soviets on prohibiting the testing of nuclear weapons. Not knowing the actual strength of the Soviet nuclear arsenal, Kennedy hesitated on this issue until he acquired additional data. The Cuban missile crisis also delayed progress. By early 1963 Kennedy acquired satellite evidence that the United States held a significant advantage over the Soviets in nuclear weapons.[4]

In July 1963 he dispatched W. Averell Harriman, under secretary of state for political affairs, to Moscow to negotiate a test ban treaty. After several weeks of deliberations and Soviet refusal to allow American inspectors to verify compliance, a limited nuclear test ban treaty was signed on August 5, 1963, in Moscow, by Secretary of State Dean Rusk, Soviet foreign minister Andrei Gromyko, and British foreign secretary Lord Alec Douglas-Home. The treaty prohibited nuclear testing in the atmosphere, in space, or under water; confined the dispersal of radioactive debris to the nation conducting the test; and pledged the three nations to work toward disarmament and world peace. Kennedy succeeded in convincing most Americans, who were skeptical of Soviet credibility, that ratification of the treaty was in their best interest. The U.S. Senate by a vote of 80 to 19 approved the treaty on September 20, 1963, and Kennedy signed it on October 7, 1963.[5]

The military and political situation in South Vietnam deteriorated during the first half of 1963. By July Kennedy was facing a crisis because, despite increased American aid, the South Vietnamese forces had failed to suppress the procommunist Vietcong. Another factor was the lack of South Vietnamese support for the government of President Ngo Dinh Diem. Diem and his brother, Ngo Dinh Nhu—both Catholics in a Buddhist nation—had been in power since the Geneva Accords of 1954. Widespread corruption and the isolation of the leaders from the people were increasingly evident. Buddhist demonstrations opposing the Diem regime were violently suppressed but did not curb the opposition. As the summer ended generals in the South Vietnamese military considered whether they could continue to tolerate the Diem government. Kennedy was undecided on what America's next steps in South Vietnam should be. Should he expand American involvement and increase the number of troops—to ensure that South Vietnam would not fall to the communists? Or should he reduce the American commitment and prepare for an eventual withdrawal? And what impact would following either of these paths have on his prospects for re-election in 1964?

In August 1963 Henry Cabot Lodge arrived in Saigon as the new American ambassador. Kennedy and Secretary of State Dean Rusk directed Lodge to persuade Diem to resign and flee South Vietnam. Diem refused to consider resignation. Lodge then countered by requesting that Diem dismiss his corrupt brother Nhu. Again, Diem refused to comply, and Lodge concluded that the only alternative was for the United States to support a coup led by army generals. In September Kennedy received conflicting assessments from the State and Defense Departments. While the military reported gains against the communists, the State Department's assessment was negative—politically and socially, trends in South Vietnam were not aligned with American interests.[6] A senior level team, led by Secretary of State Robert McNamara and General Maxwell Taylor, was sent to Saigon in October to convince Diem that he had to adopt a reform agenda or risk the loss of American aid. Again, Diem refused to co-operate. South Vietnamese army generals moved forward with their planned overthrow of the Diem regime; led by General Duong Van Minh, the coup occurred on November 1, 1963, and resulted in the assassinations of Diem and Nhu. On November 19, 1963, Kennedy was still undecided on the direction of American policy in South Vietnam, and it appeared he was planning to review all options and make a decision early in 1964.[7]

Kennedy was assassinated on Friday, November 22, 1963, in Dallas, Texas. The assassin Lee Harvey Oswald's connections with Cuba and the Soviet Union led some to believe that Khrushchev or Castro may have been involved in the plot. However, both Federal Bureau of Investigation (FBI) and CIA intelligence suggested that Oswald acted alone. Whatever Kennedy might have done in Vietnam is not relevant, and his thinking on the levels and nature of U.S. involvement there was unsettled in any case. The new president—Lyndon B. Johnson—on November 26, 1963, affirmed American support for South Vietnam's struggle against communism.[8]

Kennedy's violent death was a defining moment in American history and coincided with the arrival of a more activist American electorate that was committed to—not just interested in—substantive changes at home and abroad. The civil rights movement was at the forefront of a new politics but was closely followed by vigorous demands for women's equality and a defense of civil liberties. American culture was being transformed from the supposed conformity of the 1950s to a society that recognized the value of individuality. Accompanying such changes was a growing distrust of large bureaucratic institutions, whether governments or corporations, that wielded significant power with seemingly few checks. While the American public generally wanted a strong presidency to stand up against communism, it was wary of the concentration of too much power in the hands of any one person. Johnson thus walked on unsure ground in dealing with the Cold War and other issues. He was also unsure of himself in foreign policy, so at first he left critical thinking on those matters to advisers. On domestic matters, however, Johnson moved more confidently.

After assuming the presidency on November 22, 1963, Lyndon Johnson moved quickly to consolidate his newly acquired power.[9] He retained Kennedy's cabinet into 1964 and pledged to continue to work for civil rights. He also appeared to sustain Kennedy's foreign policies, including support of South Vietnam. Prior to leaving for Dallas, Kennedy had signed an unexecuted policy memorandum that called for the withdrawal of

1,000 American military advisers, but on November 26, 1963—just four days after Kennedy's assassination—Johnson reversed that memorandum and reaffirmed American support for South Vietnam.[10]

Prior to becoming president, Johnson had expressed little interest in or knowledge of foreign affairs. As vice president he traveled the world—including South Vietnam—as Kennedy's representative. Johnson's domestic agenda was extensive during the year after he became president and would be extended further with his Great Society and War on Poverty programs in 1965 and1966. Before the close of 1963 he appointed the Warren Commission to investigate and report on Kennedy's assassination, and he announced that passage of Kennedy's civil rights bill would be a priority in 1964. He used his knowledge of Congress's ways and of the senators there to push hard for major civil rights legislation. Johnson turned on prosegregationist southern senators, broke their filibuster in March, and signed the Civil Rights Act of 1964 into law on July 2, 1964. This act prohibited most forms of racial segregation. He followed that measure with the Voting Rights Act in 1965, which opened the voting booths to millions of blacks who had been denied the right to vote in southern states. Johnson's Justice Department expanded to enforce the implementation of these laws.

While domestic progress was achieved on many fronts, there was clear evidence that major problems existed in the United States, especially in urban areas. In July 1964 a riot occurred in Harlem (New York City); in 1965 the Watts district of Los Angeles exploded in rioting, burning, and deaths; in 1966 more than 100 American cities had riots in the summer; and in 1967 Detroit and Newark, New Jersey, suffered the loss of many lives as a result of rioting. The causes of this urban unrest and distress were economic and social injustices, high unemployment, radical ideologies, police brutality, poor educational opportunities, and the losses incurred in the Vietnam War. These factors combined to provide combustible conditions, and the suppression of these outbreaks of violence resulted in additional anguish and increasing fear throughout the country. A presidential commission to study the causes of the riots concluded that America was dividing into two societies—one black, one white—and called for significant investments in education, community development, and other programs to reverse the divide. The Vietnam War, however, would undo such efforts and, in fact, it would widen social, cultural, and racial cleavages in America.

Between July 23 and 27, 1967, 43 people were killed; 1,189 injured; and more than 7,200 arrested in the Detroit riots that were triggered by a police raid on an after-hours club. (Associated Press)

A key member of Johnson's administration who argued with confidence that the war could be won was Secretary of Defense Robert McNamara. He was a former president of Ford Motor Company and believed that he could "manage" an expanded war in Vietnam and achieve victory against the communists. His calculations failed to consider the depth of Vietnamese nationalism and the commitment of North Vietnam to unify the country under its leadership.

During 1964 Cuba pressured the United States to withdraw from the Guantánamo Naval Base by blocking access to fresh water, and Johnson responded by building an independent water system for the facility. In the same year Panamanians rioted to have the United States withdraw from the Canal Zone, and Johnson initiated negotiations that later resulted in the return of the canal to Panama. Johnson was not reluctant to use force in Latin America. On April 28, 1965, twenty thousand U.S. Marines were sent to the Dominican Republic to block the return of the elected president Juan Bosch. Johnson backed the right-wing Reid Cabral and labeled Bosch a communist and friend of Castro, which was false. The Dominican intervention was criticized worldwide and diminished Johnson's global reputation. It also might have made him more combative in his desire to fight communism.

Conditions in Vietnam deteriorated significantly during 1964 because of political instability and growing support for the communist North Vietnamese and their plan to reunify the country. Republican conservative Barry Goldwater (R-AZ) denounced Johnson's leadership and management of the conflict in Vietnam and pointed to advances that had been made by the communists. Johnson reaffirmed his belief in the domino theory and the need to hold the line against communist aggression. He also feared that pursuing an alternative course would label him weak on foreign policy and hurt his prospects for election to a full term as president.

On August 2, 1964, North Vietnamese torpedo boats attacked the destroyer USS *Maddox* in the Gulf of Tonkin, off of North Vietnam's coast. In the ensuing fight the *Maddox* was damaged by one hit from North Vietnamese torpedo boats, an American plane was damaged but not downed, and three North Vietnamese boats were severely damaged. There were no American casualties, but three North Vietnamese were killed and several others injured. Two days later, on August 4, another American destroyer, the USS *Turner Joy*, reported that it was under attack and responded. In fact, the *Turner Joy* was not under attack—but its officers thought that it was.

These two events have been known as the Tonkin Gulf incident, which proved to be a major turning point in America's involvement in the Vietnam War. On the evening of August 4, 1964, President Johnson reported to the American people on the two attacks and stated that he would request authority from Congress to respond militarily. He argued that the Tonkin incidents were part of the North Vietnamese plan to test American resolve and led his listeners to believe that the attacks occurred in international waters. Johnson pressed for congressional authority to respond. The Gulf of Tonkin Resolution was debated for two days in both the Senate and the House of Representatives before it was approved overwhelmingly. It gave the president the power to use any non-nuclear military force he thought appropriate in Southeast Asia. Its supporters believed that the two attacks against American forces were unprovoked and in international waters. In the Senate the vote was 88 to 2 in favor, with only Senators Wayne Morse (D-OR) and Ernest Gruening (D-AK) voting against it (both men opposed intervention in Vietnam). In the House of Representatives the vote was 416 to 0. However, Congressman Eugene Siler (R-KY), who could not cast his ballot because of his absence, voiced his opposition.[11] Yet American involvement in a shooting war in Vietnam, a place few Americans could then locate on a map, was not uniformly popular. Before the end of 1964 opposition to the war began to be visible. In December 600 people participated in an antiwar demonstration led by folk singer Joan Baez.[12]

In 1964 Johnson had no difficulty winning the Democratic nomination for president at the party's national convention in Atlantic City, New Jersey, from August 24 to 27. His running mate was liberal Senator Hubert Humphrey of Minnesota. At the convention a feared debate on civil rights —related to the presence of two delegations from Mississippi—did not materialize publically, though it did weaken the Democrats internally.[13] The Republicans nominated Senator Barry Goldwater of Arizona, a staunch conservative who opposed the Kennedy-Johnson agenda and feared that the United States was moving too far to the left. Goldwater also believed that the United States must oppose any additional expansion of communism, and he argued that the use of tactical nuclear weapons should be authorized if necessary. The Republican campaign never gained momentum after its convention, but it illustrated what Nixon called the "southern strategy"—Goldwater won only 52 electoral votes (from Arizona and southern states) compared to 486 for Johnson. Johnson won 61.1 percent of the popular vote versus Goldwater's 38.5 percent.

Johnson proceeded to focus his full term as president on his domestic agenda that he envisioned would extend Franklin D. Roosevelt's New Deal. His domestic achievements after his inauguration in 1965 were many and included the Voting Rights Act, Medicare, and multiple programs in support of education. But in Vietnam Johnson's policy was failing. American troop levels expanded significantly. When Kennedy died 16,300 Americans were in South Vietnam, and by the end of 1964 the number was 23,300. In subsequent years the numbers were 184,300 in 1965; 385,300 in 1966; 485,600 in 1967; and 536,100 in 1968 (Johnson's final year as president). The American death count increased significantly with the passing years. It was 206 in 1964; 1,863 in 1965; 6,144 in 1966; 11,153 in 1967; and 16,589 in 1968 (the highest level of the Vietnam war).[14] Most of these soldiers were young men who had been drafted into the army and other branches of the armed services.

Johnson attempted to direct the nation's attention to his domestic achievements and his work on arms control. In 1967 he signed an agreement with the Soviets that prohibited the use of nuclear weapons in space or on satellites circling earth. In 1968 the United States signed the Nuclear Non-Proliferation Treaty to limit the number of states with nuclear weapons. While these developments were important components of Johnson's legacy, he could not escape the mounting criticism of American policy in South Vietnam. On April 7, 1965, Johnson gave his "Peace without Conquest" address at The Johns Hopkins University in Baltimore, Maryland (Document 13). He provided his rationale for expanding the American commitment when he stated:

> ... Tonight Americans and Asians are dying for a world where each people may choose its own path to change. This is the principle for which our ancestors fought in the valleys of Pennsylvania. It is the principle for which our sons fight tonight in the jungles of Viet-Nam. Viet-Nam is far away from this quiet campus. We have no territory there, nor do we seek any. The war is dirty and brutal and difficult. And some 400 young men, born into an America that is bursting with opportunity and promise, have ended their lives on Viet-Nam's steaming soil. ... We fight because we must fight if we are to live in a world where every country can shape its own destiny. And only in such a world will our own freedom be finally secure. ... The world as it is in Asia is not a serene or peaceful place. The first reality is that North Viet-Nam has attacked the independent nation of South Viet-Nam. Its object is total conquest.[15]

Despite Johnson's efforts to rally the nation in support of the American intervention in Vietnam, protests and demonstrations against the war mounted. Johnson was plagued by a "credibility gap"—people found it increasingly difficult to believe his statements on Vietnam and other issues. During 1965 protests and teach-ins against the war occurred at dozens of colleges and universities, including the University of Michigan and the University of California, Berkeley; civil rights and feminist activists along with antipoverty protesters joined in major demonstrations in Washington, DC, and elsewhere, including overseas. Civil disobedience tactics were used (e.g., sit-ins, burning of draft cards). The anti–Vietnam

War movement expanded significantly during 1966 and 1967, and it attracted the support of significant numbers of American academics, religious leaders, reformers, and citizens. In 1967 Martin Luther King, Jr. led an antiwar protest march in Chicago, and on October 21, 1967, radicals—including Abbie Hoffman, Jerry Rubin, and Allen Ginsburg— led about 30,000 protesters in a march on the Pentagon.

The Vietnam War was polarizing American society, regional and generational differences were evident, and the war issue was frequently clouded by other political, social, and economic agendas.[16] Political opposition to the war also increased. Senator Wayne Morse (D-OR) was the war's most vocal critic in the Senate. In 1967 Senator J. William Fulbright, chair of the Senate Foreign Relations Committee, conducted hearings on the conduct of the war that were generally negative. Fulbright emerged as a major critic of the war. Antiwar leaders asked Senators Robert Kennedy (D-NY) and George McGovern (D-SD) to challenge Johnson for the presidential nomination in 1968. Both declined, and on November 30, 1967, Senator Eugene McCarthy (D-MN) announced that he would challenge Johnson for the Democratic presidential nomination in 1968, and the only issue would be the Vietnam War.

In *1968: The Year That Rocked the World*, Mark Kurlansky observed: "Despite all of this opposition, Lyndon Johnson, after five years in office, seemed a solid favorite to win another term. A Gallup poll released on January 2 [1968] showed that just less than half the population, 45 percent, believed it was a mistake to have gotten involved in Vietnam."[17] However, any confidence that Johnson may have enjoyed was shattered on January 30, 1968, when the North Vietnamese and the Vietcong launched their Tet offensive against the South Vietnamese, American, and allied forces (South Korea, Australia, New Zealand, and Thailand). The offensive consisted of multiple surprise attacks against military and civilian targets, including an assault on the American embassy in Saigon. More than 80,000 communist troops were involved in the Tet offensive. While the offensive was contained and eventually suppressed, it demonstrated a level of communist strength and commitment that was unexpected and that was at odds with the positive reports that emanated from the Johnson White House before the attack.[18]

Support for Johnson and American involvement in the war plummeted in February as the antiwar movement gained credibility and support. Until this point McCarthy's campaign in the upcoming New Hampshire Democratic primary was lackluster; after Tet it gained momentum with increased financial and volunteer help. In New Hampshire on March 12, 1968, McCarthy gained 42 percent of the Democratic primary vote to Johnson's 49 percent, which demonstrated that Johnson was vulnerable. On March 16, 1968, Senator Robert F. Kennedy (D-NY) announced that he would run for the Democratic presidential nomination as an antiwar candidate. The antiwar movement expanded and gained the support of many who were opposed to the war itself or to Johnson's leadership and management of it. On March 31, 1968, in a nationally televised speech, Johnson announced that he would not seek the 1968 Democratic presidential nomination.[19]

Throughout the spring the fighting in Vietnam intensified, as did the antiwar movement and social unrest in the United States. Martin Luther King, Jr. was assassinated on the evening of April 4, 1968, in Memphis, Tennessee. On April 12, 1968, a student riot occurred at the University of California, Berkeley, and the local police brutally suppressed it. Students in western Europe reacted by demonstrating and rioting against the war. On April 26 a million American college and high school students boycotted classes to express their antwar sentiments. It appeared that American society was unraveling. Kennedy and McCarthy opposed one another in Democratic primaries throughout the spring, and Kennedy expanded his campaign beyond the war issue and redefined himself by emerging as an advocate for a social agenda based on civil and human rights as well as civil liberties. Kennedy won primaries in Nebraska and Indiana but lost to McCarthy in Oregon. Both focused their energies on the California primary scheduled for June 4, 1968. The winner would have to defeat Vice President Hubert Humphrey, who had announced his candidacy but was not running in the primaries. Kennedy defeated McCarthy but was assassinated by a delusional lone gunman. He died early on June 6, 1968. Many who supported Kennedy did not move into the McCarthy camp. Senator George McGovern (D-SD) was urged to announce his candidacy. He hesitated but did announce that he was running on August 10 —two weeks prior to the convention. The Chicago Democratic Convention (August 26–29, 1968) coincided with the Youth International Party (Yippies) meeting that was intended to impact the Democrats. The convention was a violent spectacle with daily televised conflicts between police and demonstrators.[20] Humphrey was nominated on the first ballot.

The Republicans nominated Richard M. Nixon, who had been campaigning since early January 1968. George Wallace of Alabama received the nomination of the American Independent Party. His major issue was stopping the federal government from interfering with segregated schools in the South. While Nixon ran a campaign based on law and order and a promised but unspecified change in Vietnam, Humphrey called for a continuation of Johnson's Great Society programs. Nixon enjoyed a comfortable lead at the outset in September, but the race narrowed in October, and Humphrey attempted to separate himself from Johnson on the war issue. Given the chaos of the summer and the continued antiwar sentiment, the 1968 presidential race was closer than anticipated. Nixon won with 301 electoral votes and 43.4 percent of the popular vote to Humphrey's 191 electoral votes and 42.7 percent of the popular vote, and Wallace's 48 electoral votes and 13.5 percent of the vote.

1968 was a turbulent and memorable year. In addition to the assassinations of King and Kennedy, the Tet offensive, the withdrawal of Johnson from the presidential race, student and race riots, the election of Nixon, and a shift in popular opinion on the war, the year witnessed a crisis with North Korea over the seizure of the USS *Pueblo* and the detainment of its crew for 11 months; massive student riots in France that culminated with the "Bloody Monday" riot of May 6, 1968, and the subsequent general strike by 9 million French workers; protests by Polish students and workers in the spring; the liberal "Prague Spring" in Czechoslovakia and its suppression by the Soviet invasion of August 20, 1968; and violent student conflicts with police and military in Mexico City on October 2, 1968. In the conclusion of his *1968: The Year That Rocked the World*, Mark Kurlansky noted:

> ... Despite the thousands dead in Vietnam, the million starved in Biafra, the crushing of idealism in Poland and Czechoslovakia, the massacre in Mexico, the clubbings [sic] and brutalization of dissenters all over the world, the murder of two Americans who most offered the world hope, to many it was a year of great possibilities ... [21]

Nixon's promised law and order presidency was about to begin, and it would end with Nixon's resignation because of his illegal actions.

As indicated previously, Nixon's ascendency in American politics was based upon his alliances with conservative political forces—Whittaker Chambers, Joseph McCarthy (during the early days of 1950), midwestern and western agricultural and mining interests, and the southerners who felt betrayed by Johnson and the Democratic Party with their support of civil rights legislation and, in particular, the forced integration of their public schools. Nixon's approach to the Cold War and the direction of his foreign policy surprised many. He opened relations with China and through a policy of triangular diplomacy exploited the tensions in Soviet-Chinese relations, pursued détente (an easing of tensions) with the Soviet Union, entered into arms control agreements with the Soviet Union, brought an end to the Vietnam War, and interfered directly where he deemed it necessary—as in the Yom Kippur War and the overthrow of the elected government of Salvador Allende in Chile. His national security adviser and later secretary of state was Henry Kissinger, a former Harvard University professor, aide to New York Governor Nelson Rockefeller, and the author of A World Restored: Metternich, Castlereagh, and the Problem of the Peace, 1812–1822 (1957),[22] which analyzed the rebuilding of Europe after the generation of wars of the French Revolution and Napoleonic era. Nixon and Kissinger were ambitious and wanted to make a substantive, successful, and long-term imprint on American foreign policy.[23] They were interested in sustaining the balance of power with an edge for toward the United States. They did not envision a post–Cold War or post–Soviet Union world order.

Since the late 1950s Sino-Soviet relations had been strained over border disputes. In 1964 the relationship became aggravated when a minor skirmish occurred between the two powers, and five years later—in 1969—the violence escalated with the Zhenbao Island incident over rival claims to the island in which Soviet and Chinese soldiers were killed.[24] During this crisis Nixon sent a quiet message to the Chinese leader Mao Zedong that the United States was interested in closer relations with China. Mao responded favorably and, in the spring of 1971, arranged for an invitation to be extended to the U.S. Table Tennis team to visit China (this was known as ping-pong diplomacy). During the same time Kissinger made secret trips to Beijing, and on July 15, 1971, both powers announced that Nixon would visit China in February 1972. Reactions both in the United States and throughout the world were generally favorable.

The Soviet Union was caught off guard and recognized that a potential realignment of power could result. Within the United States the old weakened China lobby feared—correctly—that the power and prestige of the Chinese Nationalists (in Taiwan) would be jeopardized.[25]

Nixon and his wife Pat, Kissinger, Secretary of State William P. Rogers, and their entourage visited China between February 21 and 28, 1972. The staunch anticommunist Nixon met Mao Zedong, and on February 28, 1972, they issued the joint Shanghai Communiqué (Document 15), which led several years later to normalizing relations between the United States and the People's Republic of China.[26] The recognized success of Nixon's strategy and the fear that a U.S.-Chinese alliance was possible made the Soviet Union more interested in détente with the United States.[27]

Chinese communist leader Chairman Mao Zedong (left) welcomes U.S. president Richard Nixon at his house in Beijing on February 21, 1972. President Nixon urged China to join the United States in a "long march together" on different roads to world peace. (AFP/Getty Images)

Even before Nixon's election as president, the U.S. State Department was considering the value of lessening tensions with the Soviet Union (Document 14). However, Nixon and Kissinger advanced that objective in hopes of long-term agreements with the Soviets on nuclear peace. Nixon followed his triumphal trip to Beijing with a visit to Moscow on May 22, 1972, to meet with Leonid Brezhnev and other Soviet leaders to discuss arms control agreements. The results were impressive, especially to Nixon's critics. The Strategic Arms Limitation Treaty (SALT I) Agreement and the Anti-Ballistic Missile (ABM) Treaty were substantive agreements on arms control. SALT I was the initial agreement between the Soviet Union and the United States that limited nuclear weapons, and the ABM Treaty prohibited the development of defensive antimissile systems. It appeared that the Cold War was thawing and moving to a phase of peaceful coexistence.[28] Later, in 1974, Nixon again travelled to the Soviet Union and pursued additional arms control negotiations with Brezhnev. However, no additional agreements were reached, as Nixon was overwhelmed by the Watergate scandal.[29]

In South Vietnam Nixon wanted to transfer the responsibility for fighting the war to the South Vietnamese, and his goal was to withdraw American troops as soon as possible. During 1969 Nixon expanded the bombing of North Vietnam and Cambodia and opened peace talks in Paris. He visited South Vietnam in July 1969 and upon his return announced that the United States would proceed with the "Vietnamization" of the war and soon begin phased pullouts of American troops.[30] At the same time the air attacks on North Vietnam and Cambodia were intensified, and Laos was also attacked. When this air campaign proved ineffective, Nixon authorized an invasion of Cambodia on April 30, 1970, to interdict supplies and reinforcements coming from North Vietnam through Cambodia to South Vietnam. This decision enraged those who opposed the war, and demonstrations against the "Cambodian incursion" began on Friday, May 1, 1970, and continued for weeks.

At Kent State University in Kent, Ohio, students demonstrated on May 1 and became violent over the weekend, with considerable property burnt and destroyed. A state of emergency was declared, and the National Guard was ordered into the city and onto the campus. On Monday, May 4, another student demonstration was organized, and the National Guard attempted to disband it. The students refused to comply. At about 12:30 p.m.

Masked national guardsmen fire a barrage of tear gas into a crowd of demonstrators on the campus of Kent State University on May 4, 1970. When the gas dissipated, four students lay dead, and several others were injured. Hundreds of students had staged the demonstration to protest the Nixon administration's expansion of the Vietnam War into Cambodia. (Bettmann/Corbis)

national guardsmen opened fire on the students and killed four—two demonstrators and two students passing by on their way to class. The deaths at Kent State led to additional antiwar demonstrations and violence, and hundreds of colleges and universities closed because of student strikes. The nation was appalled by the Kent State massacre and more were won over to the antiwar movement.[31]

Additional opposition to the Vietnam War was generated by the appearance of excerpts of the "Pentagon Papers" in the *Washington Post* and the *New York Times*. Nixon attempted to prevent the publication of these documents (which actually revealed very little that was new), but the Supreme Court ruled in favor of the newspapers. Americans were disturbed and ashamed by the duplicity that had characterized American policy in Vietnam.[32] The war and the peace talks dragged on through 1971 and 1972. Nixon's success as president—as well as the unacceptability of Senator George McGovern, his Democratic challenger in the 1972 presidential election—resulted in a landslide victory for the incumbent. Nixon won 520 electoral votes and 60.7 percent of the popular vote to McGovern's 17 electoral votes and 37.5 percent of the vote. On January 27, 1973, an agreement was reached with the North Vietnamese in Paris calling for an immediate cease-fire, the withdrawal of all foreign (including American) troops, and the reunification of Vietnam through peaceful negotiations. On February 12, 1973, seventy-three American prisoners of war were released and by March 29, 1973, all American troops had been withdrawn from Vietnam.[33] In little over two years South Vietnam would fall to North Vietnam, and the country would be reunified.[34]

In Latin America the Nixon administration was vigilant as it sought to detect efforts by communists to gain power. Concern in Washington was elevated in September 1970 with the election of an avowed Marxist, Salvador Allende, as president of Chile. Nixon monitored numerous failed attempts to discredit Allende and supported opponents with funding to organize strikes and create economic and social disorder there. The United States welcomed the coup d'état engineered by right-wing general Augusto Pinochet on September 11, 1973, that resulted in Allende's death.[35]

Within a few weeks Nixon faced his next Cold War challenge in the unexpected Yom Kippur War. On October 6, 1973, Egypt, Syria, Iraq, and Jordan launched a surprise attack on Israel to regain lost territory and, if possible, destroy the Israeli state. They were supported by the Soviet Union, Saudi Arabia, Pakistan, and other Islamic states. During the early days of the struggle, the aggressors scored significant gains against the Israelis, by October 9 the Arab advance was contained and, by October 16 the Israelis launched successful operations that not only recovered lost territory, but also crossed into lands that Israel had not previously occupied. The Israelis lost considerable equipment that Nixon ordered replaced through an airlift. Throughout the brief war Kissinger offered to mediate a cease-fire, and the United States noted that that Soviet Union was shifting large numbers of troops to areas where they could interfere in the military activities. On October 24, Nixon ordered that all American forces be placed on a nuclear alert, and he elevated the DEFCON level from 3 to 2. The Soviets were shocked by the American action and sought to diffuse the crisis. On October 25, 1973, the warring parties agreed to a cease-fire. The Arab states responded to American intervention with an oil embargo that led to the 1973 oil crisis in the United States. Kissinger followed up on his diplomatic initiatives and established a dialogue that would eventually lead to the Camp David Accords, and in July 1974 Nixon made a state visit to Egypt.[36]

Nixon's achievements in foreign policy and the Cold War were diminished in the minds of most Americans by the Watergate scandal that not only distracted Nixon, but also came to absorb him and his administration in 1974. The cover-up of an unsuccessful burglary at the Democratic National Headquarters on June 17, 1972 and revelations of many abuses of presidential power, led to a vote on July 27, 1974, by the House Judiciary Committee to impeach Nixon. He resigned on August 8,1974 rather than face impeachment. The Watergate revelations and subsequent process eroded any optimism or energy that resulted from Nixon's foreign and domestic policies.

NOTES

1. Abd al-Karim Qasim led the successful July 14, 1958 coup that removed the pro-Western King Ahmad Mukhtan Baban.

2. Adenauer retired on October 16, 1963, and was replaced by Ludwig Erhard. Adenauer died on April 19, 1967.

3. John F. Kennedy, *Public Papers of the Presidents of the United States: John F. Kennedy, Containing the Public Messages, Speeches, and Statements of the President, January 1 to November 22, 1963* (Washington, DC: U. S. Government Printing Office, 1964), 524–25.

4. Richard Reeves, *President Kennedy: Profile of Power* (New York: Simon and Schuster, 1993), 229.

5. Ibid., 548–80.

6. Ibid., 595.

7. Ibid., 602–80. Also see Joseph Ellis, "Making Vietnam History," *Reviews in American History*, 28, no. 4 (2000): 625–29.

8. James G. Blight and Janet M. Lang, *The Fog of War: Eleven Lessons from the Life of Robert S. McNamara* (Lanham, MD: Rowman and Littlefield, 2005), 276.

9. The best source on Johnson's first months in office is Robert Caro, *The Passage of Power: The Years of Lyndon Johnson* (New York: Knopf, 2012). Also see Robert Dallek, *Lyndon B. Johnson: Portrait of a President* (New York: Oxford University Press, 2005).

10. Reeves, *President Kennedy*, 513–14.

11. Edwin E. Moise, *Tonkin Gulf and the Escalation of the Vietnam War* (Chapel Hill: University of North Carolina Press, 2004), 78–92.

12. One of the best books on the anti–Vietnam War movement is Charles DeBenedetti, *An American Ordeal: The Anti-War Movement of the Vietnam Era*, Syracuse Studies on Peace and Conflict Resolution (Syracuse, NY: Syracuse University Press, 1990).

13. Taylor Branch, *Pillar of Fire: America in the King Years, 1963–65* (New York: Simon and Schuster, 1999), 444–70.

14. Department of Defense Manpower Data Center, http://www.american library.com/vietnam/vwatl.htm.

15. Lyndon Baines Johnson, *Public Papers of the Presidents of the United States: Lyndon B. Johnson, 1965*. Vol. I (Washington, DC: Government Printing Office, 1966: entry 172), 394–99.

16. Among the best sources on the antiwar protests are Norman Mailer, *The Armies of the Night: History as a Novel, the Novel as History* (New York: Plume, 1995); Melvin Small and William D. Hoover, *Give Peace a Chance: Exploring the Vietnam Antiwar Movement: Essays from the Charles DeBenedetti Memorial Conference*, Syracuse Studies on Peace and Conflict Resolution (Syracuse, NY: Syracuse University Press, 1992); and David L. Anderson and John Ernst (eds.), *The War That Never Ends: New Perspectives on the Vietnam War* (Lexington: University Press of Kentucky, 2007).

17. Mark Kurlansky, *1968: The Year That Rocked the World* (New York: Random House/Ballantine, 2004), 13.

18. Stephen Weiss and Clark Dougan, *Nineteen Sixty-Eight* (Boston: Time/ Life Education, 1983), 22–23.

19. A very good account of Johnson's response to the tribulations of the spring of 1968 can be found in Robert Dallek, *The Flawed Giant: Lyndon Johnson and His Times, 1961–1973* (New York: Oxford University Press, 1999).

20. David Farber, *Chicago '68* (Chicago: University of Chicago Press, 1994), 167–201; Todd Gitlin, *The Sixties: Years of Hope, Days of Rage*, rev. ed. (New York: Bantam, 1993), 319–31.

21. Kurlansky, *1968*, 380.

22. Henry Kissinger, *A World Restored: Metternich, Castlereagh, and the Problems of Peace, 1812–1822* (Boston: Houghton Mifflin, 1957).

23. Without doubt the best available book on the Nixon-Kissinger partnership is Robert Dallek, *Nixon and Kissinger: Partners in Power* (New York: Harper Perennial, 2007).

24. National Archives, *The Sino-Soviet Border Conflict, 1969: U.S. Reaction Diplomatic Maneuvers*, edited by William Burr. National Security Archive

Electronic Briefing Book No. 49 (June 12, 2001), http://www.gwu.edu/~nsarchiv/NSAEBB/NSAEBB49/

25. Stephen E. Ambrose, *Nixon: The Triumph of a Politician, 1962–1972* (New York: Touchstone, 1990), 453.

26. Conrad Black, *A Life in Full: Richard M. Nixon* (New York: Public Affairs, 2007), 780–82. Also see Margaret McMillan, *Nixon and Mao: The Week That Changed the World* (New York: Random House, 2007).

27. Dallek, *Nixon and Kissinger,* 300.

28. Black, *A Life in Full,* 920–24.

29. Ibid., 963.

30. Ambrose, *Nixon,* 281–83.

31. See Scott Bills, *Kent State/May 4: Echoes through a Decade* (Kent, OH: Kent State University Press, 1988) and William W. Scranton, "The Report of the President's Commission on Campus Unrest" (Washington, DC: U.S. Government Printing Office, 1970).

32. Ambrose, *Nixon,* 446–48.

33. Ibid., 473.

34. The Vietnam War resulted in 58,282 American dead; 303,644 wounded; 1,654 missing in action; and between 65 and 119 deaths of American prisoners of war. Source: *National Archives Statistical Information about Fatal Casualties of the Vietnam War* as of January 23, 2013, http://www.archives.gov/research/militray/vietnam-war/casualty-statistics.html.

35. Black, *A Life in Full,* 921.

36. Ibid., 951–58.

CHAPTER 6

THE END OF THE COLD
WAR AND BEYOND

On December 25, 1991, the Soviet Union ceased to exist, and the Cold War ended. Many scholars and commentators have advanced varying explanations for the demise of the Soviet Union, and questions about the Soviet collapse have been multiple, far-reaching, and complex. Did the Soviet Union disintegrate because of Reagan's policies? Was it because of a lack of leadership? Was the Soviet economy so hopelessly distressed that it eroded all faith in the political structure? Did Gorbachev's reforms create a downward spiral for the Soviet Union? Were the Soviet people unable to respond positively to the reforms? Did Gorbachev's generation of Soviet leaders lose faith in their own system with its failure to realize a communist society? Was the Soviet Union inherently an "unnatural" or "artificial" state that was doomed from the outset because it lacked national cohesion?

It is not our purpose here to examine all of these issues; rather, we will consider the end of the Cold War and its impact on the United States.[1] This concluding chapter will examine the American response to Soviet expansion during the 1970s with a particular focus on the last years of the presidency of Jimmy Carter and the two terms of the Reagan administration, the multiple problems experienced by the Soviet Union—including the breakup of the Eastern Bloc and the rapid disintegration of the Soviet Union itself—and the American reaction to the end of the Cold War. Finally, the chapter will conclude with a discussion of post–Cold War U.S.-Russian relations.

In the spring of 1975 South Vietnam collapsed when the North Vietnamese launched a successful invasion of the South in violation of a pledge not to do so. This capstone failure of American policy in Vietnam followed by less than a year the Watergate political crisis and the resignation of President Richard Nixon on August 9, 1974. Vice President Gerald Ford assumed the presidency and during his brief term continued the policy of détente with the Soviet Union, signing the Helsinki Agreement on August 1, 1975, which was designed to improve East-West relations through clarifications of both state and individual rights. Many considered the Helsinki accord to be the high point of the era of détente. During the early and mid-1970s, the Soviet Union gained momentum in the Cold War over the United States. Its economy was booming because of its increased oil production, it produced more steel than the United States, and it significantly increased the size of its conventional and nuclear arms stores. The Soviet reputation throughout the underdeveloped world was improving, and Somalia, Yemen, and other nations were moving into the Soviet sphere of influence. Other than the mishandling of the writer Alexandr Solzhenitsyn, who was deported in 1974, and restrictions on human rights, the Soviet Union experienced measurable progress. All this while the United States was suffering from defeat in Asia, the worst political scandal in its history, continuing social unrest, and the worst economy since the Depression. This challenging situation was inherited by President Jimmy Carter, who defeated Ford in a close election (50.08 percent to 48.02 percent of the popular vote and 297 to 240 electoral votes) on November 2, 1976.

Carter's foreign policy focused on human rights and restoring the credibility and reputation of the United States. Carter established an investigative and reporting agency in the State Department that developed country reports on human rights policies, advances, and violations that served to determine American policy in several countries, including Argentina, Nicaragua, Cambodia, El Salvador, Panama, and Chile. Some of Carter's foreign policy experts, including his national security adviser Zbigniew Brzezinski, were more concerned with the Cold War and relations with the Soviet Union. Carter advanced the U.S.-China relationship when he recognized the People's Republic of China as the government of China; Taiwan was seen as part of China but given special status and recognition. Carter's most notable success was mediating a peace treaty between Egypt and Israel, the Camp David Accords (Document 16 on March 26, 1979). That agreement not only prevented the outbreak of another war in the

This photo taken on November 4, 1979, the first day of the occupation of the U.S. embassy in Tehran, Iran, shows American hostages being paraded by their militant Iranian captors. The hostage crisis lasted until January 20, 1981. (Bettmann/Corbis)

Middle East and the related threat of limiting American access to the region's oil, but it also restricted the Soviet Union from extending its interests in the region. The most difficult crisis of the Carter administration was the Iran hostage crisis from November 4, 1979 to January 20, 1981, when 52 Americans were held hostage in Tehran by Iranian Islamist radicals who supported the revolutionary regime of the Ayatollah Ruhollah Khomeini.

Carter stepped back from the policy of containing the Soviet Union during the early years of his administration and pursued a goal of eliminating all nuclear weapons. His proposal to initiate the process of reducing strategic nuclear delivery vehicles (ICBMs) was the centerpiece of the SALT II agreement that was signed on June 18, 1979, in Vienna by Carter and Soviet leader Leonid Brezhnev. Carter sent the agreement to the Senate for ratification, but after the Soviet invasion of Afghanistan on December 14, 1979, Carter requested that the ratification process be

delayed. Détente, already weakened by mounting suspicions by both
powers that they were returning to more aggressive policies, unraveled in
1979 and 1980 with the Soviet invasion of Afghanistan and the American
reaction to it. Additional responses to the Soviet invasion included the
pronouncement of the Carter Doctrine, which specified that the United
States would not allow a nonregional nation to gain control of the Persian
Gulf; the cessation of a proposed wheat deal with the Soviet Union;
and the prohibition of American athletes participating in the Moscow
Olympics. Carter adopted a hard line with the Soviet Union during the
last year of his presidency, and his aspirations to improve Soviet-
American relations were thwarted by the reckless adventures of an overly
confident Soviet Union.

By the summer of 1980 economic and social conditions in Poland had
deteriorated to such a level that a trade union federation (Solidarity) was
founded on August 31, 1980, at the Lenin Shipyards in Gdansk. Its leader
was Lech Walesa, an electrician who became a human rights activist, trade
union organizer, Nobel Peace laureate (1983), and president of Poland
(1990–1995). In less than a month almost two dozen other unions joined
the movement to expand the organized protest against economic conditions in Poland, and within a year more than a third of Poland's
working-age population were members. Solidarity enjoyed the support of
the Polish Catholic Church and the new pope, John Paul II. The inability
of Communist leader Wojciech Jaruzelski, who was in power from 1980 to
1989, to effectively suppress and abolish Solidarity was an clear sign that
weaknesses existed within the purportedly absolutist Polish communist
government.[2]

During the 1980 presidential election between the Democratic incumbent Carter and the Republican Ronald Reagan, Reagan called for the
restoration of America's military strength and global reputation, and he
promised to roll back Carter's windfall profit tax that impeded domestic
oil production. Carter argued that he deserved another term because he
had maintained the peace and would continue progressive policies such
as the Equal Rights Amendment (ERA). Carter was hindered by the
Iranian hostage situation, a poor economy, high unemployment, and
heightened tensions with the Soviet Union. Reagan decisively defeated
Carter on November 4, 1980, with 50.75 percent of the popular vote to
Carter's 41.01 percent (third-party challenger John Anderson received

6.61 percent). Reagan acquired 489 electoral votes to Carter's 49, and Anderson did not win any electoral votes. The 1980 presidential election constituted a realignment of electoral politics and the resurgence of the Republican Party at the national level.[3]

"Trust but verify" and "peace through strength" were two phrases that President Ronald Reagan used repeatedly to refer to his foreign policy and in particular his approach to the Soviet Union. Reagan abandoned détente and also challenged and countered the "Brezhnev Doctrine," which stated that once a nation was in the communist camp, it would never return to capitalism, with the "Reagan Doctrine," which promised logistical support and finances to anticommunist insurgents in Latin America, Africa, and Asia. The Reagan administration conducted an active anticommunist foreign policy strategy that built upon and expanded the tougher foreign policy of Carter's last 18 months in office. Carter's human rights–oriented policies were reshaped, sometimes ignored, and manipulated by Reagan to attain his objectives—the resurgence of American power and influence throughout the world and the acceleration of the decline of the Soviet Union.

During the 1980s Latin American politics were volatile and, in many instances, violent. The Reagan administration was involved in supporting prodemocracy movements in Bolivia, Honduras, Brazil, Uruguay, and Surinam. The United States also supported the post–Falkland War collapse of the Argentinian military junta and the installation of a more democratic government. The most visible American actions that were designed to feign off the advance of communism in the Western Hemisphere included the invasion of Grenada (1983) and the support of anticommunism in Guatemala, El Salvador, and Nicaragua. In 1983, fearing the expansion of communism in the Caribbean through a communist government in Grenada, Reagan denounced the New Jewel Movement's overthrow of the Grenadian government in 1979 and the establishment of the new People's Revolutionary Government of Grenada. The United States was wary of Grenada's increasingly warm relationships with Cuba and the Soviet Union under the leadership of Prime Minister Maurice Bishop. During 1983 feuding within the Grenadian government became extremely intense and led to Bishop's assassination on October 19, 1983, in a coup d'état led by Bishop's rival, Bernard Coard. The Reagan administration seized the opportunity and reported that law and order had disintegrated in Grenada, and the lives of American medical students studying at the True Blue Medical Facility in Grenada were at risk. On October 25, 1983, the United States, responding to a petition from the Organization of Eastern Caribbean States to intervene in Grenada to eliminate this threat to regional security, launched an invasion of Grenada with a force of 7,300 American troops and a few hundred Jamaican and other regional troops. Within a few weeks the American forces eliminated or captured the limited Grenadian forces and several hundred Cuban advisers who were on the island. Nineteen American troops were killed and 116 were wounded. The medical students were rescued and transported to the United States. A pro-American government was installed, and all American troops were withdrawn by December 15, 1983. The U.S. victory was applauded by most Americans but criticized by the United Nations and most nations, including American allies Great Britain and Canada.

Guatemala was embroiled in a brutal, long-standing civil war between 1960 and 1996. This struggle between the Guatemalan government and the remnants of the Mayans and the rural peasantry resulted in 140,000 to 200,000 deaths and missing persons. Since the 1954 CIA-supported coup that overthrew Jacobo Árbenz Guzmán and his leftist government, Guatemala had been led by constitutional governments dominated by the military. The Mayans and peasants pressed for reforms and fought an ongoing guerrilla war against the government. Assassinations of government leaders and others were frequent. In 1968 American ambassador John Gordon Mein was assassinated. The government increasingly fell under the right-wing influence of the military, which sought to eliminate the enemy. Genocide against the Mayans was conducted with little external criticism.

When Reagan came into office Guatemala was being led by President Fernando Romeo Lucas García, who came to power on March 7, 1978. During his regime atrocities against the Mayans, peasants, and their growing number of supporters increased. Death squads and paramilitary organizations terrorized the country and acted with the unofficial support of the government. In 1981 the insurgents launched a major offensive that resulted in the decline of the military's support for Lucas García. On March 23, 1982, junior army officers led by José Efraín Ríos Mott conducted a coup d'état and overthrew Lucas García, and Efraín Ríos Mott became the president of Guatemala. Despite stated policies to the contrary, the new regime quickly launched a terrorist and repressive strategy to eliminate what it labeled the communist opposition. Reagan stated his support for Efraín Ríos Mott during a state visit to Guatemala on December 4, 1982, and applauded him for his work on social justice. The Reagan administration provided this government with more than $10 million in military aid in 1982–1983. Efraín Ríos Mott was overthrown in another military coup on August 8, 1993, that was led by Minister of Defense Oscar Humberto Mejia Victores. Reagan continued to support right-wing Guatemalan governments in exchange for their anticommunist policies. Efraín Ríos Mott returned to power in 1995 as the leader of the Guatemalan Republican Front Party.

El Salvador experienced a civil war between 1979 and 1992 that resulted in a bloodbath that took more than 75,000 lives. Civil war broke out after the chaos following the fraudulent 1977 presidential election that resulted in the installation of General Carlos Humberto Romero as president. The protagonists were the right-wing government and a coalition of opposing groups known as the Farabundo Marti National Liberation Front. Demonstrations and violence spread, and Romero's government responded by denouncing the opposition as communists who were influenced by foreign nations. Death squads operated openly and with impunity, and more than 2,500 people were murdered during 1978 and 1979. The international community, including the United States, denounced the government's policies toward its political opposition and demanded that it cease allowing right-wing death squads to operate. A military junta replaced Romero on October 15, 1979. The Carter administration viewed this change as an opportunity for an intervention to bring the civil war to an end on terms that were favorable to the United States. This intervention was implemented with the allocation of $5.7 million in military aid in return for continuing land reforms that would appease the opposition. The Catholic Church, under the leadership of Óscar Arnulfo Romero y Galdámez, the archbishop of San Salvador, joined in the condemnations of the government and the slaughter. A death squad assassinated Archbishop Romero on March 24, 1980, as he was offering Mass. President Carter attempted to move El Salvador's government to a centrist position, but his efforts failed and resulted in an unrealized plan to kill the U.S. ambassador. In 1981 Reagan denounced the violence and threatened to terminate American aid. However, he did not suspend aid to El Salvador, fearing the establishment of another communist state in the Western Hemisphere. Finally, during the administration of President George H. W. Bush, the war came to an end with the adoption of an American-endorsed constitution that established an effective civil government.

Reagan's greatest challenge in Latin America was Nicaragua, where there was extensive anti-American sentiment. Throughout the twentieth century the United States had intervened in the domestic affairs of Nicaragua. The dictator Anastasio Somoza Debayle came to power in 1956 and courted American support by suppressing alleged communists. During the 1960s the anti-Somoza resistance (which became known as the Sandinistas) adopted a leftist orientation, and it was influenced by the success of the Cuban revolution and guerilla tactics developed by Che Guevara. Somoza was able to sustain control throughout the 1960s and into late 1970s, when the revolutionary effort scored a number of victories over the Somoza regime. On July 17, 1979, Somoza fled to Miami, Florida, but President Carter refused him entry into the United States. Somoza then travelled to Paraguay, where he was admitted and settled into exile in Ascension. However, sis exile was brief, as the Sandinistas sent a team of assassins to Ascension. On September 17, 1980, Somoza was assassinated. The new Sandinista government was led by the Junta of National Reconstruction, a committee representing a number of left-wing elements who were active in the Sandinista movement. In 1984 José Daniel Ortega Saavedra (referred to as Daniel Ortega) was elected president. The Junta and Ortega established a Marxist dictatorship in Nicaragua, property rights were abridged, and civil liberties such as freedoms of speech, the press, and to organize unions and strikes were restricted.

In 1983 the Reagan administration directed the CIA to organize a group of militants (the Contras) who would disrupt and overthrow the Sandinista regime. This action was a direct violation of the Boland Amendment that Reagan had signed on December 21, 1982, when he signed into law the Defense Appropriations Act.[4] The Boland Amendment directed that the American government could not aid the Contras in preparing for or executing the overthrow of the Sandinista regime, though it did permit other nonmilitary aid. This constituted a contradiction because the Contras were formed for the sole purpose of overthrowing the Sandinistas. In January 1984 the Contras mined Nicaraguan ports, which resulted in the sinking of several ships and widespread international condemnation of the Contras and their American sponsors. The Boland Amendment was affirmed by the American Congress. The Junta completed work on a new constitution and called for elections in 1984. Oretga was declared victorious in the elections, which were declared "fair" by some international observers. While this was a setback for Reagan, the American government continued to illegally finance the arming and training of the Contras.

Paralleling this situation in Nicaragua, another foreign affairs problem was unfolding in the Middle East, where seven Americans were being held hostage by Islamists connected to Iran. Iran was in the midst of a decade-long war with Iraq and in need of modern weapons. A scheme was devised and executed by three White House staffers (John Poindexter, Robert McFarlane, and Oliver North) whereby Israel would send weapons to Iran (the United States would restock the Israelis for the weapons sent to Iran), the Iranians would pay the Israelis for the weapons and (hopefully) arrange for the release of the American hostages, and then part of the realized funds would be used to support arming and the activities of the Contras against the Sandinistas. After the news of this circumvention of the law was revealed in November 1986, Reagan stated publicly that weapons had been sent to Iran not in exchange for hostages, but rather in hopes of developing a new strategic relationship with Iran. Congressional Iran-Contra hearings were held during the summer of 1987. This scandal was the most serious crisis of Reagan's presidency. Americans followed the Iran-Contra hearings carefully and for the most part were displeased with what they learned. Reagan denied that he ordered or even knew of the scheme of exchanging arms for hostages or the illegal use of funds raised by the sale of weapons to fund the Contras in Nicaragua. The Reagan-appointed Tower Commission (Senator John Tower, R-TX) and a congressional investigation were established to investigate the scandal, and both concluded that Reagan was not aware of many of the facets of the plan. Secretary of Defense Caspar Weinberger resigned on November 23, 1987, and he was indicted on June 16, 1992, for obstructing justice and perjury. However, he received a presidential pardon on December 24, 1992, during the last month of the presidency of George H. W. Bush. An examination of Weinberger's notes of meetings with Reagan, Poindexter, and MacFarlane indicates that Reagan was advised of all aspects of the Iran-Contra operation. In Nicaragua Ortega completed his term as president in 1990 but was defeated in his bid for another term by Violeta Barrios de Chamorro. Oretga evolved politically into a moderate, was defeated twice in presidential elections (in 1996 and 2000), and was returned to the presidency in 2006, a position in which he continues to serve.

During the 1982 Falklands War between Argentina and Great Britain, the United States was torn between two allies at war with one another. On April 2, 1982, Argentinian military units landed on the Falkland Islands, which are located several hundred miles off the Argentinian coast in the South Atlantic. Argentina claimed that the Falklands were Argentinian and not British, though Great Britain had held the islands for more than 200 years. The British government under the leadership of Prime Minister Margaret Thatcher demanded that the Argentinians withdraw their forces. When they did not she prepared an invasion force to drive them out and re-establish British control. Secretary of State Alexander Haig's unsuccessful mediation efforts conducted during April 1982 paralleled Secretary of Defense Caspar Weinberger's quiet preparations for American support for Great Britain through supplies, intelligence, and, if necessary, direct naval intervention. Weinberger was aware of Reagan's early April personal correspondence with British prime minister Margaret Thatcher in which he offered support. The Reagan administration feared that the Soviet Union would enter the conflict to support Argentina and that the struggle for these remote islands could escalate into a major conflict. Political unrest, fear, uncertainty, and distress characterized Argentinian politics during the late 1970s and 1980s. Coup d'états were frequent, and of thousands of people were murdered or went missing. The United States condemned the general violation of human rights that was caused by political and social differences, though some Argentinian right-wing leaders justified these atrocities as necessary to keep the communists from coming to power. By early May 1982 Reagan denounced the Argentinian leaders for thwarting America's mediation efforts and openly supported Great Britain. Reagan had difficulty in not directly involving the United States in the war, though eventually he was persuaded that Great Britain could handle it alone without American troops. With Reagan's public statement of support for Britain, Weinberger presented a range of options from the use of American bases to an aircraft carrier and other military assets that could be used to aid Britain. The American base on Ascension Island was used by British air and naval forces. By June 14, 1982, British forces had neutralized the Argentinian forces on the Falklands and reestablished control. In 1983 the Argentinian junta was replaced by another short-lived regime that had the temporary support of the CIA.

The Reagan administration was also active in Africa in extending American influence and countering feared expanded Soviet power and influence. In South Africa the racial policy of apartheid, which gave whites power over the majority black population, was denounced by blacks and some white South Africans and condemned by the international community. As incidents of violence increased after the assassination of Stephen Biko, an antiapartheid activist and founder of the black consciousness movement, on September 12, 1977, the international community responded with economic and diplomatic sanctions. Initially, the American response was mixed during Reagan's administration. Congress denounced the apartheid government and its repressive tactics while Reagan, who saw the South African government as a reliable ally against the Soviet Union, called for the opposing parties to enter into constructive negotiations to resolve the crisis. However, in 1985 Reagan, fearing the loss of congressional support on a range of issues, joined in the demand for sanctions, including an embargo and disinvestment in South Africa. At the same time he opposed but did not interfere with the enactment of the Comprehensive Anti-Apartheid Act in 1986. He thought that the measure was excessive in its restriction on the South African government. By 1990 South Africans were enacting reforms that ended apartheid and transformed their society.

Reagan supported the anticommunist Jonas Savimbi and his UNITA rebels against the communist Angolan government and its ally Cuba. American aid was provided through ground-to-air missiles and other military supplies. Savimbi met with Reagan in Washington and acquired the continued support of the Bush administration from 1989 to early 1993. The Angolan civil war continued until February 22, 2002, when Savimbi was killed. Shortly thereafter a cease-fire was arranged, and a tenuous peace continues today.

During the first year of the Reagan administration, relations between the United States and the Libyan government under Muammar Gaddafi were strained with the Gulf of Sidra incident. Previously Libya had announced that its territorial waters in the Gulf had been extended to 200 miles and warned other nations not to penetrate this area. The United States refused to recognize the claim. Previously, Gaddafi had established a socialist state with ties to the Soviet Union. During 1980 several potentially dangerous contacts between Libyan and American forces occurred and resulted in the Americans backing down. Reagan ordered a carrier task force to the region, and on August 19, 1981, two American fighters penetrated the disputed area in the Gulf and were attacked by two Libyan planes. The Libyan planes were destroyed over international waters, and relations between the two countries became tenuous. In April 1986 a bomb was detonated in a Berlin nightclub that was frequented by U.S. military personnel. One person was killed, and 63 were wounded. The Reagan administration quickly identified Libya as being responsible for the bombing. On April 15, 1986, American planes conducted attacks on Libyan targets, including Gaddafi residences. The United States ignored the UN resolution condemning it for the attack.

In Asia the Reagan government pursued interventionist policies in the Iran-Iraq war, Cambodia, and Afghanistan. The United States became involved quietly with both sides during the Iran-Iraq war, with the overall goals of establishing regional stability and thwarting expansion of Soviet influence or presence in the Middle East. When Iran appeared to be on the verge of victory, the Reagan administration launched a policy to restrict Iranian access to weapons. Then, reversing itself, the United States arranged for weapons to be delivered to Iran (see the earlier discussion about the Iran-Contra affair). In Cambodia Reagan provided aid to anti-Soviet/Vietnamese movements that had established a communist terrorist regime responsible for killing more than a million Cambodians—in addition to the millions killed by the Khmer Rouge during the late 1970s. Under Reagan's direction, the United States provided military and financial support to the Khmer People's National Liberation Front, whose goal was to support operations that would result in the withdrawal of Vietnamese troops. By 1991 the Soviet Union was in its last year, and Vietnam recognized that it was no longer in its interests to sustain an operation in Cambodia. Reagan's intervention in Cambodia was not a major factor in restoring peace and stability, as both Cambodians and Vietnamese recognized the meaningless of further conflict.

During Reagan's presidency the CIA intervened in Afghanistan by providing extensive military supplies that were delivered through Pakistan. The Soviet Union invaded Afghanistan in 1979 and established a pro-Soviet government. They were opposed by the mujahedeen, a disparate group of Afghan Islamic guerrilla fighters who were committed to expelling the Soviets from their country. With American weapons, the mujahedeen prevailed, and on July 20, 1987, the Soviet Union announced that it intended to withdraw its forces. All Soviet military units were removed by February 15, 1989.

When Reagan took his first oath as president of the United States on January 20, 1981, he discarded détente with the Soviet Union and introduced a new more aggressive policy that consisted of a substantive arms buildup; weakening the Soviet economy by driving down the value of its exports, especially oil, and forcing it to increase military expenditures; supporting anticommunist groups throughout the world; and restricting Soviet access to advanced technology. These actions were viewed as provocative not only by the Soviet Union and some American allies, but also by significant segments of the American public. Détente had become comfortable—the new normalcy in international affairs—and disrupting it was not only unwise, but also dangerous.[5] As the Reagan era was beginning, the age of Brezhnev was coming to a close. As Brezhnev's health declined, so did the economy of the Soviet Union. The apparent Soviet prosperity of the 1970s was in fact a fragile illusion based on the inflated price for Soviet oil. Once oil returned to a more sustained price, the weak economy became more evident. A clear indicator of the precarious condition of the Soviet economy was that it was forced to import American grain throughout the 1970s. Brezhnev died on November 10, 1982, and was replaced by Yuri Andropov, the leader of the KGB. Andropov expended considerable time and energy in placing many talented and younger managers into positions of authority, including Mikhail Gorbachev. Andropov attempted to restore more order to the Soviet system and eliminate corruption. Unlike his predecessor, Andropov lived in simplicity and hoped that others would follow his example. In foreign affairs he attempted to continue the expansionist policies of the 1970s. He denounced Reagan's anti-Soviet policies and labeled the American president as a danger to world peace. U.S.-Soviet relations continued to decline during 1983. On March 8, 1983, Reagan addressed the Annual Convention of the National

Association of Evangelicals in Orlando, Florida (see Document 17), and he used this opportunity to expand his view of the Soviet Union and American foreign policy:

> The reality is that we must find peace through strength. . . .
>
> A freeze would reward the Soviet Union for its enormous and unparalleled military buildup. It would prevent the essential and long overdue modernization of United States and allied defenses and would leave our aging forces increasingly vulnerable. And an honest freeze would require extensive prior negotiations on the systems and numbers to be limited and on the measures to ensure effective verification and compliance. And the kind of a freeze that has been suggested would be virtually impossible to verify. Such a major effort would divert us completely from our current negotiations on achieving substantial reductions. . . .
>
> [L]et us pray for the salvation of all of those who live in that totalitarian darkness—pray they will discover the joy of knowing God. But until they do, let us be aware that while they preach the supremacy of the state, declare its omnipotence over individual man, and predict its eventual domination of all peoples on the Earth, they are the focus of evil in the modern world.[6]

With these remarks Reagan buried any chance of resurrecting détente. Soviet reaction to the speech was predictable—they denounced it and also experienced increased anxiety because of concerns over their domestic economy and America's military expansion. The response of the American intellectual and academic communities was also predictable—as a group, they thought that Reagan was a relic of a bygone age and that he had embarrassed the United States. A few weeks later, on March 23, 1983, in a televised speech, Reagan discarded the concept of mutual assured destruction by announcing that the United States would pursue the Strategic Defense Initiative (SDI)—sometimes called "Star Wars"—to develop and deploy a defensive shield against an attack by nuclear armed missiles. Reagan offered the developing technology to the Soviet Union, as he wanted to eliminate any prospect of a nuclear war. The immediate reaction was negative because Reagan was upsetting the nuclear balance of power by openly discussing a nonexistent system that may or may not have been feasible. According to historian John Lewis Gaddis, "The reaction, in the Kremlin, approached panic. Andropov had concluded, while still head of the K.G.B., that the new administration in Washington might be planning a surprise attack on the Soviet Union."[7]

On September 1, 1983, a Soviet fighter shot down a South Korean Airliner that had crossed into Soviet air space. All 269 aboard were killed, including 63 Americans. From evidence available later, it was apparent that this action was based on the high alert that Andropov placed on the Soviet military after Reagan's SDI speech.[8] The stress and anxiety that Andropov's regime experienced from a fear that the West would launch a first strike against the Soviet Union reached a high point with the Able Archer '83 crisis in the fall of 1983. Able Archer '83 were the annual NATO military exercises scheduled for November 1983. Soviet intelligence reported that, compared to the past, a higher level of leadership was involved in these exercises. For several days Andropov concluded that a nuclear attack was imminent. Reagan and other NATO leaders became aware of Andropov's views through a British spy within the KGB. On January 16, 1984, Reagan gave a speech that was not provocative and that was intended to calm Andropov.[9]

Andropov, who had been suffering from adrenal disease when he assumed power, died on February 9, 1984. He was replaced by his longtime rival Konstantin Chernenko, who had emphysema and appeared ill when he was appointed Soviet leader on February 11, 1984. He abandoned Andropov's reforms and increased the suppression of dissidents. In foreign affairs Chernenko called for a resumption of détente with the United States, ordered Soviet athletes to boycott the Olympics in Los Angeles, and escalated Soviet military actions in Afghanistan. Two of Chernenko's achievements were agreeing to enter arms control talks with the United States and, with the support of Foreign Minister Andrei Gromyko, establishing support for Mikhail Gorbachev to be the next Soviet leader. Chernenko died on March 10, 1985, and on March 15, 1985, Mikhail Gorbachev was named general secretary of the Communist Party of the Soviet Union.

The challenges confronting Gorbachev included the stagnant Soviet command economy, lingering internal corruption, the increasingly unpopular war in Afghanistan, restless minority groups, a decadent and inefficient bureaucracy, and the implementation of Reagan's arms buildup and his anticommunist foreign policy throughout the world. Gorbachev argued that reform of the economy was needed to save socialism, though

in 1985 he had no intention of moving toward a market-based socialism.[10]
He replaced Foreign Minister Gromyko with the younger Eduard Shevard-
nadze, who shared many values with Gorbachev. Between 1986 and 1988
Gorbachev announced that the reforms being introduced in the Soviet
Union were guided by new principles of *perestroika* (restructuring), *glasnost*
(openness), *demokratizatsiya* (democratization), and *uskoreniye* (acceleration of economic development). In 1988 the Law on Cooperatives
allowed—indeed encouraged—private ownership of businesses. At the
same time Gorbachev was withdrawing Communist Party controls over
everyday life that it had enjoyed for decades.

Gorbachev was no less bold in foreign policy initiatives. In April 1985
he called for a resumption of arms reduction negotiations with the United
States. Reagan and Gorbachev met for the first time in Geneva at a summit meeting on November 19–20, 1985. While both elaborated at length
on their concerns with one another's national policies, neither surrendered
on any point. An important outcome of the Geneva summit was that the
two leaders developed a genuine rapport that appears to have been based
on their personalities and perhaps a willingness to trust one another—a
lack of trust between American and Soviet leaders had been an ongoing
characteristic of the Cold War. After the Geneva Summit Reagan, acting
against the counsel of his advisers, changed his approach to the Soviet
Union, as he believed that he could convince Gorbachev to adopt a free
market strategy for the Soviet Union.[11] On October 11–12, 1986, Reagan
and Gorbachev met in Reykjavik, Iceland. Reagan wanted the agenda to
include a range of issues, including arms control, Afghanistan, human
rights, and the plight of Soviet Jewry. However, Gorbachev had just one
item that it wanted to discuss—arms control. Both Reagan and Gorbachev
agreed to a bold outline that would abolish all nuclear weapons, but
Gorbachev insisted that Reagan had to abandon the SDI project. Reagan
refused, and the summit ended with disappointment on both sides.

On June 12, 1987, Reagan visited Berlin to mark the city's 750th anniversary. He used the visit to push Gorbachev to loosen Soviet controls in
the Eastern Bloc (see Document 18). Referring to recently "openness" of
Soviet society, Reagan stated:

> Are these the beginnings of profound changes in the Soviet state? Or are
> they token gestures, intended to raise false hopes in the West, or to

Soviet leader Mikhail Gorbachev (second from right) and U.S. president Ronald Reagan (second from left) shake hands at the start of a series of talks on October 11, 1986, in Reykjavik, Iceland. The other men are unidentified. The meeting did not result in an arms agreement, but it did pave the way for such a treaty that was signed on December 8, 1987. (AP Photo/Ron Edmonds)

strengthen the Soviet system without changing it? We welcome change and openness; for we believe that freedom and security go together, that the advance of human liberty can only strengthen the cause of world peace. There is one sign the Soviets can make that would be unmistakable, that would advance dramatically the cause of freedom and peace.

General Secretary Gorbachev, if you seek peace, if you seek prosperity for the Soviet Union and Eastern Europe, if you seek liberalization: Come here to this gate! Mr. Gorbachev, open this gate! Mr. Gorbachev, tear down this wall![12]

Reagan wanted to achieve a major nuclear arms reduction treaty before the end of his term. Negotiations continued on arms control through the next year that resulted in the Intermediate-Range Nuclear Forces Treaty between the United States and the Soviet Union, which was signed on December 8, 1987, during Gorbachev's visit to Washington, DC. Under its terms, all short- and intermediate-range missiles were to be withdrawn from Europe (see Document 19). The Washington Summit was followed by another meeting in Moscow between May 25 and June 3, 1988, where the two sides ratified the terms that were agreed to on December 8, 1987. Reagan and Gorbachev discussed human rights and other issues, but no additional agreements were signed.[13] During his last six months in office, Reagan continued to prod Gorbachev and offer advice, but still no additional agreements were signed.

In the 1988 presidential election Vice President George H. W. Bush was the Republican candidate, and Governor Michael Dukakis of Massachusetts led the Democratic ticket. Bush enjoyed the benefits of having served as the vice president to the outgoing and popular president, a good economy, and the restored international preeminence of the United States. Bush also ran a strong and effective campaign. Dukakis, who received a strong but short-lived post-convention bounce, ran a dismal campaign in which he did not respond to Bush's attacks and made a series of mistakes that the Bush campaign manipulated to its advantage. On Tuesday, November 8, 1988, Bush defeated Dukakis by 53.4 percent to 45.7 percent in the popular vote and 426 to 111 in electoral votes.[14] During his single term as president, Bush ordered successful military actions in Panama (December 1989) and Iraq (January 1991), and he initiated an action in Somalia (December 1992) that the new administration of President William Clinton inherited in January 1993.

On November 9, 1989, the East German government announced that it would no longer restrict access between East Berlin and West Berlin, and East Germany and West Germany. That same day, German citizens began to dismantle the wall that had separated them since August 13, 1961, and most of the wall was taken down during 1990. This dramatic action led to the rapid reunification of Germany on October 2, 1990.[15] Shortly after these developments in Germany, Bush and Gorbachev held a summit meeting on the island of Malta on December 2–3,1989. While no agreements were reached or treaties signed, the two leaders declared that the Cold War was over. Although some considered that announcement premature, there was no question that tensions between the former adversaries had been reduced significantly. They reviewed the rapidly changing geopolitical situation in Europe and discussed anticipated issues that would emerge in the future.[16] On July 31, 1991, Bush and Gorbachev met in Moscow and signed the START I (Strategic Arms Reduction Treaty) agreement that constituted the largest and most extensive nuclear arms treaty ever signed. Later the new Russian government committed itself to the treaty, and it became effective on December 5, 1994, which resulted in the elimination of about 80 percent of all Soviet/Russian and American nuclear weapons. START I expired on December 5, 2009, and was extended by START II (sometimes referred to as New START) that was signed by President Barack Obama and Russian president Dmitry Medvedev in Prague on April 8, 2010. It became operational on January 26, 2011.[17]

Gorbachev's liberalization programs, which had unleashed nationalist movements in Soviet-dominated states, accelerated changes during 1989 both within and outside of the Soviet Union. On March 26, 1989, the first democratic elections in Soviet history were conducted, and more than 89.8 percent of eligible voters participated in voting for membership in the Congress of People's Deputies. A majority of those elected had the official endorsement of the Communist Party. Despite that result, the new Congress was quickly transformed into a mechanism for open and critical debate on the future of the Soviet Union and the myriad problems and issues that confronted its citizens. Russian nationalists and liberals found a leader in Boris Yeltsin. On May 30, 1989, Gorbachev proposed nationwide local elections for November 1989. His intent was to decentralize political power and sustain local communist parties. However, these elections were postponed until 1990 because of the absence of approved procedures and the fear that local communists would be defeated. There was also a mounting—and valid—concern that local republics and national groups would use the elections to break with the central government.[18]

The "Revolutions of 1989" occurred from June through December 1989, with peaceful political sea changes taking place in Poland, East Germany, Czechoslovakia, Hungary, and Bulgaria. The Soviet Union and its army did not interfere with these developments, as Gorbachev believed that it was no longer in the Soviet Union's interests or capability to continue to dominate Eastern Europe as it had been doing since the end of World War II. A violent revolution in Romania resulted in the executions of President Nicolae Ceausescu and his wife as they attempted to escape on

December 16, 1989. Yugoslavia began the process of disintegration that resulted in the appearance of new national states in the early 1990s. Between May 4 and June 4, 1989, the People's Republic of China was challenged by thousands of student demonstrators in Tiananmen Square in Beijing demanding reforms until the army was ordered to crush the demonstration.

Of greater concern was the emergence of vibrant nationalist movements within the Soviet Union. The Baltic states of Estonia, Latvia, and Lithuania had been seized in 1940 and incorporated into the Soviet Union. On August 23, 1989—the fiftieth anniversary of the Soviet Union's nonaggression pact with Hitler's Germany that paved the way for the attack on Poland on September 1, 1939—2 million Estonians, Latvians, and Lithuanians linked hands on their previous borders with the Soviet Union in a nationalist demonstration designed to restore the independence of their countries.[19] In December Gorbachev approved the independence of the Lithuanian Communist Party from that of the Soviet Union, and in January 1990 he attempted unsuccessfully to ensure that Lithuanians would not seek to form an independent state. Soviet republics Lithuania, Moldova, Estonia, Latvia, Armenia, and Georgia broke with the centralized Communist Party of the Soviet Union during 1990 and began to pursue their own nationalist agendas. From the perspective of the continuity of the Soviet Union, one of the most radical developments that occurred in 1990 was the emergence of the Russian independence movement within the Soviet Union as Boris Yeltsin led the struggle between the Russian Republic[20] and the Soviet Union. Between May and July 1990 Yeltsin was elected president of the Russian Republic, achieved approval for a declaration of sovereignty (which questioned Russia's place within the Soviet Union), and resigned from the Communist Party.[21] Soviet authority was also challenged in Azerbaijan and Ukraine during 1990, and Gorbachev's efforts to keep them within the Soviet system failed.

The separatist movements gained momentum in 1991 but faced opposition from staunch supporters of the Soviet Union and the Communist Party of the Soviet Union. These elements opposed the approval of the New Union Treaty that was to be signed on August 20, 1991, which would transform the Soviet Union into a federation of independent republics, that is, the Soviet central government would control foreign policy and the armed forces and be led by an elected president. The opponents of the New Union Treaty—including Vice President Gennady Yannayev, Defense Minister Dmitry Yazov, and KBG leader Vladimir Kryuchkov—attempted a coup d'état on August 19, 1991. Gorbachev was arrested, the proposed treaty was denounced, and units of the military were deployed. The leaders of the coup had expected public support for their action, but that did not materialize. Most military units refused to take orders from them, and Yeltsin seized the moment to emerge as the Russian leader who was committed to a new democratic future, not a return to the dismal and failed past. The coup was defeated in three days, and Gorbachev was restored as president of the Soviet Union, though he had little power.[22]

Bush and the leadership of the American government were admittedly astonished by the acceleration of an already swift and dynamic process that was unfolding in the Soviet Union, and every statement was carefully measured to avoid being accused of intervention.[23] During the summer and fall of 1991, the disintegration of the Soviet Union continued unabated. In a free election on December 1, 1991, more than 90 percent of voters declared for Ukrainian independence. On December 8, 1991, Yeltsin, along with leaders of Ukraine and Belarus, met and agreed to the Belavezha Accords, which declared the end of the Soviet Union and the establishment of a new Commonwealth of Independent States. Gorbachev denounced the agreement but had no power to stop it. Eleven other republics signed the Accords on December 21, 1991, and with the exception of Estonia, Latvia, Lithuania, and Georgia, effectively ratified the end of the Soviet Union. Early on December 25, 1991, Gorbachev resigned as leader from the now-defunct Soviet Union. That evening in a televised address to the American people, President George H. W. Bush stated that the Cold War had ended with the demise of the Soviet Union. On January 28, 1992, before a joint session of the Congress (See Document 20), Bush remarked:

> We gather tonight at a dramatic and deeply promising time in our history and in the history of man on Earth. For in the past 12 months, the world has known changes of almost Biblical proportions. And even now, months after the failed coup that doomed a failed system, I'm not sure we've absorbed the full impact, the full import of what happened. But communism

died this year. . . . Even as President, with the most fascinating possible vantage point, there were times when I was so busy managing progress and helping to lead change that I didn't always show the joy that was in my heart. But the biggest thing that has happened in the world in my life, in our lives, is this: By the grace of God, America won the cold war. . . . I mean to speak this evening of the changes that can take place in our country, now that we can stop making the sacrifices we had to make when we had an avowed enemy that was a superpower. Now we can look homeward even more and move to set right what needs to be set right. I will speak of those things. But let me tell you something I've been thinking these past few months. It's a kind of roll call of honor. For the cold war didn't end; it was won. And I think of those who won it, in places like Korea and Vietnam. And some of them didn't come back. Back then they were heroes, but this year they were victors.[24]

The Cold War was over and a new, perhaps even more dangerous, era was beginning.

After collapse of the Soviet Union, one of Gorbachev's most volatile, gifted, and energetic critics—Boris Yeltsin—emerged as the voice of reform in Russia. At first a supporter of Gorbachev's reform initiatives, Yeltsin became one of his most visible critics during the last years of the Soviet Union. In 1991 Yeltsin was elected the first president of Russia in an open election, and he remained in office until December 31, 1999, when the newly elected president Vladimir Putin took over. Encouraged by American governments led by Presidents George H. W. Bush and William Clinton, Yeltsin's Russia rushed into political, economic, and social reforms that resulted in internal chaos. Poverty and unemployment increased significantly, the life span declined dramatically, public order appeared to be near collapse, corruption was rampant, and a new class of rich oligarchs emerged to take advantage of the volatility and lack of order in Russian society.

In 1993 the fragile Russian government was threatened when Yeltsin dissolved the Russian parliament, which responded by removing Yeltsin as president. The crisis was resolved when army units backed Yeltsin and attacked the parliament building, killing almost 200 opponents. Yeltsin scrapped the two-year-old constitution and replaced it with a new constitution that strengthened presidential power but imposed a limit of two consecutive terms. The new constitution was ratified in a referendum on December 12, 1993. Economic and social progress was slow and appeared to be beyond the reach of Yeltsin's leadership. From the American perspective, the most pressing matter that had to be addressed was reaching an agreement on the removal of nuclear weapons that were now in the new nations that had emerged from the collapse of the Soviet Union. After successful negotiations these weapons were dismantled and neutralized by applying extensive American funds and expertise. In 1999 Yeltsin condemned American involvement in the Kosovo war in Serbia, a traditional Russian ally, though Russia did not possess the ability or the will to intervene on Serbia's behalf. On December 31, 1999, Yeltsin surprised everyone when he resigned. His vice president Vladimir Putin replaced him and won the 2000 presidential election for a full term.

Putin restored political and social stability, confidence, and economic growth to Russia during his first two terms as president (2000–2008), and he was more critical of the United States. He denounced America's war in Iraq but allowed American planes that were providing supplies to NATO forces in Afghanistan to fly over Russian territory. A major point of contention has been the deployment of an antimissile system in Poland and a radar installation in the Czech Republic. U.S.-Russian relations appeared to improve during the first term of President Barack Obama. President Dmitry Medvedev (2008–2012) and Obama signed a new disarmament treaty (New START) on April 8, 2010, in Prague. This treaty modified an earlier agreement of 2002 and specified that both powers would reduce the number of ICBM nuclear weapons to 1,500.

The current question is whether the historic mistrust between the powers will be overcome to allow the development of a new partnership, or will that mistrust prevail and a new cold war begin.

In 2007 Mark MacKinnon, a respected correspondent (the *Globe and Mail*) and recognized foreign policy expert, published *The New Cold War: Revolutions, Rigged Elections and Pipeline Politics in the Former Soviet Union*. MacKinnon argued that a new cold war between Russia and the United States was already underway and that the United States was responsible for it. He declared that American intervention in the Russian economy and border states has enhanced Russian mistrust of the United States, and American criticism of Putin and his internal policies has resulted in a backlash that has limited the development of democracy in Russia.[25] In a 2008 study titled *The New Cold War: Putin's Russia and the*

Threat to the West, Edward Lucas (the *Economist*) blamed Russia for increased tensions and the new cold war with the United States because it continued to interfere in the affairs of Eastern European states, used its oil supplies to intimidate energy-dependent countries, and attempted to weaken and disrupt the European Union. Lucas argued that the West must accept the reality that the struggle with Russia will continue for decades.[26] In 2011 an important report was released by the Belfer Center for Science and International Affairs at Harvard University. *Russia and U.S. National Interests: Why Should Americans Care?* was developed by the Task Force on Russia and U.S. National Interests, which was chaired by Graham Allison and Robert D. Blackwill; Dimitri K. Simes served as the project director, and Paul J. Saunders as senior advisor and editor. This report identified American and Russian national interests as well as areas of mutual interest and, indeed, interdependence. Both possess nuclear weapons that could destroy the each other, and both need to cooperate with one another to limit the spread of nuclear weapons. Both need to protect their people from terrorist attacks, and both need to secure adequate energy supplies. Both want to preserve their spheres of influence in Europe, Asia, and Latin America, and, at the same time, the balance of geopolitical power. Each needs to respect the other's sovereignty, and both require flexibility to sustain continued economic growth. The problems emerge when Russia and the United States differ in their approaches to attaining and sustaining these interests. The determining factor in U.S.-Russia relations is mutual trust. Without it, a cooperative relationship will be most difficult to achieve.[27]

NOTES

1. The literature on the collapse of the Soviet Union and the end of the Cold War is extensive and continues to expand. Among the more notable works to consider are *Lenin's Tomb: The Last Days of the Soviet Empire* by David Remnick (New York: Vintage, 1994); two books by Peter Schweizer, *Victory: The Reagan Administration's Secret Strategy That Hastened the Collapse of the Soviet Union* (New York: Atlantic Monthly, 1996) and *Reagan's War: The Epic Story of His Forty-Year Struggle and Final Triumph over Communism* (New York: Anchor, 2003); *The Rebellion of Ronald Reagan: A History of the End of the Cold War* by James Mann (New York: Viking, 2009); *The Soviet Tragedy: A History of Socialism in Russia, 1917–1991* by Martin Malia (New York: Free Press, 1995); *Age of*

Delirium: The Decline and Fall of the Soviet Union by David Satter (New Haven, CT: Yale University Press, 2001); *Dismantling Utopia: How Information Ended the Soviet Union* by Scott Shane (Chicago: Ivan R. Dee, 1995); and useful partisan accounts such as *With Reagan: The Inside Story* by Edward Meese, 2nd ed. (Washington, DC: Regnery Gateway, 1992).

2. See George Weigel, *The Final Revolution: The Resistance Church and the Collapse of Communism* (New York: Oxford University Press, 2003); and Maryjane Osa, *Solidarity and Contention:Networks of Polish Opposition*. Social Movements, Protest and Contention Series (Minneapolis: University of Minnesota Press, 2003).

3. See Andrew E. Busch, *Reagan's Victory: The Presidential Election of 1980 and the Rise of the Right* (Lawrence: University Press of Kansas, 2005); John Ehrman, *The Eighties: America in the Age of Reagan* (New Haven, CT: Yale University Press, 2005); and Gerald M. Pomper (ed.), *The Election of 1980: Reports and Interpretations* (Chatham, NY: Chatham Press, 1981).

4. The Boland Amendment was named for Representative Edward Patrick Boland (D-MA).

5. John Lewis Gaddis, *The Cold War: A New History* (New York: Penguin, 2005), 221–44.

6. Ronald Reagan, *Public Papers of the Presidents of the United States: Ronald Reagan, 1983*, Bk. 1 (Washington, DC: U.S. Government Printing Office, 1984), 359–64.

7. Gaddis, *The Cold War*, 226–28.

8. Ibid., 227.

9. Ibid., 227–28.

10. Blaier Seweryn and Joan Afferica, "The Genesis of Gorbachev's World," *Foreign Affairs*, 64, no. 3 (1985): 605–44.

11. See Jack Mattock, *Reagan and Gorbachev: How the Cold War Ended* (New York: Random House, 2004) and Lou Cannon, *President Reagan: The Role of a Lifetime* (New York: Public Affairs, 2000).

12. Ronald Reagan, *Public Papers of the Presidents of the United States, Ronald Reagan, 1987*, Bk. 1 (Washington, DC: U. S. Government Printing Office, 1989), 634–38.

13. Gaddis, *The Cold War*, 225–28.

14. See J. David Goppian, "Image and Issues in the 1988 Presidential Election," *Journal of Politics*, 55, no. 1 (February 1993): 151–66.

15. See Frederick Taylor, *The Berlin Wall: 13 August 1961–9 November 1989* (London and New York: Bloomsbury, 2006); and William F. Buckley, Jr., *The Fall of the Berlin Wall* (Hoboken, NJ: John Wiley and Sons, 2004).

16. Anatoly S. Chernyaev, *My Six Years with Gorbachev*, edited by Robert English and Elizabeth Tucker (University Park: Pennsylvania State University Press, 2000), 237–38.

17. See David Treisman, *The Return: Russia's Journey from Gorbachev to Medvedev* (New York: Free Press, 2011); James Baker, *The Politics of Diplomacy: Revolution, War, and Peace, 1989–1992* (New York: Putnam, 1995); George H. W. Bush and Brent Scowcroft, *A World Transformed* (New York: Vintage, 1999); and David F. Schmitz, *Brent Scowcroft: Internationalism and Post–Vietnam War American Foreign Policy*, Biographies in American Foreign Policy Series (Lanham, MD: Rowman and Littlefield, 2011).

18. Sharon L. Wolchik and Jane Leftwich Curry, *Central and East European Politics: From Communism to Democracy* (Lanham, MD: Rowman and Littlefield, 2007), 237–38.

19. Alfred E. Senn, *Gorbachev's Failure in Lithuania* (New York: Palgrave Macmillan, 1995), 78.

20. The Russian Soviet Republic was the most significant political component of the Soviet Union.

21. Leon Aron, *Boris Yeltsin, A Revolutionary Life* (New York: HarperCollins, 2000), 738–41.

22. Gaddis, *The Cold War*, 256–58; Ronald Suny, *The Soviet Experiment: Russia, the USSR, and the Successor States*, 2nd ed. (New York: Oxford University Press, 2010), 480–82; Mikhail Gorbachev, *Memoirs* (New York: Doubleday, 1996), 626–45.

23. Gaddis, *The Cold War*, 256–59.

24. George H. W. Bush, "Address before a Joint Session of the Congress on the State of the Union," George H. W. Bush, January 28, 1992, *Public Papers of the President, George Bush, I: 1992–93* (Washington, DC: U.S. Government Printing Office, 1993), 156–58.

25. Mark MacKinnon, *The New Cold War: Revolutions, Rigged Elections and Pipeline Politics in the Former Soviet Union* (New York: Carroll and Graf, 2007), 4–5, 255–75; Bohdan Harasymiw, "Russia, the United States, and the New Cold War," *Military and Strategic Studies*, 12, no. 2 (Winter 2010): 1–31.

26. Edward Lucas, *The New Cold War: Putin's Russia and the Threat to the West* (New York: Palgrave Macmillan, 2008), 3, 210–15.

27. Graham Allison, Robert D. Blackwill, Dimitri K. Simes, and Paul J. Saunders, *Russia and U.S. National Interests: Why Should Americans Care?* (Cambridge, MA and Washington, DC: Jointly published by the Belfer Center for Science and International Affairs, Harvard University, and the Center for the National Interest, 2011), 1–38.

BIOGRAPHIES

DEAN ACHESON (1893–1971)

Dean Gooderham Acheson served as secretary of state during the Truman administration and was a dominant force in establishing the American policy of containment during the early years of the Cold War. Acheson replaced George C. Marshall in 1949 and was succeeded by John Foster Dulles in 1953. Acheson's tenure as secretary of state witnessed the implementation of the Marshall Plan and the Truman Doctrine, the establishment of the North Atlantic Treaty Organization (NATO), the victory of the communists in China, the outbreak of the Korean War, and the emergence of McCarthyism.

Dean G. Acheson was born on April 11, 1893, in Middletown, Connecticut, and graduated from Yale College (1915) and Harvard Law School (1918). During World War I he served in the Army National Guard but was not deployed overseas. With the recommendation of Felix Frankfurter, a Harvard Law School professor and later associate justice of the U.S. Supreme Court, Acheson served as a clerk to Supreme Court associate justice Louis Brandeis from 1919 to 1921. During the 1920s he developed an excellent reputation in international law at the Washington law firm of Covington and Burling. Acheson served briefly as President Franklin D. Roosevelt's undersecretary of the treasury in 1933. He resigned when Roosevelt announced plans to devalue the dollar. He returned to his law firm and remained there until 1941, when Roosevelt named him assistant secretary of state. Acheson organized the Lend-Lease Program to assist Great Britain and the provocative oil embargo against Japan that contributed to the Japanese decision to attack the United States. He also developed and organized a strategy for conducting economic warfare against Germany and Italy. Acheson represented the State Department at the Bretton Woods Conference in 1944 and contributed to the Allied plan for the postwar economic system that included the establishment of the World Trade Organization, the World Bank, and the International Monetary Fund.

As under secretary of state in the Truman administration (1945–1949), Acheson supported the emerging containment policy against the Soviet Union and drafted the Truman Doctrine (see Document 3) and the Marshall Plan (see Document 5). After Truman's election to a full term as president, Acheson replaced George C. Marshall as secretary of state and remained in that position through January 20, 1953. He sustained the containment policy through his leadership in establishing the North Atlantic Treaty Organization (NATO) in 1949, which was designed to deter Soviet aggression in Europe. Acheson was also very concerned about the imminent collapse of China to the communists. He formed a study group that produced a white paper known as *United States Relations with China with Special Reference to the Period 1944–1949* (August 5, 1949), which was an indictment of American policy and recognized the coming success of Mao Zedong's communists. Combined with Truman's announcement on September 23, 1949, that the Soviet Union had detonated an atomic bomb, the information in the white paper contributed to the mounting criticism of Truman's foreign policy by those who were not satisfied with containment or with the administration's ineptitude in implementing it. On October 1, 1949, as expected, Mao Zedong proclaimed the establishment of the People's Republic of China. On January 12, 1950, Acheson presented a speech before the National Press Club in which he reviewed American foreign policy objectives and the "defense perimeter." He omitted Korea. Domestic critics have argued that his omission contributed to the communists' decision to invade South Korea on June 25, 1950.

On February 9, 1950, Senator Joseph McCarthy gave his infamous speech in Wheeling, West Virginia, in which he accused Acheson and the State Department of employing more than 200 communists. Acheson would later comment that this speech began the "attack of the primitives." Acheson was attacked for his continuing support of his friend Alger Hiss, even after his conviction for perjury. Hiss had worked in the federal government during the 1930s and 1940s and was involved in the diplomacy that led to the creation of the United Nations. Accused of being a Soviet agent by Whittaker Chambers, Hiss mounted a strong defense but was found guilty of perjury (but not treason). Acheson's postconviction support provided more material for McCarthy and his followers in their denunciation of Acheson and the State Department. Sentiment against Acheson was so extensive that the Republicans in the House of Representatives passed a motion on December 15, 1950, calling for his dismissal as secretary of state. However, Truman retained Acheson until the end of his term.

Acheson left office on January 20, 1953, and returned to his legal practice. During the next two years he continued to be attacked by McCarthy. During the Cuban missile crisis in October 1962, President John F. Kennedy invited Acheson to join an executive committee that coordinated American policy. Acheson was sent to Paris to gain the support of President Charles de Gaulle for the quarantine policy that Kennedy would soon announce against the Soviet Union and Cuba. Acheson resigned from the executive committee when it was revealed that the quarantine was the only component in Kennedy's planned response. Initially Acheson supported American policy in Vietnam but later reversed himself. He died on October 12, 1971.

For additional information, see *Dean Acheson: A Life in the Cold War* by Robert L. Beisner (New York: Oxford University Press, 2006) and Acheson's *Present at the Creation: My Years in the State Department* (New York: W. W. Norton, 1969).

ELIZABETH T. BENTLEY (1908–1963)

Elizabeth T. Bentley was an American-born Soviet spy during the years before and during World War II (1938–1945). Fearing that she would be assassinated by Soviet agents, Bentley confessed to the FBI in 1945 that she was a spy. When her testimony about her spying activities was made public in 1948—in which she exposed and implicated many individuals in and out of the government for their work on behalf of the Soviet Union—the American public was shocked, and many were convinced that there existed an internal threat from Soviet agents and sympathizers.

Bentley was born on January 1, 1908, into a middle-class family in New Milford, Connecticut. During her childhood and youth the family moved to Ithaca, New York, then to McKeesport, Pennsylvania, and finally they settled in Rochester, New York. She graduated from Vassar College (B.A. in English, 1930) and Columbia University (M.A., 1933) and then, with the aid of a fellowship, pursued additional studies at the University of Florence, Italy, where her knowledge of French and Italian helped her adapt to European life and her later espionage activities.

Bentley's earliest known political activities occurred at Columbia, where she joined a communist club. While in Italy she expressed support for Mussolini's fascist government but soon denounced that regime and resumed her activities in support of communism. Upon her return to the United States, Bentley joined the Communist Party of the United States in 1935 and in 1938 began working at the Italian Library of Information in New York. As an agency of the Italian government, the Italian Library promoted the image and interests of Mussolini's government.

Soon Bentley began providing secret information to the Communist Party USA. Her initial handler was Jacob Golos, with whom she became intimate and who was involved in plans to assassinate Leon Trotsky in Mexico. Bentley did not realize the she was serving as a Soviet agent until 1940, when she left the Italian Library and was made vice president of the United States Service and Shipping Corporation, a pro-Soviet front organization. Bentley's real duty was to serve as a courier for the transfer of secret information from the Silvermaster spy ring, which was led by Nathan Gregory Silvermaster, to the Soviet Union. The Silvermaster ring included Alger Hiss, Donald Hiss, and Harry Dexter White. By 1944 Bentley understood the extensive control of the Soviet Union over the Communist Party USA, and at the same time she recognized her precarious position and became increasingly fearful that she would be killed— she had heard that the Soviets had eliminated others who had been in similar situations.

That anxiety combined with the impact of failed relationships, excessive alcohol abuse, and paranoia led Bentley to consider defecting from the communist cause. In August 1945 she contacted the FBI in New Haven, Connecticut, and had a preliminary conversation. In October the defection of Louis Budenz, one of Bentley's communist contacts, became public. Fearing that Budenz would implicate and denounce her before she could defect, Bentley accelerated her planned process and defected on November 7, 1945. In her statements to the FBI, Bentley named more than 150 members in the spy networks with which she had experience and knowledge. At first the FBI wanted Bentley to serve as a double agent, but the FBI dropped the plan because of leaks on her defection and a developing understanding of her emotional and drinking problems. In 1948 she testified before a federal grand jury, made public statements on her spying activities, and provided information to the House Un-American Activities Committee. She corroborated Whittaker Chambers's testimony that Harry Dexter White, William Remington, and others were Soviet agents. During the 1950s and 1960s Bentley, because of her deepening depression and continuing alcohol abuse, had employment difficulties. She died on December 3, 1963. After the opening of the Soviet archives in the 1990s, Bentley's testimony was confirmed as accurate.

For additional information, see *Red Spy Queen: A Biography of Elizabeth Bentley* by Kathryn S. Olmsted (Chapel Hill: University of North Carolina Press, 2002) and *Clever Girl: Elizabeth Bentley, the Spy Who Ushered in the McCarthy Era* by Lauren Kessler (New York: Harper, 2003).

CHARLES E. BOHLEN (1904–1974)

Charles E. "Chip" Bohlen was an American diplomat who was a Soviet specialist and who served as U.S. ambassador to the Soviet Union (1953–1957), the Philippines (1957–1959), and France (1962–1968). From his entrance into the U.S. Foreign Service in 1929 until his appointment as ambassador to the Soviet Union, Bohlen served in numerous posts in Czechoslovakia, France, Latvia, the Soviet Union, and Japan. He also worked as an adviser to Presidents Franklin D. Roosevelt, Harry Truman, and John F. Kennedy, and as an interpreter for Roosevelt at the Tehran and Yalta Conferences during World War II.

Charles Eustis Bohlen was born on August 30, 1904, in Clayton, New York, into a wealthy family—he was related to the Krupp family that produced many German weapons and was a grandson of James Biddle Eustis, a judge advocate in the Confederate Army, U.S. senator (D-LA), and ambassador to France during President Grover Cleveland's second term. Bohlen graduated from Harvard University with a B.A. in history in 1927 and spent the next year touring the world. In 1929 he entered the Foreign Service and, with a fluency in Russian, quickly became a Russian specialist. Bohlen's early assignments took him to Latvia, Czechoslovakia, France, and in 1934 to the Soviet Union as vice-consul under Ambassador William C. Bullitt. He travelled extensively in the Soviet Union and returned to Washington, DC, where he was debriefed. In 1940 Bohlen was assigned to be second secretary at the American embassy in Tokyo. After the Japanese attack on Pearl Harbor, Bohlen was interned until the late spring of 1942, when an exchange of diplomats was arranged. During World War II Bohlen served as assistant chief of European affairs (1943), first secretary at the American embassy in Moscow (1943–1944), chief of the Division of Eastern European Affairs (1944), and assistant to the secretary of state for the White House liaison (1944–1946). In addition, Bohlen served as interpreter and advisor to Harry Hopkins in his Moscow meetings with Josef Stalin. He developed a personal relationship with Roosevelt when he was the president's interpreter at the Tehran and Yalta Conferences. Bohlen also served as President Truman's interpreter at the Potsdam Conference in July 1945.

Unlike George Kennan and Paul Nitze, Bohlen—while arguing for a nonpartisan foreign policy—recognized the impact of domestic politics on foreign affairs. Generally, he was identified with the liberals and became a target of McCarthyism. After the war Bohlen disagreed with Kennan's containment policy and suggested that the United States adopt a policy that accommodated Soviet interests and recognized their hegemony in Eastern Europe. However, when the decision was made in favor of containment, Bohlen supported that policy. During the Truman administration Bohlen served as a counselor of the Department of State, was involved in the development of the Marshall Plan (see Document 5), and became an adviser to Truman. After Kennan could no longer serve as U.S. ambassador to the Soviet Union because of statements that he made in September 1952 that the Soviets found offensive, President Dwight D. Eisenhower appointed Bohlen as his replacement in April 1953. He held that post through 1957—years that witnessed the rise of Nikita Khrushchev, insurrections in Poland and Hungry, the Suez crisis, and Secretary of State John Foster Dulles's doctrine of "massive retaliation" (see Document 9). Upon Dulles's recommendation, Bohlen was removed from the Moscow assignment in 1957, demoted, and appointed U.S. ambassador to the Philippines (1957–1959). Dulles had been consistently critical of Bohlen's performance in the Soviet Union.

In 1959 the new secretary of state, Christian Herter, brought Bohlen back to Washington to serve as special assistant to the secretary of state. He continued in that position in the Kennedy administration and served Secretary of State Dean Rusk until he was appointed U.S. ambassador to France in 1962. Bohlen held that difficult position, which centered on the policies of President Charles de Gaulle—including American-Franco tensions relating to French membership in NATO—until 1968. Bohlen retired from the Foreign Service in 1969 and died on January 1, 1974, in Washington.

For additional information, see *The Wise Men: Six Friends and the World They Made; Acheson, Bohlen, Harriman, Kennan, Lovett, McCoy* by Walter Isaacson and Evan Thomas (New York: Simon and Schuster, 1986) and *The Cautious Diplomat: Charles E. Bohlen and the Soviet Union, 1929–1969* by T. Michael Ruddy (Kent, OH: Kent State University Press, 1987).

JOHN FOSTER DULLES (1888–1959)

John Foster Dulles served as secretary of state under President Dwight D. Eisenhower from 1953 until his resignation in 1959 that was due to a terminal illness. During his five years as secretary of state, Dulles expanded American Cold War alliances to isolate and "roll back" the influence and power of the Soviet Union and Communist China, worked to overthrow regimes in Iran and Guatemala, advanced the policy of massive retaliation, supported the French in Indochina, opposed the British and French actions in the Suez crisis (1956), endorsed the Eisenhower doctrine, and misread the causes and significance of anti-Soviet developments in Poland and Hungary.

Dulles was born on February 25, 1888, in Washington, DC, to the Reverend Allen Macy and Edith Foster Dulles. His paternal father and grandfather were Presbyterian ministers, and his maternal grandfather, John W. Dulles, served as secretary of state, as did his uncle, Robert Lansing. His brother, Allen Welsh Dulles, served as the first director of the Central Intelligence Agency, and his sister, Eleanor Lansing Dulles, worked at the State Department for decades and played a significant role in the economic recovery of Europe after World War II. Dulles graduated from Princeton University, where he was a student of Woodrow Wilson in 1908, studied at the Sorbonne in Paris, and then received a law degree from George Washington University in 1911. During World War I he served as a U.S. army major on the War Industries Board. President Woodrow Wilson appointed Dulles as a legal counsel to the American delegation at the Versailles Peace Conference, where he served under his uncle, Secretary of State Robert Lansing, who led the delegation when Wilson was not present. After the conference Dulles was appointed to the War Reparations Committee, where he opposed excessive demands on the Germans. During the 1920s and 1930s Dulles returned to the private practice of law and advanced the agenda of the Presbyterian Church at many conferences. His law firm, Sullivan and Cromwell, managed accounts for the Nazi Party during the late 1920s and early 1930s. Dulles was a vocal supporter of Adolf Hitler during 1933 and 1934, though he ceased his firm's relationship with the Hitler regime in 1935 when his brother Allen and other partners in the firm threatened to act against Dulles if he did not close their Berlin office. In 1939 Dulles wrote *War, Peace and Change*, which denounced fascism.

During World War II Dulles's conservatism, commitment to international institutions, and intense Christian beliefs were evident. He supported the war effort and chaired President Roosevelt's Commission to Study the Bases of a Just and Durable Peace, which advocated the establishment and use of international organizations in resolving disputes and which defended the fundamental freedoms of all peoples in politics, religion, and speech. Dulles supported Governor Thomas Dewey's (R-NY) 1944 presidential campaign, opposed the use of the atomic bomb against Japan, and worked to establish the United Nations. Dulles assisted Senator Arthur H. Vandenberg (R-MI) at the San Francisco Conference in 1945 and served as an American delegate to the UN General Assembly for three sessions between 1946 and 1950. In 1949 Dulles served briefly (July–November 1949) as a senator from New York—he was appointed by Governor Thomas Dewey upon the death of Senator Robert Wagner (D-NY) but was defeated by Herbert Lehman in a special election. With the emergence of the Cold War with the Soviet Union and Communist China, Dulles became a critic of Truman's containment policy. In 1950 Dulles published *War or Peace* and argued that "liberation" rather than "containment" should be the cornerstone of American policy. This militant position attracted the attention of moderates and conservatives alike.

Dulles was appointed secretary of state by President Eisenhower in 1953 and for the next six years became the voice of American Cold War policy. Diplomatically, Dulles strengthened the North Atlantic Treaty Organization (NATO) and initiated the establishment of the Southeast Asia Treaty Organization (SEATO) in 1954. Through SEATO, Australia, France, New Zealand, Pakistan, the Philippines, Thailand, the United Kingdom, and the United States pledged collective action against aggression. Dulles, along with his brother Allen, also was directly involved in the overthrow of the government of Iranian prime minister Mohammed Mossadegh in 1953 and the installation of Mohammad Reza Pahlavi, the shah of Iran, as ruler. In 1954 the Dulles brothers worked successfully to topple the government of Jacobo Árbenz Guzmán in Guatemala. Like Eisenhower, Dulles was concerned with the financing of the Cold War with the Soviet Union and at the same time fearful of nuclear war. Nonetheless, on January 12, 1954, Dulles announced that the United States would protect itself and its allies with "massive retaliation" (i.e., they would rely on nuclear weapons) in the event of war with the Soviet Union (see Document 9). This policy led to diplomacy known as brinkmanship. In 1956 Dulles condemned the British and French for their attack on Egypt in the Suez Crisis, and he did not support the Hungarians in their revolt against the Soviets, which occurred at about the same time. Dulles became increasingly annoyed with states that were neutral—to Dulles, you either supported the United States or you were an enemy. During the fall of 1956 Dulles was diagnosed with colon cancer, and despite aggressive treatments that temporarily arrested the cancer, Dulles died on May 24, 1959. Christian Herter succeeded Dulles as secretary of state.

For additional information, see *John Foster Dulles: Piety, Pragmatism, and Power in U.S. Foreign Policy* by Richard H. Immerman (Lanham, MD: Rowman and Littlefield, 1998) and *John Foster Dulles and the Diplomacy of the Cold War* edited by Richard H. Immerman (Princeton, NJ: Princeton University Press, 1992).

J. WILLIAM FULBRIGHT (1905–1995)

J. William Fulbright was a dominant force in the U.S. Senate for three decades during the Cold War. He chaired the Senate Foreign Relations

Committee and was instrumental in the passage of many Cold War–related acts and treaties. In 1964 he supported passage of the Tonkin Gulf Resolution, which resulted in expanding the American commitment in South Vietnam. By 1967, however, he had became an ardent critic President Lyndon Johnson's Vietnam policy.

J. [James] William Fulbright was born on April 9, 1905, in Sumner, Missouri, to Jay and Roberta Fulbright. His parents relocated to Fayetteville, Arkansas, in 1906 and developed an extensive successful and multifaceted business that included a bank, newspaper, manufacturing, and a lumberyard. Fulbright had an extraordinary education. He earned a B.A. in history (1925) from the University of Arkansas and also participated in its experimental programs as a child and during his teen years. Recipient of a Rhodes scholarship, Fulbright received another B.A. (1928) and a M.A. (1931) from Oxford University. He traveled extensively in central and southeastern Europe during his years studying at Oxford. Fulbright returned to Arkansas in 1931 and then went to Washington, DC, where he earned a law degree from George Washington University in 1934. He served in President Franklin D. Roosevelt's Justice Department and at the National Recovery Administration until it was declared unconstitutional. Fulbright taught law at George Washington University before accepting a teaching position at the Law School at the University of Arkansas in 1936. In 1939, at the age of 34, Fulbright was named president of the University of Arkansas (his mother had arranged the appointment). Two years later, when the board of trustees came under the control of anti-Fulbright forces, Fulbright lost that position.

In 1942, he was elected to the U.S. Congress. Fulbright was an internationalist and an ardent supporter of the new United Nations. In 1944 he was elected to the U.S. Senate and began a 30-year senatorial tenure that witnessed his willingness to change positions while at the same time consistently protecting the interests of his constituents, Arkansas, and the United States. In 1946 Fulbright established the Fulbright Exchange Program to sponsor international educational opportunities that he hoped would result in a new generation of global leaders who would be equipped to better understand the world and its people and to live in peace.

Recognized for his intelligence, wit, and sophistication, Fulbright supported the containment policy, the Truman Doctrine, the Marshall Plan, and the establishment of NATO. Outraged by Senator Joseph McCarthy's behavior and reckless accusations, Fulbright assisted in organizing Senate colleagues in the censure of Senator Joseph McCarthy on December 4, 1954. However, in 1956 Fulbright signed the "Southern Manifesto," which was a pledge to support segregation in spite of the decisions of the Supreme Court. During the 1957 integration crisis at Little Rock (Arkansas) High School, Fulbright was touring Europe. Upon his return he attacked Governor Orval Faubus for mismanaging the crisis and embarrassing the people of Arkansas. Fulbright's civil rights record was at best mixed, and he opposed civil rights bills until 1970. While primarily motivated by political considerations, Fulbright—an elitist—considered himself surrounded, for the most part, by inferiors.

In 1959 Fulbright was appointed chair of the Senate Foreign Relations Committee on which he had served since 1949. He chaired that committee until 1974. In that capacity he received information of the planned Bay of Pigs invasion in April 1961. He voiced his opposition to President Kennedy, but the plan went ahead anyway. In response to reported attacks on U.S. naval units in the Tonkin Gulf off the coast of Vietnam, on August 7, 1964, Fulbright, along with 94 other senators and at the request of President Lyndon Johnson, voted for the Gulf of Tonkin resolution, which expanded the war in Vietnam through presidential fiat. When Johnson used the resolution to greatly increase the number of American troops in Vietnam, Fulbright regretted his vote and became a vocal critic of the war, denouncing the argument that the Vietnam intervention was required by Cold War geopolitics. In 1966 Fulbright published *The Arrogance of Power*, which expanded the arguments that he advanced in the Senate and in public. Fulbright's Senate Foreign Relations Committee held hearings on American policy and actions in Vietnam during the late 1960s and early 1970s. Some of these hearings were televised and resulted in extending the debate on American policy. Fulbright's Senate career ended in 1974 when he was defeated in the Arkansas Democratic primary by a strong challenger, Governor Dale Bumpers, who was supported by the right-wing forces that had come to despise Fulbright because of his criticism of the Vietnam War. During the next 20 years Fulbright practiced law in Washington, DC, and he died on February 9, 1995.

For additional information, see *William Fulbright and the Vietnam War: The Dissent of a Political Realist* by William C. Berman (Kent, OH: Kent State University Press, 1988); *J. William Fulbright, Vietnam, and the Search for a Cold War Foreign Policy* by Randall Bennett Woods (New York: Cambridge University Press, 1998); *Fulbright: A Biography* by Randall Bennett Woods (New York: Cambridge University Press, 1995); and *The Arrogance of Power* by J. William Fulbright (New York: Random House, 1967).

WILLIAM FRANKLIN "BILLY" GRAHAM, JR. (1918–)

Billy Graham's career as a preeminent American Christian evangelist paralleled the Cold War. Graham opposed the atheism of communism and gave spiritual, and sometimes political, advice to American presidents. The secularism of the Soviet world was repugnant to Graham. When he concluded that there was no biblical rationale for segregation, he supported the emerging civil rights movement during the 1950s. When Graham appeared in New York at his 1957 crusade, he reinforced Martin Luther King, Jr.'s argument that Christianity required supporting the civil rights movement. In 1963 Graham provided the bail that resulted in King's release from jail in Birmingham, Alabama.

Graham was born on November 7, 1918, near Charlotte, North Carolina. Raised by loving but strict parents who opposed all alcohol consumption, Graham was influenced and "born again" in 1934 by Mordecai Fowler Ham, Jr. (1877–1961). Ham was an American Independent Baptist evangelist and temperance movement leader. After a semester at Bob Jones University, Graham enrolled at the Florida Bible Institute (now Trinity Bible College) and received a diploma in 1940. In 1943 he was awarded a B.A. in anthropology from Wheaton College in Illinois, and in the same year he married a Wheaton student, Ruth Bell (1920–2007), who had been born in China to Presbyterian missionaries.

Graham served as a minister to several congregations during the mid-1940s, and he was president of the Northwestern Bible College in Minneapolis between 1948 and 1952. During this time he developed a national reputation as a leader of youth and an American patriot. In 1949 Graham organized a revival meeting in Los Angeles that gained media support from William Randolph Hearst, who saw Graham as a potential conservative anticommunist leader. With the additional assistance of Henry Luce, Graham became a nationally known personality. He had close relationships with Dwight D. Eisenhower and Richard M. Nixon, and he developed contacts with all American presidents from

Eisenhower to Barack Obama. He was involved in a secret effort among evangelical Protestants to undermine the presidential bid of the Catholic John F. Kennedy in 1960. When this effort became known, it weakened Graham's position and made him less inclined to become entangled in political interests.

Unlike others who opposed communism and other aspects of the Soviet regime, Graham did not make that the core of his message or life. He approached the Cold War as a moral conflict—the godless communists were evil while God fearing and loving America was good. He remained fixed on a biblically based Christianity, which was a consistent theme of his more that 400 crusades. Beginning in 1977 in Budapest, Hungary, Graham was the first Christian preacher to be allowed to conduct crusades behind the Iron Curtain.

He established the Billy Graham Evangelistic Association in North Carolina in 1950, which evolved into a multimedia empire that retained focus on the Christ as savior message. During the 1950s Graham spoke out against segregation and racism, but he was not in the forefront of the civil rights movement. He supported and identified with King but avoided political entanglements. After the close of the Cold War, Graham continued his evangelization work and expanded his international reputation. His preaching style and convictions, and the well-organized crusades he ran, drew tens of thousands to his revivals, which featured highly orchestrated yet passionate singing, praying, and sermonizing that concluded with calls to come forward to make a public commitment to Christ. The Graham crusades became staples of Christian television, even in reruns, which extended his influence and reach. His last major speaking engagement was in 2006, when he spoke at a religious crusade in Baltimore, Maryland, that was organized by his son Franklin Graham.

For additional information, see *Billy Graham: His Life and Influence* by David Aikman (New York: Thomas Nelson, 2010) and *Billy Graham and the Rise of the Republican South* by Steven P. Miller (Philadelphia: University of Pennsylvania Press, 2009).

THOMAS EMMET HAYDEN (1939–)

Thomas "Tom" Hayden emerged as a leader of the antiwar movement during the 1960s, and he became visible as a national advocate of civil rights and as a social activist. Hayden led the Students for a Democratic Society, worked as a freedom rider in the South, wrote the "Port Huron Statement," founded the Indochina Peace Campaign, and became an ardent critic of American policy in Vietnam. Later he served in the California State Assembly (1982–1992) and Senate (1992–2000), and he co-founded the Peace and Justice Resource Center in Culver City, California, which he currently directs.

Born on December 11, 1939, in Detroit, Michigan, Hayden attended the University of Michigan, where he developed a reputation as an antiestablishment student activist. He edited the *Michigan Daily* and was a member of the Students for a Democratic Society (SDS). During the early 1960s Hayden became a freedom rider in the southern states defending the civil rights of African Americans. In 1962 he clarified SDS objectives with the "Port Huron Statement: An Agenda for a Generation," which stated that its two major objectives were to actively pursue and support civil rights for all and to combat the culture of the Cold War, which could lead to the end of humanity. These objectives would be realized through a radical activism that rejected the past. Hayden became president of the SDS in 1962 and served a one-year term. In 1965 Hayden travelled to North Vietnam with Staughton Lynd, a peace activist affiliated with the Society of Friends, and Herbert Aptheker, a member of the Communist Party USA. While there they denounced the anticommunism of the American government and society. Hayden participated in the antiwar protests at the Chicago Democratic National Convention in 1968, where he was arrested and convicted for inciting a riot. However, the conviction was overturned on appeal. Hayden emerged as one of the leaders of the new left and attracted a following of dissidents, mostly from his own generation. Hayden made additional trips to North Vietnam, including one in 1972 with actress Jane Fonda, whom he married in 1973. Also in 1972 Hayden established the Indochina Peace Campaign to oversee national and regional antiwar efforts in the United States. In 1976 Hayden undertook an unsuccessful primary campaign for the Democratic nomination the U.S. Senate against incumbent Senator John V. Tunney (D-CA). Tunney was upset in the general election by Republican S. I. Hayakawa, the president of San Francisco State University. Hayden continued to work for social and economic justice and against war through his Campaign for Economic Democracy. A prolific author, Hayden has published more than 20 books and currently serves as the director of the Peace and Justice Center.

For additional information, see *The Other Side* by Staughton Lynd and Thomas Hayden (New York: Signet/New American Library, 1967) and *Tom Hayden* edited by Jesse Russell and Ronald Cohn (Stoughton, WI: Books on Demand, 2012).

J. [JOHN] EDGAR HOOVER (1895–1972)

J. Edgar Hoover served as director of the Federal Bureau of Investigation for 37 years (1935–1972) and played an important role in the first and second Red Scares as well as the Cold War. He nurtured the reputation of the FBI at the same time that he used legal and illegal investigative techniques in amassing data in secret files on Americans he suspected of holding left-wing views or who could pose an internal security threat to the United States.

Born on January 1, 1895, in Washington, DC, Hoover earned a law degree from the George Washington University School of Law in 1916 and became a special assistant to the U.S. attorney general in 1917. With seemingly tireless energy, solid organizational skills, and a deep-seated commitment to the security of the United States, Hoover advanced rapidly in the Justice Department and was appointed to direct the General Intelligence Division. This appointment coincided with the Red Scare that followed World War I. Disillusioned with the failings of capitalism, the war, and prevailing American values, dissenters—communists, anarchists, and others not aligned with a political philosophy—wanted dramatic political, economic, and social change. While many in these minority groups were content to confine their aspirations to writing and speaking, a few resorted to violence. With the support of Attorney General A. Mitchell Palmer, Hoover built a database on radicals and tracked down those who were involved in bombings of Wall Street and other sites. Hoover directed much of his attention to the new Communist Party of the United States, which he considered a danger to the country.

In 1924 Hoover was appointed the director of the Bureau of Investigation, which was renamed the Federal Bureau of Investigation in 1935. In the midst of a wave of lawlessness that was related to the culture of the Depression and increased anxiety over the growth of the Communist Party

USA, Hoover succeeded in expanding the mission, responsibilities, and size of the FBI. He argued that the FBI had to be free from political pressures in its investigations, and he succeeded in increasing the budget and adding forensic facilities.

As the United States entered World War II, Hoover not only was concerned with the prospect of Nazi and Japanese sabotage and spying, but also with the infiltration and spying activities of an ally, the Soviet Union. Along with the British government, the FBI joined in the Venona Project during the 1930s. In this effort Soviet codes were broken, and an extensive espionage network was revealed in both countries. Hoover never informed President Truman of the Venona Project or that he possessed the valuable intercepts. In 1945 Hoover became increasingly concerned with the impact of Soviet spying. He supported the loyalty programs (See Document 4) introduced by the Truman administration and provided federal agencies with a constant flow of information. During the late 1940s Hoover introduced a process in which an FBI file on an individual not only included the assessed and validated report, but also "field notes" that were not verified. As Hoover became increasingly concerned with internal subversion, the field notes, were used frequently to intimidate individuals and gain support among political leaders in and out of government.

Deeply influenced by the deterioration of U.S.-Soviet relations, the Soviet detonation of an atomic bomb, communist successes in Eastern Europe and China, and—perhaps most significantly—by the revelations provided by Elizabeth Bentley and Whittaker Chambers on the activities within and on behalf of the Communist Party and the Soviet Union, Hoover expanded the FBI's investigations of internal subversion. With the ascendency of Senator Joseph McCarthy in the spring 1950 as a leader of anticommunism, Hoover quietly supported McCarthy's Senate investigations by providing information, research assistance, and personnel. Hoover maintained a distance in his relationship with McCarthy, and with the failure of the Army-McCarthy hearings, the denunciation of McCarthy by Edward R. Murrow, and the Senate censure of McCarthy in December 1954, Hoover withdrew all assistance. In June 1950 the Korean War started, and Hoover submitted a plan to detain more than 12,000 Americans suspected of disloyalty. However, Truman declined to follow through with the plan. In the post-McCarthy 1950s the Supreme Court rendered decisions that limited the government's power in investigations and prosecutions. Hoover adjusted to these constraints but continued to pursue his anticommunist agenda. He also instituted the secret "Cointelpro" program, a covert operation that ignored the law and violated individual liberties.

During the 1950s and 1960s Hoover began to develop "secret" files on major political and social leaders, most notably President John F. Kennedy and Martin Luther King, Jr. Informed rumors spread about the existence of these files, and Hoover alluded to their existence in private conversations with some of the presidents he served. As the Cold War developed in the 1960s, Hoover's fear of internal subversion expanded. He considered the civil rights, free speech, and feminist movements dangerous and potential sources for Soviet exploitation. Racial riots, the activities of the Ku Klux Klan, acts of political violence, and the assassinations of President John F. Kennedy; Martin Luther King, Jr.; and Senator Robert F. Kennedy exacerbated his concerns and affected his leadership of the FBI when questions arose about his abilities as a principal law enforcement officer. Hoover remained in office until his death on May 2, 1972.

For additional information, see *Young J. Edgar: Hoover, the Red Scare, and the Assault on Civil Liberties* by Kenneth D. Ackerman (New York: Carroll and Graf, 2007) and *Secrecy and Power: The Life of J. Edgar Hoover* by Richard Gid Powers (New York: Free Press, 1988).

GEORGE F. KENNAN (1904–2005)

George F. Kennan served as a diplomat and foreign policy adviser to many presidents prior to, during, and after the Cold War. Author of "The Long Telegram" (1946) (see Document 2) and a related article, "The Sources of Soviet Conduct" in *Foreign Affairs* (1947), Kennan had a significant impact on the development of American foreign policy after World War II. He became a critic of the application of his earlier thoughts on containment, served briefly as U.S. ambassador to the Soviet Union during the Truman administration and as U.S. ambassador to Yugoslavia in the Kennedy administration. For the last 50 years of his life, he was affiliated with the Institute of Historical Studies in Princeton, New Jersey, where he wrote and lectured. Kennan was an independent thinker who approached diplomacy as a realist—he did not support the use of American power to advance democracy or in the process of nation-building. Nonetheless, he was revered and recognized by many who pursued policies that Kennan condemned, such as the war in Kosovo (1998) and the Iraq war (2003), because of his historic role during the early years of the Cold War.

Kennan was born on February 16, 1904, in Milwaukee, Wisconsin. He graduated from Princeton University in 1925 and joined the U.S. Foreign Service. Initially assigned as a vice consul in Switzerland, Kennan was transferred in 1927 to the U.S. consulate in Hamburg, Germany. From 1929 to 1931 he studied Russian and related subjects at the University of Berlin. These studies were subsidized by the U.S. State Department. In 1931 Kennan was assigned to Riga, Latvia, and expanded his knowledge of and interest in all aspects of Soviet affairs. In 1933 the United States opened diplomatic relations with the Soviet Union. Kennan, along with Charles E. Bohlen, was assigned to the Moscow embassy, which was headed by Ambassador William C. Bullitt. Kennan's views on the Soviet Union and its leader, Josef Stalin, were transformed by the horrors of the Great Purge that resulted in the execution of more than a million people between 1936 and 1938. Ambassador Joseph E. Davies replaced Bullitt in 1936 and almost immediately found himself at odds with Kennan. Davies argued that the purge was of no concern to the United States. Kennan considered leaving the Foreign Service but was transferred to the Moscow desk at the State Department in Washington. In September 1938 Kennan was dispatched to Prague in the midst of the Munich Crisis between Germany, Britain, and France over the Sudetenland, Czechoslovakia.

After the subsequent fall of Czechoslovakia in the spring 1939, Kennan was assigned to the Berlin embassy. Between 1939 and 1941 Kennan persisted in arguing that the United States should not provide any support to the Soviet Union because of its unpredictability and unreliability. After Germany declared war against the United States on December 11, 1941, Kennan and other American diplomats were interned in Germany until an exchange of diplomats was arranged in June 1942. During the war he held positions in Lisbon, London, and Moscow, where he remained after the war and quickly became dissatisfied with the direction of American policy related to the Soviet Union. In 1945 the Truman administration indicated that it desired to cooperate with the Soviet Union, and Kennan countered that such cooperation was not in America's interests. On February 22, 1946, as deputy head of the American mission in Moscow, he sent a telegram ("The Long Telegram") (see Document 2) to Secretary of State James Byrnes that provided a detailed explanation of Soviet motivation and sense of history, along with guidelines for appropriate relations with the Soviet Union. Kennan argued that Russian insecurity was the fundamental driving force of Soviet policies and that Stalin's continuance in power was dependent on a worldview in which the Soviet Union was threatened by imperialists and capitalists. The solution was to strengthen the West and contain the Soviets until they adopted a new international perspective. In 1946 Kennan returned to Washington to work at the National War College. In the July 1947 issue of *Foreign Affairs*, Kennan—using the pseudonym "X"—published "The Sources of Soviet Conduct." In this article he stated that Soviet policy was founded upon Marxist-Leninist ideology, rather than the element of insecurity that he stressed in the "Long Telegram." Kennan assisted Secretary of State George Marshall with the development of the Marshall Plan (see Document 5) for the economic recovery of Europe.

His influence at the State Department declined after Marshall, who was suffering from poor health, resigned and was replaced by Dean Acheson. Kennan believed that the Soviets were exhausted by World War II and were not in any position to get involved in a major conflict. However, Acheson viewed the Soviet Union as a direct and imminent military threat. As the decade closed with the Soviets acquiring nuclear capability, the fall of China to the communists, and the outbreak of the Korean War, Kennan joined in the consensus that the United States had to be prepared for military action when needed. American hawks such as Paul Nitze gained the ascendency and formulated a National Security Council Report (NSC-68) (see Document 7), which was endorsed by Truman and Acheson as the defining statement on American foreign policy in waging the Cold War. Only Kennan and Bohlen opposed it.

The rift between Kennan and Acheson expanded when they differed on Korea and the development of the hydrogen bomb. In spite of this, Truman appointed Kennan as ambassador to the Soviet Union in December 1951. His tenure was brief, as the Soviets refused to allow Kennan to return to the Soviet Union in September 1952 after he made a statement comparing his Moscow residence to the more favorable conditions that he experienced while interned in Germany in 1941–1942. Kennan's relationship with Acheson's successor, John Foster Dulles (Eisenhower's secretary of state, 1953–1959), was strained from the outset because of Dulles's personality and because Kennan questioned the means through which Dulles planned to "roll back" communist advances.

At the invitation of J. Robert Oppenheimer, Kennan became affiliated with the Institute of Advanced Studies in Princeton, New Jersey, as a resident scholar in 1950. By 1956 Kennan was a member of the institute's School of Historical Studies, where he remained for almost a half-century. Other than serving rather unsuccessfully as U.S. ambassador to Yugoslavia during the Kennedy administration (1961–1963), Kennan settled in at Princeton to write and lecture on American foreign policy. He produced numerous books and articles, and he won two Pulitzer Prizes, two National Book Awards, the Bancroft Prize from Columbia University, and the Parkman Prize conferred by the Society of American Historians. Kennan died on March 17, 2005, in Princeton, New Jersey.

For additional information, see *George F. Kennan: An American Life* by John Lewis Gaddis (New York: Penguin, 2011) and *George Kennan: A Study of Character* by John Lukacs (New Haven, CT: Yale University Press, 2009).

ROBERT F. KENNEDY (1925–1968)

Robert F. Kennedy served as U.S. attorney general (1961–1964) and U.S. senator (D-NY) (1965–1968). As one of the primary advisers to his brother, President John F. Kennedy, he was deeply involved in the formulation of American policy during the Berlin crisis (1961) and the Cuban missile crisis with the Soviet Union and Cuba (1962). After his election to the Senate, Robert Kennedy emerged as a critic of President Lyndon Baines Johnson's Vietnam strategy (see Document 13).

Robert F. Kennedy was born on November 20, 1925, in Brookline, Massachusetts, into one of the most politically influential families in twentieth-century America. Initially enrolled in the Harvard University naval officer program, he was released from that program and served as an enlisted seaman in the navy during the last months of World War II. In May 1946 he was discharged from the navy and matriculated at Harvard, from which he graduated in 1948. Kennedy travelled in Europe and the Near East for several months after graduation and wrote several articles for the *Boston Post*. He visited Palestine and predicted the outbreak of war with the establishment of an Israeli state. Upon his return Kennedy enrolled in the University of Virginia's Law School, and he was awarded his law degree in 1951. In October 1951 John Kennedy (then a U.S. congressman), their sister Patricia, and Robert made a tour of Israel, India, Vietnam (at that time still part of French Indo-China), and Japan. After the trip Robert Kennedy moved his family to Washington, DC, where he started working as counsel for the Justice Department. He was involved in investigating those suspected of being Soviet agents, which was his direct entry to the Cold War.

Shortly thereafter he was assigned to a group that focused on fraud. In 1952 he left the Justice Department to lead his brother's campaign for the U.S. Senate. John Kennedy succeeded in defeating the incumbent Henry Cabot Lodge, Jr. In December 1952 Robert Kennedy was appointed as assistant counsel to Senator Joseph McCarthy's (R-WI) Permanent Subcommittee on Investigations. Kennedy's father, Joseph, was an ardent anticommunist and personal friend of McCarthy's, and he provided the necessary influence to obtain the appointment for his son. Robert Kennedy served seven months in that position before resigning to accept a position as counsel to the Senate Democratic minority leadership. In 1956 he was an aide in the presidential campaign of Governor Adlai Stevenson (D-IL), though Kennedy was not impressed with Stevenson and later reported that he voted for President Eisenhower. Between 1957 and 1959 Robert Kennedy developed a national reputation as a tough investigator on the Senate Labor Rackets Committee, which was chaired by John L. McClellan (D-AR). While on this committee Kennedy's most notable target was the teamster leader James Hoffa. In 1959 he resigned from the committee to organize John Kennedy's presidential campaign.

In 1961 the Senate approved President Kennedy's appointment of his brother Robert as U.S. attorney general. While Robert Kennedy continued his work against organized crime, he also served as his brother's confidant and adviser on other matters, including the Cold War. During the Berlin crisis in 1961–1962, which resulted from the impasse over the military occupation of Berlin and the construction of the Berlin Wall by the East German government, Robert Kennedy acted as a conduit between the United States and Soviet Union. During the Cuban missile crisis in October 1962, he was first a hawk in his recommendations in confronting the Soviets, but the discussions of his brother's executive committee on the crisis led him to modify his views and seek a peaceful resolution through the quarantine policy (see Document 11).

He also agreed with his brother's decision not to expand America's commitment in Vietnam by assuming responsibility and launching a land war. President Lyndon Johnson, using the rationale of the domino theory, expanded the war in 1965 (see Document 13) by committing large numbers of American troops. By 1967 Kennedy was a vocal critic of American involvement in Vietnam and argued that human rights must be a major factor in formulating American foreign policy. In the fall of 1967 Senator Eugene McCarthy (D-MN) announced that he would seek the Democratic nomination for president. McCarthy gained strength as the antiwar movement expanded. On March 12, 1968, McCarthy came in a strong second to the incumbent Johnson in the New Hampshire primary, where he demonstrated Johnson's vulnerability and led Kennedy to announce his own candidacy on March 16, 1968. In a televised address to the nation on March 31, 1968, Johnson announced that he would not continue to seek re-election. The next months witnessed the assassination of Martin Luther King, Jr.; Kennedy's victories in the Indiana and Nebraska primaries; McCarthy's victory in Oregon; and then on June 4, 1968, Kennedy's victory in the California primary. Early on June 5, after his victory speech, Kennedy was shot. He died the next day, on June 6, 1968.

For additional information, see *Robert Kennedy and His Times* by Arthur Schlesinger, Jr. (New York: Mariner Books, 2002) and *The Last Campaign: Robert F. Kennedy and the Eighty-Two Days That Inspired America* by Thurston Clarke (New York: Holt, 2009).

HEINZ ALFRED "HENRY" KISSINGER (1923–)

Henry Kissinger served as national security advisor and secretary of state under President Richard M. Nixon (1969–1974) and as secretary of state under President Gerald Ford (1974 and 1977). In those capacities Kissinger advanced the policy of détente with the Soviet Union (see Document 14), redirected relations with China, and negotiated an end to American participation in the Vietnam War. He also supported Nixon during the Watergate crisis until he recognized the inevitable need for the president's resignation, at which time he worked to facilitate Nixon's departure.

Kissinger was born on May 23, 1923, in Fürth, in Bavaria, Germany, into a family of Jews. Fearing Hitler's Nazi regime, the Kissinger family fled Germany in 1938 and took up residence in New York. Kissinger attended the City College of New York until 1943, when he was drafted into the army. He was involved in combat during the Battle of the Bulge in December 1944 and, with his language skills, became involved with administration and intelligence as the army penetrated Germany. After the war Kissinger studied political science at Harvard, where he earned A.B., M.A., and Ph.D. degrees. His dissertation focused on the diplomacy associated with the Congress of Vienna after the defeat of Napoleon. This study—which advanced the values of *realpolitik*—was published in 1954 as *A World Restored: Metternich, Castlereagh, and the Problems of Peace, 1812–1822*.

Kissinger approached diplomacy as a pragmatist. He remained at Harvard University on the faculty and became affiliated with the Council on Foreign Relations in 1955 and the Rockefeller Brothers Fund in 1956. He supported Governor Nelson Rockefeller of New York in his efforts to acquire the Republican presidential nomination in 1960, 1964, and 1968. After the election of Richard Nixon in 1968, Kissinger was named national security advisor, and on September 22, 1973, he became secretary of state, a position in which he remained after Nixon's resignation. He continued to serve until President Gerald Ford left office on January 20, 1977. As National security advisor and secretary of state, Kissinger exerted extensive influence on American foreign policy. While his major achievements were détente with the Soviet Union, the reorientation of American foreign policy with China and the success of triangulation, and the end of the Vietnam War, Kissinger was also involved with the India-Pakistan War in 1971, the Yom Kippur War in 1973, the overthrow of the Allende regime in Chile in 1973, and African conflicts in Angola and Rhodesia.

Implementing Nixon's policy of détente with the Soviet Union, Kissinger led the stalled (because of the Soviet invasion of Czechoslovakia during the Prague Spring in 1968) negotiations with Soviet leader Leonid Brezhnev that resulted in the SALT I (Strategic Arms Limitations Talks) and the ABM (Anti-Ballistic Missile) Treaty. Negotiations were conducted over several years, with both sides approaching them in a productive manner. These talks and the subsequent agreements were accompanied by a general relaxation of tension between the two powers.

Arriving at an agreeable number of ICBMs was rendered difficult by technological advances—with MIRVs (multiple independently targetable re-entry vehicles) each ICBM could launch multiple warheads directed at different targets.

Détente with the Soviet Union paralleled a new initiative with China that was intended to exert pressure on the Soviet Union and at the same time to develop direct diplomatic relations between Washington and Beijing that would improve their relationship. Kissinger made a secret trip to China in July 1971 that was followed by a publicly revealed trip in October 1971. On both occasions he met with Chinese premier Zhou Enlai. These meetings resulted in a presidential visit to China from February 21 to 28, 1972 (see Document 15), when Nixon and his entourage visited Beijing, Shanghai, and Hangzhou. Nixon met Mao Zedong and had several meetings with Zhou Enlai. Kissinger's arrangements and work during the visit proved productive, as direct communications with China were assured and China's concerns of a potential threat from the Soviet Union were diminished. However, full diplomatic relations were not restored until 1979 during President Jimmy Carter's administration.

While advancing détente and the opening of China, Kissinger was charged by Nixon to bring about an end to the Vietnam War. Nixon's policy of "Vietnamization" required time for the South Vietnamese to prepare to assume full responsibility for their defense. Initial conversations on a peace agreement started in March 1968 during Johnson's term. Nixon and Kissinger continued the dialogue with the North Vietnamese at the same time that they expanded military operations. Kissinger was an advocate of the Cambodian incursion in May 1970 and the expanded bombing campaign against North Vietnam while he was conducting negotiations with Le Duc Tho of North Vietnam in Paris. The North Vietnamese, fearing isolation in the new U.S.-Soviet-Chinese diplomatic dynamic that resulted from the Nixon-Kissinger triangulation initiative, altered their negotiating position on October 8, 1972, when Tho announced that North Vietnam would agree to the continued existence of South Vietnam and that separate negotiations between North and South Vietnam could lead to a peace treaty. Kissinger used this opening as the basis for a January 27, 1973, agreement between the United States, North Vietnam, and South Vietnam that included a cease-fire, the withdrawal of American troops, the return of American prisoners of war, and the North Vietnamese pledge to continue negotiations with the South on a permanent settlement for Vietnam.

In the India-Pakistan War of 1971, Kissinger supported the independence of Bangladesh that resulted from the struggle. In 1973 Kissinger negotiated the end of the Yom Kippur War between Israel and Egypt, Syria, and their Arab allies, though the state of war between Israel and Egypt did not end until the Camp David Accords were achieved in 1978 under President Jimmy Carter. In Latin America Kissinger's involvement in overthrowing Chilean president Salvador Allende on September 11, 1973—and supporting the military coup led by General Augusto Pinochet—resulted in later investigations in Chile, Spain, France, and Argentina. Kissinger has avoided all legal summons in these countries. Two cases that charged Kissinger with wrongful behavior associated with the Chilean coup were filed in the United States, but both were dismissed because of diplomatic immunity and the issue of sovereignty.

Since leaving office in 1977 Kissinger has maintained an active academic, public, and business life. Such work has included affiliations with Columbia and Georgetown Universities, service on federal study groups and committees, and serving as the head of Kissinger Associates and writing his memoirs and other works—including two important books, *Diplomacy* (1994) and *On China* (2011).

For additional information, see *Kissinger: A Biography* by Walter Isaacson (New York: Simon and Schuster, 1992) and *Nixon and Kissinger: Partners in Power* by Robert Dallek (New York: Harpers, 2007).

FULTON LEWIS, JR. (1903–1966)

Fulton Lewis, Jr. worked as a nationally syndicated radio commentator from the 1930s to his death in 1966. Lewis championed Senator Joseph McCarthy's investigations of communist influence inside the American government and Senator Barry Goldwater's 1964 presidential campaign.

Fulton Lewis, Jr. was born on April 30, 1903, in Washington, DC, into a wealthy family. He attended the University of Virginia and the George Washington School of Law but did not graduate from either institution. During the 1920s he worked at the *Washington Herald* as a reporter and then as city editor. In 1928 Lewis joined the Universal News Service, which was owned by the conservative William Randolph Hearst. Lewis was well connected and knew most of the prominent leaders of the Republican presidential administrations during the 1920s and early 1930s. On June 28, 1930, for example, many members of the Hoover administration attended Lewis's wedding to Alice Huston, daughter of Claudius Hart Huston, a Tennessee businessman and politician who had been the chairman of the Republican National Committee but had been forced to resign earlier that year because of his involvement in a scandal over oil pipelines in Tennessee.

Lewis tried unsuccessfully to develop a reputation as an investigative reporter. As a Hearst reporter, he gathered incriminating information on both Democrats and Republicans to satisfy the Hearst papers' interest in scandal. In his position he also travelled to Cuba during 1933 and interviewed the outgoing president, Geraldo Machado. Many viewed Lewis as an intellectual lightweight who possessed neither the intelligence nor the knowledge required of a first-class journalist. Also in 1933 Lewis began writing a column entitled "The Washington Sideshow" for the King Features syndicate. He began appearing on radio with commentaries related to items in the news, and his conservative arguments and conversational presentation attracted the interest of the Mutual Broadcasting Network. By 1936 Lewis had a national nightly 15-minute program that eventually was broadcast on more than 500 radio stations and claimed an audience of more that 15 million listeners.

Lewis liked the personable President Franklin D. Roosevelt but opposed his liberal New Deal policies. In 1936 Lewis continued moving to the right, as evidenced by his article "How the Republicans Hope to Beat Roosevelt," which appeared in the right-wing *Liberty Magazine*. Ignoring the human distress caused by the Depression, Lewis argued that the essential key to economic recovery was a balanced budget. With the outbreak of war in Europe in 1939, Lewis joined the isolationists and supported the America First Committee to keep the United States out of the war. After the attack on Pearl Harbor, Lewis gave enthusiastic support to the war effort. He also argued unsuccessfully that Roosevelt should be denied a fourth term as president in 1944.

After the war Lewis used his radio program to denounce Soviet aggression in Eastern Europe. He provided uncritical support for Senator Joseph McCarthy and his anticommunist movement during the 1950s, and he continued this support even after McCarthy's censure by the Senate in

1954. During that time Lewis gained notoriety for his reports and comments on the Julius and Ethel Rosenberg atomic spy case, and his arguments were later vindicated when the Venona papers were released. During the late 1950s Lewis's audience declined, but he continued his radio program until his death on August 20, 1966, in Washington, DC.

For additional information, see *Political Commentators in the United States in the Twentieth Century: A Bio-Critical Sourcebook* by Dan D. Nimmo and Chevelle Newsome (Westport, CT: Greenwood, 1997) and *News for Everyone: Radio and Foreign Affairs in Thirties America* by David Holbrook Culbert (Westport, CT: Greenwood, 1976).

GEORGE C. MARSHALL (1880–1959)

George Catlett Marshall, American soldier and public servant, served the United States as a military officer in the Philippines War, World War I, and World War II. During the latter, he became the nation's first chief of staff. After the war he became directly involved with the beginning of the Cold War, serving as President Harry S. Truman's secretary of state and secretary of defense. He advocated American support for the economic recovery of Europe after World War II as a means to curtail the expansion of communism; the Marshall Plan (see Document 5) succeeded but resulted in alienating the Soviet Union. Marshall was awarded the Nobel Peace Prize in 1953 for his efforts to bring about European economic recovery.

Born in December 31, 1880, in Uniontown, Pennsylvania, Marshall came from a middle-class family. When he graduated from the Virginia Military Institute in 1901, he was commissioned a second lieutenant in the U.S. Army. Marshall's first deployment was to the Philippines War, where he served as an infantry commander. In 1906 he was assigned to Fort Leavenworth, Kansas, where he studied and taught contemporary warfare. At this time American military investments were directed to the navy rather than the army. Marshall's strengths in organization and planning were recognized early. During World War I he was assigned to the 1st Infantry Division in France and soon was working directly with General John J. Pershing, commander of the American Expeditionary Forces. Marshall's planning for the Meuse-Argonne offensive in 1918 won acclaim as a major tactical achievement that contributed to winning the war. After the war Marshall served as an aide to Pershing and a strategist in the War Department, commanded an American regiment in China and an army base in Georgia, and was on the faculty of the Army War College in Carlisle, Pennsylvania. In 1936 Marshall was promoted to brigadier general, and in 1939 he was appointed as the army's chief of staff and promoted to general.

During World War II Marshall excelled at organization as the United States prosecuted the two-front war in Europe and the Pacific; however, he had mixed success on strategic and leadership issues. President Franklin D. Roosevelt was expected to appoint Marshall as commander of the invasion force in France; however, he appointed Dwight Eisenhower instead. Marshall was elevated to five-star general of the army rank on December 16, 1944, and he stepped down as chief of staff after the war. In December 1945 President Harry Truman dispatched Marshall to China to settle the dispute between the Nationalists and the Communists. The Nationalists, who were supported by the United States, refused to cooperate, and the Chinese civil war was resumed. Marshall returned to the United States early in 1947 and was soon appointed secretary of state. It was in this position that he advocated American assistance in the economic recovery of Europe. On June 5, 1947, at Harvard University, Marshall offered an American plan that became known as the Marshall Plan (see Document 5). The Soviet Union viewed it as a threat to their interests and refused to allow their subject states to participate in the program.

Truman and Marshall held opposing views on American recognition of the new Israeli state. Marshall maintained that such an action was not in America's interest and would result in a prolonged period of conflict in the Middle East between the Arabs and the Israelis. Nonetheless, Truman recognized Israel in 1948. In January 1949 Marshall resigned as secretary of state because of failing health. With Marshall's health somewhat improved, in September 1950 Truman appointed him as secretary of defense. During his year in this position, Marshall secretly directed General Douglas MacArthur, the American and UN field commander in Korea, to expand the war into North Korea, an action that exacerbated the later difficulties between Truman and MacArthur. At the same time Marshall was attacked by Senator Joseph McCarthy (R-WI) as an ineffective diplomat who played into the hands of the Chinese Communists between 1945 and 1947, when Marshall, serving as Truman's agent in

China, tried to force the Nationalists to negotiate; also, he limited American military aid to the Nationalists because of their corruption in handling American funds and weapons. Truman and others defended Marshall and condemned McCarthy for his reckless and unfounded statements. In September 1951 Marshall resigned as secretary of defense. Most of his remaining years were spent at his home in Leesburg, Virginia. He died on October 16, 1959.

For additional information, see *General of the Army: George C. Marshall, Soldier and Statesman* by Ed Cray (New York: Cooper Square Press, 2000) and *Soldier, Statesman, Peacemaker: Leadership Lessons from George C. Marshall* by Jack Uldrich (New York: American Management Association, 2005).

JOSEPH R. MCCARTHY (1908–1957)

Joseph R. McCarthy represented Wisconsin in the U.S. Senate from 1947 to 1957. During the early years of his Senate tenure, he was a low-profile and rather inactive member who "discovered" internal subversion as a means of acquiring notoriety and reelection. McCarthy became a nationally prominent politician after his Wheeling, West Virginia, speech on February 9, 1950, when he announced that more than 200 State Department employees were communists. He enjoyed considerable support from the political right until 1954, when his arbitrary and capricious techniques and behavior were exposed through the televised Army-McCarthy hearings, challenged by journalist broadcaster Edward R. Murrow, and denounced through a Senate censure.

McCarthy was born in Grand Chute, Wisconsin, on November 14, 1908. From 1930 to 1935 he was a student at Marquette University and acquired a degree in law. In 1939 he was elected as the 10th District Wisconsin circuit judge. In 1942 McCarthy enlisted in the marines and during the next two years served in the South Pacific as an intelligence officer. He submitted unwarranted claims that he was in combat and wounded, and that he deserved recognition through commendations and medals. His ploy worked, and he returned to Wisconsin as a war hero. In 1944, still in the marines, he unsuccessfully sought the Republican nomination for the U.S. Senate. In 1945 he resigned from the marines and was reelected to his previous position as 10th District circuit judge.

At the same time he initiated his campaign to gain the Republican nomination for the Senate seat that was held by the longtime Progressive-
Republican Robert M. LaFollette, Jr. McCarthy prevailed and won the
1946 election against Democrat Howard McMurry.

During his early years in the Senate, McCarthy did not emerge as a
leader or an industrious legislator. Previously a loyal supporter of workers,
McCarthy supported the Taft-Hartley Act and became an advocate for
business interests. As 1950 approached McCarthy was concerned that his
performance and lack of achievements would cause him difficulty in gaining re-election in 1952. His assessment of the current political environment focused on the Cold War developing with the Soviet Union and
the new Communist China. Dominating the national political agenda
were external events such as the fall of China, the acquisition of the
atomic bomb by the Soviet Union, the deployment of opposing NATO
and Warsaw Pact troops in Europe, and the Berlin blockade. Internally,
the national political agenda focused on the case of Alger Hiss, the
expanding activities of the House Committee on Un-American Activities,
and mounting concerns over the policies and actions of Secretary of State
Dean Acheson. On February 9, 1950, in a Lincoln's Day speech to the
Republican Women's Club of Wheeling, West Virginia (see Document
6), McCarthy claimed that there were enemies within our government
and that he had a list of 205—soon to be reduced to 57—communists
who were employed by the Department of State.

Within days McCarthy became a national figure. He quickly polarized
American politics through additional speeches and remarks that recklessly
denounced not only Secretary of State Dean Acheson, but also President
Harry Truman and Secretary of Defense George C. Marshall. The Senate
formed a committee to consider McCarthy's accusations. Led by Senator
Millard Tydings (D-MD), the committee determined that there was no
evidence to support any of McCarthy's charges. Nonetheless, McCarthy
denounced Tydings and continued to make unsubstantiated statements
against individuals. His rhetoric destroyed the reputations as well as the
professional and personal lives of many, but he found himself applauded
by some aenators and large segments of the American public. However,
some Republican senators, led by Margaret Chase Smith (R-ME), viewed
McCarthy and his methods as a threat to American political values and
the civility of Senate proceedings. On June 1, 1950, several Republican

senators supported her "Declaration of Conscience" (see Document 8), which beseeched all members of the Senate to act rationally and appropriately. Smith's plea had no impact on McCarthy—he continued his attacks on the Truman administration and anyone who criticized him.

The term "McCarthyism" emerged with both positive and negative connotations, though only the negative meaning, relating to an anti-intellectual witch hunt, remains. Critics spoke out in a variety of forms. For example, playwright Arthur Miller wrote *The Crucible* (1953), which was centered on the Salem witch trials of the seventeenth century but was a not so veiled condemnation of McCarthyism. On March 9, 1954, Edward R. Murrow of CBS radio and television, broadcasted a critique of McCarthy and his methods. The Army-McCarthy hearings started in April 1954 and provided the nation with an opportunity to see McCarthy in action. The result was a sharp decline in public support and an emboldening of resolve among senators who had had enough of McCarthy and his unacceptable means of investigating subversion. McCarthy found himself increasingly isolated and frequently resorted to excessive use of alcohol. On June 11, 1954, Senator Ralph Flanders (R-VT) asked the Senate to censure McCarthy and strip him of his chairmanship of all committees. After a report recommending censure was received from committee, the Senate voted on December 2, 1954, to censure McCarthy for his abuse of his Senate Subcommittee on Rules and Administration and his unfounded charges of deception and fraud against three members of the committee that recommended his censure. After the censure McCarthy retained his seat, but his influence all but disappeared. Health problems plagued him for more than two years, and he died in the Bethesda Naval Hospital in Maryland on May 2, 1957.

For additional information, see *The Life and Times of Joe McCarthy: A Biography* by Thomas C. Reeves (New York: Stein and Day, 1982) and *McCarthyism and the Red Scare: A Reference Guide* by William T. Walker (Santa Barbara, CA: ABC-CLIO, 2011).

GEORGE MCGOVERN (1922–2008)

An icon of twentieth-century American liberalism, George McGovern was recognized as a courageous citizen-intellectual during and after his terms in the U.S. House of Representatives and Senate. In 1972

McGovern, the Democratic candidate for president, lost decisively to Richard M. Nixon. McGovern was the champion of the anti–Vietnam War movement, curtailing military expenditures, amnesty for draft evaders, civil rights, and extending liberal policies. After this defeat McGovern continued to represent South Dakota in the Senate until 1981, at which point he became devoted to the issue of world hunger and launched unsuccessful and short-lived efforts to secure the Democratic presidential nomination in 1984, 1988, and 1992.

Born on July 19, 1922, in Avon, South Dakota, George McGovern was the son of a Methodist minister and a Canadian-born mother whose family had relocated to South Dakota from Calgary. Between the ages of three and six, McGovern lived in Calgary and then moved to Mitchell, South Dakota. As a member of a family living at or near poverty, McGovern developed sympathy for workers and the unemployed. A good student, McGovern excelled in debating. He graduated from high school in 1940, enrolled in Dakota Wesleyan University, and learned to be a pilot. In 1943 McGovern joined the U.S. Army Air Corps and by November 1944 was flying B-24s in Europe. He was deeply affected by the hunger and disease that resulted from the war. After the war he returned to Dakota Wesleyan University, where he completed his undergraduate degree in 1946. He then left Wesleyan Methodism for orthodox Methodism and studied for the ministry at Garrett Theological Seminary in Evanston, Illinois. In 1947 he abandoned the ministry and undertook graduate studies in history at Northwestern University, where he earned a master's degree (1949) and a doctorate (1953). He was appointed to the faculty at Dakota Wesleyan.

Politically, McGovern migrated from his family's Republican allegiance to Franklin Roosevelt's Democratic Party. Never a communist, McGovern understood that postwar political difficulties in Asia and parts of Eastern Europe resulted from local socioeconomic conditions. He flirted with Henry A. Wallace's Progressive campaign for president in 1948 but was alarmed by the leftist radicals who dominated that movement, which led him to support Truman's campaign. During the early 1950s McGovern became a leader of the South Dakota Democratic Party, actively supported Adlai Stevenson's 1952 campaign for the presidency, and developed an interest in holding public office. Despite attempts to identify him as a left-wing radical, McGovern was elected to the U.S. House of Representatives in 1956. During his first term he supported government aid for education, farm policies that provided producers with increased income, and additional protection for labor. He was reelected in 1958 but was defeated in his race for the Senate in 1960.

McGovern had been a strong advocate for John F. Kennedy in the presidential election, so the new president appointed McGovern to serve as director of the Food for Peace Program and as a special assistant to the president, a capacity in which he served during 1961 and 1962. In 1962 with strong support from young voters and the South Dakota Farmers Union, McGovern narrowly won the race for the Senate, where he served from 1963 until 1981. During 1963 McGovern emerged as a critic of America's Cuba policy, called for substantive cuts to the defense budget, targeted the funding of new missile systems, and in September 1963 questioned the expanding American commitment in Vietnam. He supported Kennedy's Alliance for Progress program, along with a wide range of agricultural programs that would aid farmers and alleviate hunger throughout the world.

While McGovern became increasingly concerned with the situation in Vietnam, he succumbed to pressure from Senator J. William Fulbright (D-AK) and supported the Gulf of Tonkin Resolution (August 1964) that gave President Lyndon B. Johnson extensive authority to increase America's involvement in Vietnam. McGovern quickly realized his error and moved closer to the antiwar stance of Senator Wayne Morse (D-OR). During 1964 and 1965 McGovern became increasingly convinced that the American strategy in Vietnam was not only politically and militarily wrong, but that it was immoral. In 1965 he visited Vietnam and witnessed the inhumanity of the struggle. While McGovern continued until 1967 to vote for military appropriations that supported equipment for American troops, he emerged as a leading and vocal critic of the continued American presence in Vietnam.

By 1967 critics of the war had formed a movement that challenged not only President Johnson's Vietnam policy, but also his continuance in office. After Senator Robert F. Kennedy (D-NY) turned down an offer of support to campaign against the war and unseat Johnson, McGovern was approached in September 1967 and asked to run for the Democratic nomination for president. He declined, thinking that the effort would be unsuccessful and that it would cost him re-election to the Senate in 1968. Later, in the fall of 1967, the antiwar movement settled on Senator

Eugene McCarthy (D-MN) as its choice to unseat Johnson. McCarthy mounted a strong campaign, and Johnson announced that he would not seek re-election. Robert Kennedy entered the race and challenged McCarthy for the presidential nomination. After Kennedy was assassinated (he died on June 6, 1968), McGovern was approached again but delayed announcing for the presidency until August 10, 1968—too late to prevail over Vice President Hubert Humphrey, who became the standard-bearer for the Democrats. While Humphrey was defeated by Republican Richard M. Nixon, McGovern was re-elected to the Senate. He returned to the Senate and quickly became a critic of Nixon's Vietnam policy. He also became chair of the new Senate Select Committee on Nutrition and Human Needs and co-chair of a commission that expanded the number of Democratic presidential primaries. Through McGovern's work in reforming the rules and procedures of the Democratic Party, the people gained power in the selection of their candidates and the composition of the party's platform, a notable achievement that was accomplished at the expense of the old political "machines."

In 1969 McGovern became a leading force in the antiwar movement and called for the withdrawal of all American forces by 1970. He sponsored legislation that would eliminate all funding for American forces remaining in Vietnam after 1971. This legislation did not become law, and McGovern became fully engulfed in the antiwar, anti-Nixon fervor. In January 1971 McGovern announced that he was seeking the 1972 Democratic presidential nomination. He overcame his numerous rivals—Senators Edmund Muskie (D-ME) and Hubert Humphrey (D-MN)—as well as the fierce opposition of the delegates from the South and was nominated on July 12, 1972, at the Democratic National Convention in Miami Beach, Florida. From its outset, the McGovern campaign was distracted from presenting its liberal and antiwar agenda by its own internal problems, foremost of which was the change in the vice presidential candidate from Thomas Eagleton (D-MO) to Ambassador R. Sargent Shriver because of Eagleton's history of mental illness and the mounting perception that McGovern was too radical. Nixon was re-elected by a wide margin with 520 electoral votes and 61 percent of the popular vote to McGovern's 17 electoral votes and 37 percent of the popular vote. McGovern remained in the Senate and was re-elected in 1974 to what would be his last term. During the 1970s he expended much effort on national public health and women's issues, he was criticized for ignoring concerns important to South Dakota, and he was defeated in 1980 Senate race. His post-Senate years were spent teaching, writing, pursuing unsuccessful bids for the presidency, and an unfortunate attempt to run an inn. In 1998 McGovern was appointed by President William Clinton as U.S. ambassador to the UN Agencies for Food and Agriculture (1998–2001). McGovern continued to speak and write until two weeks prior to his death on October 21, 2012.

For additional information, see *The Liberals' Moment: The McGovern Insurgency and the Identity Crisis of the Democratic Party* by Brice Miroff (Lawrence: University Press of Kansas, 2007) and *George McGovern: A Political Life, A Political Legacy* by Robert P. Watson (Pierre: South Dakota State Historical Society Press, 2004).

ARTHUR A. MILLER (1915–2005)

Arthur A. Miller, a leading American playwright and author during the Cold War, refused to identify writers and artists who may have had an affiliation with the Communist Party USA. His play *The Crucible*, which focused on the Salem witch trials of 1692, was really a denunciation of McCarthyism and the activities of the House Un-American Activities Committee. Miller's most notable plays were *All My Sons* (1947), *Death of a Salesman* (1949), *The Crucible* (1953), *Incident at Vichy* (1964), and *The Price* (1968).

Miller was born in New York on October 17, 1915. His family was devastated by the Depression, but Miller managed to raise enough funds to attend the University of Michigan, and he graduated in 1938 with a B.A. in English. After graduation Miller was employed by the Federal Theatre Project (FTP), a New Deal program intended for out-of-work dramatists and actors. Congress abolished the FTP in 1940 because of the fear that communists were being supported with public funds. Politically, Miller expressed leftist views—he was a vocal critic of Father Charles Coughlin's anticommunist, anti-Jewish, and pro-Nazi rhetoric. During World War II Miller, who was not eligible to serve in the military because of physical ailments, launched his career as a playwright in New York. It was during the mid-1940s that Miller supported petitions and appeals endorsing such communist efforts as the World Youth Festival in Prague, condemning a proposal to outlaw the Communist Party USA, criticizing the House Committee on Un-American Activities, supporting relief work in Communist China, and opposing the Smith Act, which prohibited advocating the overthrow of the American government. Miller was not a revolutionary, but he was very concerned with freedom of expression.

His career was not successful until after the war, when his play *All My Sons* received critical acclaim and was awarded the New York Drama Critics' Circle Award in 1947. In 1949 the success of *Death of a Salesman* elevated Miller to the first rank of American playwrights. It was directed by Elia Kazan, who had also directed *All My Sons*, and won numerous awards, including the Pulitzer Prize for Drama (1949). During the early 1950s the House Un-American Activities Committee expanded its investigation into supposed communist influence in film and theatre. In 1952 Kazan, fearing that he would be blacklisted and possibly face imprisonment, agreed to testify before the committee and identified eight artists and writers of the Group Theatre—Clifford Odets, J. Edward Bromberg, Lewis Leverett, Morris Carnovsky, Phoebe Brand, Tony Kraber, Ted Wellman, and Paula Miller, who later married Lee Strasberg—as members of the Communist Party USA during the1930s. Kazan, who admitted that he had been a member of the Communist Party USA during the early 1930s, saved himself and his employment opportunities but was denounced by many former colleagues and friends for his betrayal and his failure to support basic human freedoms. Miller's outrage over Kazan's testimony led to *The Crucible*, a play that he wrote in 1952 in which he attacked McCarthyism through focusing on the Salem witch trials of 1692. *The Crucible* was produced in 1953 and received mixed reviews, though it did draw the committee's attention to Miller, who received a subpoena to appear before it. In his testimony Miller provided details about his involvement with communist groups—he was never a member of the Communist Party USA—but refused to identify anyone else. In May 1957 Miller was found guilty of contempt of Congress and was fined, denied a passport, and blacklisted. In 1958 this verdict was overturned. On June 25, 1956, Miller married Marilyn Monroe, a noted film actress and celebrity. The marriage, which brought Miller into the Hollywood social network, ended in divorce in 1961. During the 1960s Miller's career as a first-rank playwright was restored with *Incident at Vichy* (1964) and *The Price* (1968). Miller went on to write more than a dozen more plays and his autobiography *Timebends*. He died on February 10, 2005, in Roxbury, Connecticut.

For additional information, see *Arthur Miller: His Life and Work* by Martin Gottfried (New York: Da Capo, 2004) and *Arthur Miller* by Christopher Bigsby (Cambridge, MA: Harvard University Press, 2010).

EDWARD R. MURROW (1908–1965)

Edward R. Murrow, a renowned radio and television producer and commentator, revolutionized the delivery of information to the American people. Murrow opposed authoritarianism and threats to basic liberties, from the left as well as the right. In 1954 Murrow took on the bombastic Senator Joseph R. McCarthy (R-WI), who attacked political enemies and innocent citizens without evidence to gain acclaim as a political leader opposed to communism and its alleged agents in the United States. Murrow risked his reputation and position in publicly attacking McCarthy. In December 1954 McCarthy was censured by the Senate and was a broken man, and Murrow was applauded for his courage and method in defending the First Amendment and due process.

Born on April 25, 1908, in Guilford County, North Carolina, Murrow and his family moved in 1914 to a farm near Blanchard, Washington, a few miles from the Canadian border. As a student in public schools, Murrow emerged as a leader and a gifted debater. In 1926 he enrolled at Washington State College (now University), where he continued to demonstrate leadership skills and where he was elected president of the National Student Federation of America in 1929. Murrow graduated from Washington State in 1930 and moved to New York. Interested in international affairs and communications, Murrow, while working at the Institute of International Education between 1932 and 1935, assisted émigré German scholars find positions and accommodations. A key opportunity in Murrow's career came in 1935 when he was offered the position of director of Talks and Education at CBS (Columbia Broadcasting System), and he remained at CBS for most of his professional career. In 1937 Murrow was named director of European Operations for CBS. He worked from London to arrange for presentations on CBS radio by prominent Europeans, and he hired William L. Shirer as an assistant on the continent. These assignments for Murrow and Shirer coincided with the expansion of Nazi Germany in Austria, Czechoslovakia, and Poland. Murrow revolutionized broadcast journalism by using existing technology to create a multicity network into a single broadcast as they reported on the mounting European crisis. Murrow and Shirer became the on-air voices of CBS's coverage of European diplomacy and politics. After World War II began in 1939, Murrow developed an international reputation through his sometimes roof-top coverage of the German bombing of London in 1940–1941. After the United States entered the war in 1941, Murrow flew and reported on combat missions over Germany, and he was one of the first journalists to see the horrors of the Buchenwald death camp. Murrow's reporting throughout the war years reflected a commitment to democracy as well as human rights and values. After the war Murrow was appointed vice president of CBS, but his tenure was short-lived because he wanted to continue to be directly involved in broadcasting. During the 1950s Murrow worked as the principal in several CBS radio and television news programs such as *This I Believe*, *Hear It Now*, *See It Now*, and *Person to Person*.

On February 9, 1950, Senator Joseph R. McCarthy (R-WI) surfaced as a national political force when he condemned the State Department for employing communists (see Document 6). Despite the absence of evidence, McCarthy continued his baseless onslaught against the Truman administration, the First Amendment, and innocent Americans for several years, enjoying the support of millions of Americans who were attracted by his outrageous charges against elements in the establishment. Publically, Murrow did not respond to McCarthyism until the spring 1954, by which time McCarthy's reckless arrogance had led his investigative committee to take on the U.S. Army. On March 9, 1954, prior to the Army-McCarthy Hearings (April 22–June 17, 1954), Murrow and his producer, Fred Friendly, aired a 30-minute report entitled "A Report on Senator Joseph McCarthy" on *See It Now*. This report utilized McCarthy's own speeches and written statements to illustrate his contradictions, falsehoods, and demeaning methods in assaulting his victims. While Murrow believed McCarthy and McCarthyism were dangers to American values and freedoms, he allowed McCarthy to indict himself. McCarthy accepted Murrow's invitation to respond, but his response backfired and confirmed the criticism that Murrow advanced in the initial program. Murrow's broadcast contributed to the erosion of McCarthy's popularity and power.

The Senate censured McCarthy on December 2, 1954. While McCarthy was a broken man without power, a diminished McCarthyism continued to be evident in American society for many years. During the late 1950s Murrow became embroiled in difficulties with CBS management. His most significant achievement was an episode for the new *CBS Reports* program called "Harvest of Shame," in which Murrow reported on the difficulties and inhumane migrant farm labor in the United States. This episode aired immediately after Thanksgiving in 1960. In 1961 Murrow accepted President John F. Kennedy's invitation to serve as director of the U.S. Information Agency (USIA). However, while Murrow appeared in propaganda films and reorganized the agency, his illness from cancer imposed limitations on his plans. Murrow resigned in 1964 and died on April 27, 1965, in Pawling, New York.

For additional information, see *Edward R. Murrow and the Birth of Broadcast Journalism* by Bob Edwards (New York: Wiley, 2004) and *Edward R, Murrow: An American Original* by Joseph Persico (New York: Da Capo, 1997).

PAUL H. NITZE (1907–2004)

Between 1944 and 1989 Paul H. Nitze held a range of positions in the administrations of Presidents Franklin D. Roosevelt, Harry Truman, Dwight D. Eisenhower, John F. Kennedy, Lyndon B. Johnson, Richard Nixon, Gerald Ford, and Ronald Reagan. Nitze directed the development of and wrote most of the important Cold War document NSC-68, which was published in 1950 (see Document 7), and he served as vice chair and author of the U.S. Strategic Bombing Survey (1944–1946); director of policy planning for the State Department (1950–1953); assistant secretary of defense for international security affairs (1953); secretary of the navy (1963–1967); deputy secretary of defense (1967–1969); member of the U.S. delegation to the Strategic Arms Limitation Talks (1969–1973); assistant secretary of defense for international affairs (1973–1976); and special adviser to the president and secretary of state on arms control (1984–1989).

Born on January 16, 1907, in Amherst, Massachusetts, Nitze graduated from Harvard University with a degree in economics in 1928. He launched his career as an investment banker in Chicago and prospered during the

1930s. He became independently wealthy during the 1930s as a result of the sale of a science laboratory that he had acquired. During World War II Nitze served on the White House staff under James V. Forrestal and the office on Inter-American Affairs. He also led a section of the Board of Economic Warfare. In 1943 Nitze, along with his friend Congressman Christian Herter (R-MA), established the School of Advanced International Studies (SAIS) in Washington, DC. Within a few years it became affiliated with The Johns Hopkins University and provided Nitze with a facility for his research and writing until his death. In 1944 he was appointed to manage and author the Strategic Bombing Survey, a position in which he remained until 1946; he travelled to Japan to assess the impact of atomic bombs. In that same year he became the deputy director of the Office of International Trade Policy at the State Department.

Along with other members of the Truman administration, Nitze was concerned with the apparent Soviet expansionism. He contributed to the development of the Marshall Plan (see Document 5) in 1947 and accepted George Kennan's argument on containment. However, where Kennan focused on diplomacy to manage the Soviet threat, Nitze argued for a strong American military. In 1949 Nitze became Kennan's deputy and then succeeded Kennan as director of policy planning. Differing from Kennan, Nitze supported the development of the hydrogen bomb and was the primary author of the National Security Council's report (NSC-68) in 1950 that argued for a large conventional military. With Truman's approval, NSC-68 became a cornerstone of American policy for more than a decade. With the arrival of the Republican president Dwight D. Eisenhower, Nitze was appointed assistant secretary of defense for inter-national security affairs; however, because of pressures brought by Republican senators who wanted a Democrat in that position, Nitze resigned. Between 1953 and 1957 Nitze expanded SAIS by establishing the Washington Center of Foreign Policy Research. In 1957 Nitze returned to government as an adviser to a committee studying American civil defense.

In 1960 Nitze joined the presidential campaign of Senator John F. Kennedy as a national security adviser, and in 1961 he was appointed assistant secretary of defense for international security affairs in the new Kennedy administration. Nitze advised Kennedy on the Berlin crisis of 1961 and served on the executive committee of the National Security Council during the Cuban missile crisis in October 1962. Kennedy appointed Nitze secretary of the navy in 1963, and he continued in that position under President Lyndon B. Johnson until he was appointed deputy secretary of defense in 1967. Privately, Nitze did not support Johnson's Vietnam policy because he feared that the United States was being diverted from addressing a more substantive threat—the Soviet Union. During the 1960s Nitze developed the expertise on arms control that would sustain his public career for decades.

During the administration of President Richard M. Nixon, Nitze assisted in negotiating the Anti-Ballistic Missile (ABM) Treaty and the interim Strategic Arms Limitation Agreement Treaty (SALT I) in 1972. Nitze opposed the arms control policies of President Jimmy Carter, in particular the SALT II agreement, which Nitze considered inherently flawed and not in the interests of the United States. In 1981 President Ronald Reagan appointed Nitze as head of the American negotiation team for the Intermediate Range Nuclear Forces (INF) talks that were held in Geneva, Switzerland. In spite of a personal agreement between Nitze and the Soviet lead negotiator Yuli Kvitsinsky, no agreement resulted. Nitze became an ambassador-at-large and special adviser to Reagan. With the ascendency of the reformer Mikhail Gorbachev as leader of the Soviet Union, Reagan moved to resume arms control negotiations. At the Reykjavik, Iceland, summit meeting between Reagan and Gorbachev, an agreement seemed to be within reach when Nitze and the Soviet negotiator Sergei Akhromeyev came to a tentative arrangement, but the Soviet leadership was not prepared to agree to a treaty at that time. However, the momentum achieved in Iceland was sustained, and a treaty was signed in December 8, 1987 (see Document 19) that limited medium- and short-range missiles in Europe and committed to not building new nuclear warheads as well as working to eliminate existing nuclear weapons. In 1988 Nitze initiated negotiations to reduce both Soviet and American stockpiles of nuclear weapons. The START agreement realized that goal, but Nitze had left the government by that time. In 1989 President George H. W. Bush invited Nitze to continue serving the government as an ambassador-at-large emeritus, but Nitze declined and returned to SAIS, where he wrote his memoirs and continued to lecture. Paul Nitze died on October 19, 2004, at the age of 97.

For additional information, see *The Hawk and the Dove: Paul Nitze, George Kennan, and the History of the Cold War* by Nicholas Thompson

(New York: Henry Holt, 2009) and *From Hiroshima to Glasnost: At the Center of Decision* by Paul Nitze, Ann M. Smith, and Steven L. Reardon (New York: Grove Weidenfeld, 1989).

FULTON JOHN SHEEN (BORN PETER JOHN SHEEN) (1895–1979)

Born on May 8, 1895, in El Paso, Illinois, Fulton Sheen was a member of a devout Roman Catholic farming family. The family relocated to Peoria, Illinois, during his youth. Sheen attended St. Viator College before graduating from Saint Paul Seminary School of Divinity in 1919. He was ordained a priest on September 20, 1919, and after a brief assignment to a parish in Peoria, he was sent to the Catholic University of America, where he received a doctorate in theology. Recognized for his intelligence, scholarship, and industrious work ethic, Sheen was assigned to the Catholic University of Leuven in Belgium, where he received a doctorate in philosophy in 1923. From there he went to Rome to study at the Pontificium Collegium Internationale Angelicum, where he earned yet another doctorate (in sacred theology) in 1924. During 1925 and 1926 Sheen taught in England and served as an assistant pastor at St. Patrick's Church in London. In 1926 he returned to Peoria and assumed the duties of pastor at St. Patrick's Parish, though in less than a year Sheen was back in Washington, DC, to teach philosophy at the Catholic University of America. While teaching there, Sheen started a weekly radio program, *The Catholic Hour*, which began in 1930 and eventually had an audience of more than 4 million. In 1951 Sheen was elevated to bishop and was assigned to be an auxiliary bishop in the Archdiocese of New York. In that same year his television program *Life Is Worth Living* began airing. It made the telegenic priest a national celebrity.

He used his new podium to condemn communism and warn of the threat from the Soviet Union and its leaders. The atheism and materialism of the Soviet Union were frequent targets of Sheen's programs and rhetoric. He frequently linked religion and patriotism as the key elements of America's distinctive national character that warranted its global leadership. A few weeks before Stalin's death on March 5, 1953, Sheen, using the framework of William Shakespeare's *Julius Caesar*, denounced Stalin and his inner circle as vile Satanists. Sheen's Emmy-winning *Life Is Worth*

Living continued until 1957. In 1961 Sheen launched another television program, *The Fulton Sheen Program,* which ran until 1968.

Sheen was appointed bishop of Rochester, New York, in 1966. For three years as leader of this diocese he confronted the issues that impacted his congregation. He denounced the war in Vietnam, supported the civil rights movement, and endorsed programs for the poor. In 1969 Sheen resigned and was appointed an archbishop of the Titular See of Newport, Wales, by Pope Paul VI. He had few specific duties and returned to writing. Sheen died on December 9, 1979, in New York.

For additional information, see *America's Bishop: The Life and Times of Fulton J. Sheen* by Thomas C. Reeves (New York: Encounter, 2001); *Treasure in Clay: The Autobiography of Fulton J. Sheen* by Fulton J. Sheen (New York: Image, 1982); and "Religion, Culture, and the Cold War: Bishop Fulton J. Sheen and America's Anti-Communist Crusade of the 1950s," by Irvin Winsboro and Michael Epple, *Historian,* 71 (June 2009): 209–233.

PRIMARY DOCUMENTS

DOCUMENT 1
Yalta Agreement, February 11, 1945

In February 1945 President Franklin D. Roosevelt of the United States, Soviet premier Josef Stalin, and British prime minister Winston Churchill met at Yalta in the Crimea to discuss a range of topics relating to the postwar era. The establishment of the United Nations, the role of the Soviet Union in the war against Japan, and numerous other issues were settled. The most contentious items on the agenda related to the future of Germany, Poland, and Eastern Europe. Many Americans thought that Roosevelt and Churchill were too generous to the Soviets and "sold out" the Poles and other Eastern Europeans by conceding Soviet dominance in the region and that the Soviets acquired too much for their brief war against Japan. For decades the right wing in American politics continued to blame Roosevelt for betraying Eastern Europeans at Yalta.

... The Premier of the Union of Soviet Socialist Republics, the Prime Minister of the United Kingdom and the President of the United States of America have consulted with each other in the common interests of the people of their countries and those of liberated Europe. They jointly declare their mutual agreement to concert during the temporary period of instability in liberated Europe the policies of their three Governments in assisting the peoples liberated from the domination of Nazi Germany and the peoples of the former Axis satellite states of Europe to solve by democratic means their pressing political and economic problems.

The establishment of order in Europe and the rebuilding of national economic life must be achieved by processes which will enable the liberated peoples to destroy the last vestiges of nazism and fascism and to create democratic institutions of their own choice. This is a principle of the *Atlantic Charter*—the right of all people to choose the form of government under which they will live—the restoration of sovereign rights and self-government to those peoples who have been forcibly deprived to them by the aggressor nations.

To foster the conditions in which the liberated people may exercise these rights, the three governments will jointly assist the people in any European liberated state or former Axis state in Europe where, in their judgment conditions require,

- (a) to establish conditions of internal peace;
- (b) to carry out emergency relief measures for the relief of distressed peoples;
- (c) to form interim governmental authorities broadly representative of all democratic elements in the population and pledged to the earliest possible establishment through free elections of Governments responsive to the will of the people; and
- (d) to facilitate where necessary the holding of such elections.

The three Governments will consult the other United Nations and provisional authorities or other Governments in Europe when matters of direct interest to them are under consideration. . . .

By this declaration we reaffirm our faith in the principles of the *Atlantic Charter*, our pledge in the Declaration by the United Nations and our determination to build in cooperation with other peace-loving nations world order, under law, dedicated to peace, security, freedom and general well-being of all mankind. . . .

III. DISMEMBERMENT OF GERMANY

It was agreed that Article 12 (a) of the Surrender terms for Germany should be amended to read as follows:

"The United Kingdom, the United States of America and the Union of Soviet Socialist Republics shall possess supreme authority with respect to Germany. In the exercise of such authority they will take such steps, including the complete dismemberment of Germany as they deem requisite for future peace and security." ...

It was agreed that a zone in Germany, to be occupied by the French forces, should be allocated France. This zone would be formed out of the British and American zones and its extent would be settled by the British and Americans in consultation with the French Provisional Government. ...

VII. POLAND

The following declaration on Poland was agreed by the conference:

A new situation has been created in Poland as a result of her complete liberation by the Red Army. This calls for the establishment of a Polish Provisional Government which can be more broadly based than was possible before the recent liberation of the western part of Poland. The Provisional Government which is now functioning in Poland should therefore be reorganized on a broader democratic basis with the inclusion of democratic leaders from Poland itself and from Poles abroad. This new Government should then be called the Polish Provisional Government of National Unity.

M. Molotov, Mr. Harriman and Sir A. Clark Kerr are authorized as a commission to consult in the first instance in Moscow with members of the present Provisional Government and with other Polish democratic leaders from within Poland and from abroad, with a view to the reorganization of the present Government along the above lines. This Polish Provisional Government of National Unity shall be pledged to the holding of free and unfettered elections as soon as possible on the basis of universal suffrage and secret ballot. In these elections all democratic and anti-Nazi parties shall have the right to take part and to put forward candidates.

When a Polish Provisional of Government National Unity has been properly formed in conformity with the above, the Government of the U.S.S.R., which now maintains diplomatic relations with the present Provisional Government of Poland, and the Government of the United Kingdom and the Government of the United States of America will establish diplomatic relations with the new Polish Provisional Government National Unity, and will exchange Ambassadors by whose reports the respective Governments will be kept informed about the situation in Poland.

The three heads of Government consider that the eastern frontier of Poland should follow the Curzon Line with digressions from it in some regions of five to eight kilometers in favor of Poland. They recognize that Poland must receive substantial accessions in territory in the north and west. They feel that the opinion of the new Polish Provisional Government of National Unity should be sought in due course of the extent of these accessions and that the final delimitation of the western frontier of Poland should thereafter await the peace conference. . . .

AGREEMENT REGARDING JAPAN

The leaders of the three great powers—the Soviet Union, the United States of America and Great Britain—have agreed that in two or three months after Germany has surrendered and the war in Europe is terminated, the Soviet Union shall enter into war against Japan on the side of the Allies on condition that:

1. The status quo in Outer Mongolia (the Mongolian People's Republic) shall be preserved.
2. The former rights of Russia violated by the treacherous attack of Japan in 1904 shall be restored, viz.:
   (a) The southern part of Sakhalin as well as the islands adjacent to it shall be returned to the Soviet Union;
   (b) The commercial port of Dairen shall be internationalized, the pre-eminent interests of the Soviet Union in this port being safeguarded, and the lease of Port Arthur as a naval base of the U.S.S.R. restored;
   (c) The Chinese-Eastern Railroad and the South Manchurian Railroad, which provide an outlet to Dairen, shall be jointly operated by the establishment of a joint Soviet-Chinese company, it being understood that the pre-eminent interests of the Soviet Union shall be safeguarded and that China shall retain sovereignty in Manchuria;
3. The Kurile Islands shall be handed over to the Soviet Union.

It is understood that the agreement concerning Outer Mongolia and the ports and railroads referred to above will require concurrence of Generalissimo Chiang Kai-shek. The President will take measures in order to maintain this concurrence on advice from Marshal Stalin.

The heads of the three great powers have agreed that these claims of the Soviet Union shall be unquestionably fulfilled after Japan has been defeated.

For its part, the Soviet Union expresses it readiness to conclude with the National Government of China a pact of friendship and alliance between the U.S.S.R. and China in order to render assistance to China with its armed forces for the purpose of liberating China from the Japanese yoke.

Source: A Decade of American Foreign Policy: Basic Documents, 1941–49. Prepared at the request of the Senate Committee on Foreign Relations by the staff of the Committee and the Department of State. Washington, DC: U.S. Government Printing Office, 1950, 27–33.

DOCUMENT 2
"The Long Telegram"
George F. Kennan, February 22, 1946

In response to an inquiry from the U.S. Treasury Department about the Soviet Union's intransience in supporting the new World Bank, George F. Kennan, deputy chief at the American embassy in Moscow, responded with his "Long Telegram" on February 22, 1946. In it he provided an analysis of Soviet values, sense of history, and goals. This is a key document in the development of the American containment policy of the Soviet Union and laid the foundation for Kennan's seminal article, "The Sources of Soviet Conduct," which was published in Foreign Affairs *in July 1947.*

. . . Part 1: Basic Features of Post War Soviet Outlook, as Put Forward by Official Propaganda Machine Are as Follows:

(a) USSR still lives in antagonistic "capitalist encirclement" with which in the long run there can be no permanent peaceful coexistence. . . .

(b) Capitalist world is beset with internal conflicts, inherent in nature of capitalist society. These conflicts are insoluble by means of peaceful compromise. Greatest of them is that between England and US.

(c) Internal conflicts of capitalism inevitably generate wars. Wars thus generated may be of two kinds: intra-capitalist wars between two capitalist states, and wars of intervention against [the] socialist world. Smart capitalists, vainly seeking escape from inner conflicts of capitalism, incline toward latter.

(d) Intervention against USSR, while it would be disastrous to those who undertook it, would cause renewed delay in progress of Soviet socialism and must therefore be forestalled at all costs.

(e) Conflicts between capitalist states, though likewise fraught with danger for USSR, nevertheless hold out great possibilities for advancement of socialist cause, particularly if USSR remains militarily powerful, ideologically monolithic and faithful to its present brilliant leadership.

(f) It must be borne in mind that [the] capitalist world is not all bad. In addition to hopelessly reactionary and bourgeois elements, it includes (1) certain wholly enlightened and positive elements united in acceptable communistic parties and (2) certain other elements (now described for tactical reasons as progressive or democratic) whose reactions, aspirations and activities happen to be "objectively" favorable to interests of USSR. These last must be encouraged and utilized for Soviet purposes.

(g) Among negative elements of bourgeois-capitalist society, most dangerous of all are those whom Lenin called false friends of the people, namely moderate-socialist or social-democratic leaders (in other words, non-Communist left-wing). These are more dangerous than out-and-out reactionaries, for [the] latter at least march under their true colors, whereas moderate left-wing leaders confuse people by employing devices of socialism to seine [the network of] interests of reactionary capital.

So much for premises. To what deductions do they lead from [the] standpoint of Soviet policy? To following:

(a) Everything must be done to advance relative strength of USSR as [a] factor in international society. Conversely, no opportunity must be missed to reduce strength and influence, collectively as well as individually, of capitalist powers.

(b) Soviet efforts, and those of Russia's friends abroad, must be directed toward deepening and exploiting of differences and conflicts between capitalist powers. If these eventually deepen into an "imperialist" war, this war must be turned into revolutionary upheavals within the various capitalist countries.

(c) "Democratic-progressive" elements abroad are to be utilized to [the] maximum to bring pressure to bear on capitalist governments along lines agreeable to Soviet interests.

(d) Relentless battle must be waged against socialist and social-democratic leaders abroad. . . .

At [the] bottom of Kremlin's neurotic view of world affairs is traditional and instinctive Russian sense of insecurity. Originally, this was insecurity of a peaceful agricultural people trying to live on vast exposed plain in neighborhood of fierce nomadic peoples. To this was added, as Russia came into contact with economically advanced West, fear of more competent, more powerful, more highly organized societies in that area. But this latter type of insecurity was one which afflicted rather Russian rulers than Russian people; for Russian rulers have invariably sensed that their rule was relatively archaic in form fragile and artificial in its psychological foundation, unable to stand comparison or contact with political systems of Western countries. For this reason they have always feared foreign penetration, feared direct contact between Western world and their own, feared what would happen if Russians learned truth about world without or if foreigners learned truth about world within. And they have learned to seek security only in [a] patient but deadly struggle for total destruction of rival power, never in compacts and compromises with it. . . .

Basically this [aggression] is only the steady advance of uneasy Russian nationalism, a centuries old movement in which conceptions of offense and defense are inextricably confused. But in [the] new guise of international Marxism, with its honeyed promises to a desperate and war torn outside world, it is more dangerous and insidious than ever before. . . . It should not be thought from [the] above that [the] Soviet party line is necessarily disingenuous and insincere on part of all those who put it forward. Many of them are too ignorant of outside world and mentally too dependent to question [apparent omission] self-hypnotism, and who have no difficulty making themselves believe what they find it comforting and convenient to believe. Finally, we have the unsolved mystery as to who, if anyone, in this great land, actually receives accurate and unbiased information about outside world. In [the] atmosphere of oriental secretiveness and conspiracy which pervades this Government, possibilities for distorting or poisoning sources and currents of information are infinite. The very disrespect of Russians for objective truth—indeed, their disbelief in its existence—leads them to view all stated facts as instruments for furtherance of one ulterior purpose or another. There is good reason to suspect that this Government is actually a conspiracy within a conspiracy; and I for one am reluctant to believe that Stalin himself receives anything like an objective picture of outside world. Here there is ample scope for the type of subtle intrigue at which Russians are past masters. Inability of foreign governments to place their case squarely before Russian policy makers —extent to which they are delivered up in their relations with Russia to good graces of obscure and unknown advisors whom they never see and cannot influence—this to my mind is most disquieting feature of diplomacy in Moscow, and one which Western statesmen would do well to keep in mind if they would understand nature of difficulties encountered here. . . .

We have now seen nature and background of Soviet program. What may we expect by way of its practical implementation?

Soviet policy, as Department implies in its query under reference, is conducted on two planes: (1) official plane represented by actions undertaken officially in name of Soviet Government; and (2) subterranean plane of actions undertaken by agencies for which Soviet Government does not admit responsibility. . . .

On [the] official plane we must look for following:

(a) Internal policy devoted to increasing in every way strength and prestige of Soviet state: intensive military-industrialization; maximum development of armed forces; great displays to impress outsiders; continued secretiveness about internal matters, designed to conceal weaknesses and to keep opponents in dark.

(b) Wherever it is considered timely and promising, efforts will be made to advance official limits of Soviet power. For the moment, these efforts are restricted to certain neighboring points conceived of here as being of immediate strategic necessity, such as Northern Iran, Turkey, . . . However, other points may at any time come into question, if . . . Soviet political power is extended to new areas. . . .

(c) Russians will participate officially in international organizations where they see opportunity of extending Soviet power or of inhibiting or diluting power of others. . . .

(d) Toward colonial areas and backward or dependent peoples, Soviet policy, even on official plane, will be directed toward weakening of power and influence and contacts of advanced Western nations, on theory that in so far as this policy is successful, there will be created a vacuum which will favor Communist-Soviet penetration. . . .

(e) Russians will strive energetically to develop Soviet representation in, and official ties with, countries in which they sense strong possibilities of opposition to Western centers of power. . . .

(f) In international economic matters, Soviet policy will really be dominated by pursuit of autarchy for Soviet Union and Soviet-dominated adjacent areas taken together. . . .

(g) With respect to cultural collaboration, lip service will likewise be rendered to desirability of deepening cultural contacts between peoples, but this will not in practice be interpreted in any way which could weaken security position of Soviet peoples. . . .

(h) Beyond this, Soviet official relations will take what might be called "correct" course with individual foreign governments, with great stress being laid on prestige of Soviet Union and its representatives and with punctilious attention to protocol as distinct from good manners.

Part 4: Following May Be Said as to What We May Expect by Way of Implementation of Basic Soviet Policies on Unofficial, or Subterranean Plane, i.e. on Plane for Which Soviet Government Accepts no Responsibility

Agencies utilized for promulgation of policies on this plane are following:

1. Inner central core of Communist Parties in other countries . . . a concealed Comintern tightly coordinated and directed by Moscow. It is important to remember that this inner core is actually working on underground lines, despite legality of parties with which it is associated.

2. Rank and file of Communist Parties. . . .

3. A wide variety of national associations or bodies which can be dominated or influenced by such penetration. These include: labor unions, youth leagues, women's organizations, racial societies, religious societies,

social organizations, cultural groups, liberal magazines, publishing houses, etc.

4. International organizations which can be similarly penetrated through influence over various national components. Labor, youth and women's organizations are prominent among them. Particular, almost vital importance is attached in this connection to international labor movement. . . .

5. Russian Orthodox Church, with its foreign branches, and through it the Eastern Orthodox Church in general.

6. Pan-Slav movement and other movements (Azerbaijan, Armenian, Turcoman, etc.) based on racial groups within Soviet Union.

7. Governments or governing groups willing to lend themselves to Soviet purposes in one degree or another, such as present Bulgarian and Yugoslav Governments, North Persian regime, Chinese Communists, etc. . . .

It may be expected that component parts of this far-flung apparatus will be utilized in accordance with their individual suitability, as follows:

(a) To undermine general political and strategic potential of major western powers. Efforts will be made in such countries to disrupt national self confidence, to hamstring measures of national defense, to increase social and industrial unrest, to stimulate all forms of disunity. . . . Here poor will be set against rich, black against white, young against old, newcomers against established residents, etc.

(b) On unofficial plane particularly violent efforts will be made to weaken power and influence of Western Powers of [on] colonial backward, or dependent peoples. . . .

(c) Where individual governments stand in path of Soviet purposes pressure will be brought for their removal from office. . . .

(d) In foreign countries Communists will, as a rule, work toward destruction of all forms of personal independence, economic, political or moral. Their system can handle only individuals who have been brought into complete dependence on higher power. . . .

(e) Everything possible will be done to set major Western Powers against each other. . . .

(f) In general, all Soviet efforts on unofficial international plane will be negative and destructive in character, designed to tear down sources of strength beyond reach of Soviet control. . . .

In summary, we have here a political force committed fanatically to the belief that with US there can be no permanent *modus vivendi* that it is desirable and necessary that the internal harmony of our society be disrupted, our traditional way of life be destroyed, the international authority of our state be broken, if Soviet power is to be secure. ....

[But] I think we may approach calmly and with good heart [the] problem of how to deal with Russia. As to how this approach should be made, I only wish to advance, by way of conclusion, following comments:

(1) Our first step must be to apprehend, and recognize for what it is, the nature of the movement with which we are dealing. We must study it with same courage, detachment, objectivity, and same determination not to be emotionally provoked or unseated by it, with which doctor studies unruly and unreasonable individual.

(2) We must see that our public is educated to realities of Russian situation. I cannot over-emphasize importance of this. Press cannot do this alone. It must be done mainly by Government, which is necessarily more experienced and better informed on practical problems involved. In this we need not be deterred by [the ugliness?] of [the] picture ....

(3) Much depends on health and vigor of our own society. World communism is like malignant [a] parasite which feeds only on diseased tissue. This is point at which domestic and foreign policies meets every courageous and incisive measure to solve internal problems of our own society, to improve self-confidence, discipline, morale and community spirit of our own people, is a diplomatic victory over Moscow worth a thousand diplomatic notes and joint communiqués. If we cannot abandon fatalism and indifference in face of deficiencies of our own society, Moscow will profit—Moscow cannot help profiting by them in its foreign policies.

(4) We must formulate and put forward for other nations a much more positive and constructive picture of [the] sort of world we would like to see than we have put forward in past. It is not enough to urge people to develop political processes similar to our own. Many foreign peoples, in Europe at least, are tired and frightened by experiences of past, and are less interested in abstract freedom than in security. They are seeking guidance rather than responsibilities. We should be better able than [the] Russians to give them this. And unless we do, Russians certainly will.

(5) Finally we must have courage and self-confidence to cling to our own methods and conceptions of human society. After all, the greatest danger that can befall us in coping with this problem of Soviet communism, is that we shall allow ourselves to become like those with whom we are coping.

Source: George F. Kennan Telegram, U.S. Department of State Files, 861.00/2-2246, National Archives, College Park, Maryland. February 22, 1946.

DOCUMENT 3
The Truman Doctrine, March 12, 1947

The expansion of communism in Greece and Turkey was feared because of Great Britain's inability to provide effective support for the Greek and Turkish governments' efforts to defeat the communist insurgencies there. In this speech before a joint session of the Congress, President Harry S. Truman advanced a plan for the United States to assume a more direct role in this anticommunist effort. The Truman Doctrine was a defining moment during the early years of the Cold War and demonstrated American willingness to act to contain the spread of communism. It also signaled the end of the traditional return to isolationism that followed the closure of previous American foreign wars.

... The gravity of the situation which confronts the world today necessitates my appearance before a joint session of the Congress.

The foreign policy and the national security of this country are involved.

One aspect of the present situation, which I present to you at this time for your consideration and decision, concerns Greece and Turkey.

The United States has received from the Greek Government an urgent appeal for financial and economic assistance. Preliminary reports from the American Economic Mission now in Greece and reports from the American Ambassador in Greece corroborate the statement of the Greek Government that assistance is imperative if Greece is to survive as a free nation.

I do not believe that the American people and the Congress wish to turn a deaf ear to the appeal of the Greek Government.

Greece is not a rich country. Lack of sufficient natural resources has always forced the Greek people to work hard to make both ends meet.

Since 1940, this industrious, peace loving country has suffered invasion, four years of cruel enemy occupation, and bitter internal strife.

When forces of liberation entered Greece they found that the retreating Germans had destroyed virtually all the railways, roads, port facilities, communications, and merchant marine. More than a thousand villages had been burned. Eighty-five percent of the children were tubercular. Livestock, poultry, and draft animals had almost disappeared. Inflation had wiped out practically all savings.

As a result of these tragic conditions, a militant minority, exploiting human want and misery, was able to create political chaos which, until now, has made economic recovery impossible.

Greece is today without funds to finance the importation of those goods which are essential to bare subsistence. Under these circumstances the people of Greece cannot make progress in solving their problems of reconstruction. Greece is in desperate need of financial and economic assistance to enable it to resume purchases of food, clothing, fuel and seeds. These are indispensable for the subsistence of its people and are obtainable only from abroad. Greece must have help to import the goods necessary to restore internal order and security so essential for economic and political recovery. . . .

The very existence of the Greek state is today threatened by the terrorist activities of several thousand armed men, led by Communists, who defy the government's authority at a number of points, particularly along the northern boundaries. A Commission appointed by the United Nations Security Council is at present investigating disturbed conditions in northern Greece and alleged border violations along the frontier[s] between Greece on the one hand and Albania, Bulgaria, and Yugoslavia on the other.

Meanwhile, the Greek Government is unable to cope with the situation. The Greek army is small and poorly equipped. It needs supplies and equipment if it is to restore authority to the government throughout Greek territory.

Greece must have assistance if it is to become a self-supporting and self-respecting democracy.

The United States must supply this assistance. We have already extended to Greece certain types of relief and economic aid but these are inadequate.

There is no other country to which democratic Greece can turn.

No other nation is willing and able to provide the necessary support for a democratic Greek government.

The British Government, which has been helping Greece, can give no further financial or economic aid after March 31. Great Britain finds itself under the necessity of reducing or liquidating its commitments in several parts of the world, including Greece.

We have considered how the United Nations might assist in this crisis. But the situation is an urgent one requiring immediate action, and the United Nations and its related organizations are not in a position to extend help of the kind that is required.

It is important to note that the Greek Government has asked for our aid in utilizing effectively the financial and other assistance we may give to Greece, and in improving its public administration. It is of the utmost importance that we supervise the use of any funds made available to Greece, in such a manner that each dollar spent will count toward making Greece self-supporting, and will help to build an economy in which a healthy democracy can flourish.

No government is perfect. One of the chief virtues of a democracy, however, is that its defects are always visible and under democratic processes can be pointed out and corrected. The government of Greece is not perfect. Nevertheless it represents 85 percent of the members of the Greek Parliament who were chosen in an election last year. Foreign observers, including 692 Americans, considered this election to be a fair expression of the views of the Greek people.

The Greek Government has been operating in an atmosphere of chaos and extremism. It has made mistakes. The extension of aid by this country does not mean that the United States condones everything that the Greek Government has done or will do. We have condemned in the past, and we condemn now, extremist measures of the right or the left. We have in the past advised tolerance, and we advise tolerance now. Greece's neighbor, Turkey, also deserves our attention.

The future of Turkey as an independent and economically sound state is clearly no less important to the freedom-loving peoples of the world than the future of Greece. The circumstances in which Turkey finds itself today are considerably different from those of Greece. Turkey has been spared the disasters that have beset Greece. And during the war, the United States and Great Britain furnished Turkey with material aid.

Nevertheless, Turkey now needs our support.

Since the war Turkey has sought additional financial assistance from Great Britain and the United States for the purpose of effecting that modernization necessary for the maintenance of its national integrity.

That integrity is essential to the preservation of order in the Middle East.

The British Government has informed us that, owing to its own difficulties, it can no longer extend financial or economic aid to Turkey.

As in the case of Greece, if Turkey is to have the assistance it needs, the United States must supply it. We are the only country able to provide that help.

I am fully aware of the broad implications involved if the United States extends assistance to Greece and Turkey, and I shall discuss these implications with you at this time.

One of the primary objectives of the foreign policy of the United States is the creation of conditions in which we and other nations will be able to work out a way of life free from coercion. This was a fundamental issue in the war with Germany and Japan. Our victory was won over countries which sought to impose their will, and their way of life, upon other nations.

To ensure the peaceful development of nations, free from coercion, the United States has taken a leading part in establishing the United Nations. The United Nations is designed to make possible lasting freedom and independence for all its members. We shall not realize our objectives, however, unless we are willing to help free peoples to maintain their free institutions and their national integrity against aggressive movements that seek to impose upon them totalitarian regimes. This is no more than a frank recognition that totalitarian regimes imposed upon free peoples, by direct or indirect aggression, undermine the foundations of international peace and hence the security of the United States.

The peoples of a number of countries of the world have recently had totalitarian regimes forced upon them against their will. The Government of the United States has made frequent protests against coercion and intimidation, in violation of the Yalta agreement, in Poland, Rumania, and Bulgaria. I must also state that in a number of other countries there have been similar developments.

At the present moment in world history nearly every nation must choose between alternative ways of life. The choice is too often not a free one.

One way of life is based upon the will of the majority, and is distinguished by free institutions, representative government, free elections, guarantees of individual liberty, freedom of speech and religion, and freedom from political oppression.

The second way of life is based upon the will of a minority forcibly imposed upon the majority. It relies upon terror and oppression, a controlled press and radio, fixed elections, and the suppression of personal freedoms.

I believe that it must be the policy of the United States to support free peoples who are resisting attempted subjugation by armed minorities or by outside pressures.

I believe that we must assist free peoples to work out their own destinies in their own way.

I believe that our help should be primarily through economic and financial aid which is essential to economic stability and orderly political processes.

The world is not static, and the status quo is not sacred. But we cannot allow changes in the status quo in violation of the Charter of the United Nations by such methods as coercion, or by such subterfuges as political infiltration. In helping free and independent nations to maintain their freedom, the United States will be giving effect to the principles of the Charter of the United Nations.

It is necessary only to glance at a map to realize that the survival and integrity of the Greek nation are of grave importance in a much wider situation. If Greece should fall under the control of an armed minority, the effect upon its neighbor, Turkey, would be immediate and serious. Confusion and disorder might well spread throughout the entire Middle East.

Moreover, the disappearance of Greece as an independent state would have a profound effect upon those countries in Europe whose peoples are struggling against great difficulties to maintain their freedoms and their independence while they repair the damages of war.

It would be an unspeakable tragedy if these countries, which have struggled so long against overwhelming odds, should lose that victory for which they sacrificed so much. Collapse of free institutions and loss of independence would be disastrous not only for them but for the world. Discouragement and possibly failure would quickly be the lot of neighboring peoples striving to maintain their freedom and independence.

Should we fail to aid Greece and Turkey in this fateful hour, the effect will be far reaching to the West as well as to the East.

We must take immediate and resolute action.

I therefore ask the Congress to provide authority for assistance to Greece and Turkey in the amount of $400,000,000 for the period ending June 30, 1948. In requesting these funds, I have taken into consideration the maximum amount of relief assistance which would be furnished to Greece out of the $350,000,000 which I recently requested that the Congress authorize for the prevention of starvation and suffering in countries devastated by the war.

In addition to funds, I ask the Congress to authorize the detail of American civilian and military personnel to Greece and Turkey, at the request of those countries, to assist in the tasks of reconstruction, and for the purpose of supervising the use of such financial and material assistance as may be furnished. I recommend that authority also be provided for the instruction and training of selected Greek and Turkish personnel.

Finally, I ask that the Congress provide authority which will permit the speediest and most effective use, in terms of needed commodities, supplies, and equipment, of such funds as may be authorized.

If further funds, or further authority, should be needed for the purposes indicated in this message, I shall not hesitate to bring the situation before the Congress. On this subject the Executive and Legislative branches of the Government must work together. . . .

The seeds of totalitarian regimes are nurtured by misery and want. They spread and grow in the evil soil of poverty and strife. They reach their full growth when the hope of a people for a better life has died.

We must keep that hope alive. . . .

Source: Harry S. Truman, *Public Papers of the Presidents of the United States: Harry S. Truman, 1947.* Washington, DC: U.S. Government Printing Office, 1963, 176–180.

DOCUMENT 4
Truman Loyalty Oath, March 21, 1947

In response to the mounting concerns over communists working for the U.S. government and the pressures from the Republican-controlled Congress to root out alleged disloyal workers in his administration, President Harry S. Truman instituted a loyalty oath requirement for all federal employees (Executive Order 9835). This policy illustrates the impact of the Cold War on the internal operations of the American government and reflects the fear of internal subversion. The loyalty oath preceded Senator Joseph R. McCarthy's accusations of February 9, 1950, concerning communists being employed in the Department of State.

PART I—INVESTIGATION OF APPLICANTS

1. There shall be a loyalty investigation of every person entering the civilian employment of any department or agency of the executive branch of the Federal Government.

2. Investigations of persons entering the competitive service shall be conducted by the Civil Service Commission, except in such cases as are covered by a special agreement between the Commission and any given department or agency.

3. Investigations of persons other than those entering the competitive service shall be conducted by the employing department or agency. Departments and agencies without investigative organizations shall utilize the investigative facilities of the Civil Service Commission.

4. The investigations of persons entering the employ of the executive branch may be conducted after any such person enters upon actual employment therein, but in any such case the appointment of such person shall be conditioned upon a favorable determination with respect to his loyalty.

5. Investigations of persons entering the competitive service shall be conducted as expeditiously as possible; provided, however, that if any such investigation is not completed within 18 months from the date on which a person enters actual employment, the condition that his employment is subject to investigation shall expire, except in a case in which the Civil Service Commission has made an initial adjudication of disloyalty and the case continues to be active by reason of an appeal, and it shall then be the responsibility of the employing department or agency to conclude

such investigation and make a final determination concerning the loyalty of such person.

6. An investigation shall be made of all applicants at all available pertinent sources of information and shall include reference to:

Federal Bureau of Investigation files.
Civil Service Commission files.
Military and naval intelligence files.
The files of any other appropriate government investigative or intelligence agency.
House Committee on Un-American Activities files.
Local law-enforcement files at the place of residence and employment of the applicant, including municipal, county, and State law-enforcement files.
Schools and colleges attended by applicant.
Former employers of applicant.
References given by applicant.
Any other appropriate source.

Whenever derogatory information with respect to loyalty of an applicant is revealed a full investigation shall be conducted. A full field investigation shall also be conducted of those applicants, or of applicants for particular positions, as may be designated by the head of the employing department or agency, such designations to be based on the determination by any such head of the best interests of national security.

PART II—INVESTIGATION OF EMPLOYEES

1. The head of each department and agency in the executive branch of the Government shall be personally responsible for an effective program to assure that disloyal civilian officers or employees are not retained in employment in his department or agency.

2. He shall be responsible for prescribing and supervising the loyalty determination procedures of his department or agency, in accordance with the provisions of this order, which shall be considered as providing minimum requirements.

3. The head of a department or agency which does not have an investigative organization shall utilize the investigative facilities of the Civil Service Commission.

4. The head of each department and agency shall appoint one or more loyalty boards, each composed of not less than three representatives of the department or agency concerned, for the purpose of hearing loyalty cases arising within such department or agency and making recommendations with respect to the removal of any officer or employee of such department or agency on grounds relating to loyalty, and he shall prescribe regulations for the conduct of the proceedings before such boards.

5. An officer or employee who is charged with being disloyal shall have a right to an administrative hearing before a loyalty board in the employing department or agency. He may appear before such board personally, accompanied by counsel or representative of his own choosing, and present evidence on his own behalf, through witnesses or by affidavit.

6. The officer or employee shall be served with a written notice of such hearing in sufficient time, and shall be informed therein of the nature of the charges against him in sufficient detail, so that he will be enabled to prepare his defense. The charges shall be stated as specifically and completely as, in the discretion of the employing department or agency, security considerations permit, and the officer or employee shall be informed in the notice (1) of his right to reply to such charges in writing within a specified reasonable period of time, (2) of his right to an administrative hearing on such charges before a loyalty board, and (3) of his right to appear before such board personally, to be accompanied by counsel or representative of his own choosing, and to present evidence on his behalf, through witness or by affidavit.

7. A recommendation of removal by a loyalty board shall be subject to appeal by the officer or employee affected, prior to his removal, to the head of the employing department or agency or to such person or persons as may be designated by such head, under such regulations as may be prescribed by him, and the decision of the department or agency concerned shall be subject to appeal to the Civil Service Commission's Loyalty Review Board, hereinafter provided for, for an advisory recommendation.

8. The rights of hearing, notice thereof, and appeal therefrom shall be accorded to every officer or employee prior to his removal on grounds of disloyalty, irrespective of tenure, or of manner, method, or nature of appointment, but the head of the employing department or agency may suspend any officer or employee at any time pending a determination with respect to loyalty.

9. The loyalty boards of the various departments and agencies shall furnish to the Loyalty Review Board, hereinafter provided for, such reports as may be requested concerning the operation of the loyalty program in any such department or agency.

Source: Executive Order No. 9835, March 21, 1947, Prescribing Procedures for the Administration of an Employees Loyalty Program in the Executive Branch of the Government, *Code of Federal Regulations*, Title 3: The President 1943–1948 Compilation or 3 CFR, 1943–1948 Comp.

DOCUMENT 5
The Marshall Plan, June 5, 1947

The economic recovery of Europe from the impact of World War II was more sluggish than expected, and the leaders of the democratic governments feared that continued unemployment and the scarcity of consumer products would assist the communists in expanding their power within Western governments and societies. After failing to reach an agreement with the Soviet Union on an economic recovery program, Secretary of State George C. Marshall, in a speech at Harvard University, advanced a proposal for an American-led European Economic Recovery Program, which, when instituted, became known as the Marshall Plan. It was implemented over several years, accelerated the economic recovery of Western Europe, and stabilized democratic governments.

I need not tell you gentlemen that the world situation is very serious. That must be apparent to all intelligent people. . . .

In considering the requirements for the rehabilitation of Europe the physical loss of life, the visible destruction of cities, factories, mines and railroads was correctly estimated, but it has become obvious during recent months that this visible destruction was probably less serious than the dislocation of the entire fabric of European economy. For the past ten years conditions have been highly abnormal. The feverish preparation for war and the more feverish maintenance of the war effort engulfed all aspects of national economies. Machinery has fallen into disrepair or is entirely obsolete. Under the arbitrary and destructive Nazi rule, virtually every possible enterprise was geared into the German war machine. Long-standing commercial ties, private institutions, banks, insurance companies and shipping companies disappeared, through loss of capital, absorption through nationalization or by simple destruction. In many countries, confidence in the local currency has been severely shaken. The breakdown of the business structure of Europe during the war was complete. Recovery has been seriously retarded by the fact that two years after the close of hostilities a peace settlement with Germany and Austria has not been agreed upon. But even given a more prompt solution of these difficult problems, the rehabilitation of the economic structure of Europe quite evidently will require a much longer time and greater effort than had been foreseen. . . .

The town and city industries are not producing adequate goods to exchange with the food-producing farmer. Raw materials and fuel are in short supply. Machinery is lacking or worn out. The farmer or the peasant cannot find the goods for sale which he desires to purchase. So the sale of his farm produce for money which he cannot use seems to him an unprofitable transaction. He, therefore, has withdrawn many fields from crop cultivation and is using them for grazing. He feeds more grain to stock and finds for himself and his family an ample supply of food, however short he may be on clothing and the other ordinary gadgets of civilization. Meanwhile people in the cities are short of food and fuel. So the governments are forced to use their foreign money and credits to procure these necessities abroad. This process exhausts funds which are urgently needed for reconstruction. This a very serious situation [that] is rapidly developing [and] which bodes no good for the world. The modern system of the division of labor upon which the exchange of products is based is in danger of breaking down.

The truth of the matter is that Europe's requirements for the next three or four years of foreign food and other essential products—principally from America—are so much greater than her present ability to pay that she must have substantial additional help, or face economic, social and political deterioration of a very grave character.

The remedy lies in breaking the vicious circle and restoring the confidence of the European people in the economic future of their own countries and of Europe as a whole. . . .

It is logical that the United States should do whatever it is able to do to assist in the return of normal economic health in the world, without which there can be no political stability and no assured peace. Our policy is directed not against any country or doctrine but against hunger, poverty, desperation and chaos. Its purpose should be the revival of a working economy in the world so as to permit the emergence of political and social conditions in which free institutions can exist. Such assistance, I am convinced, must not be on a peacemeal basis as various crises develop. Any assistance that this Government may render in the future should provide a cure rather than a mere palliative. Any government that is willing to assist in the task of recovery will find full cooperation, I am sure, on the part of the United States Government. Any government which maneuvers to block the recovery of other countries cannot expect help from us. Furthermore, governments, political parties or groups which seek to perpetuate human misery in order to profit therefrom politically or otherwise will encounter the opposition of the United States. ...

[T]here must be some agreement among the countries of Europe as to the requirements of the situation and the part those countries themselves will take in order to give proper effect to whatever action might be undertaken by this Government. It would be neither fitting nor efficacious for this Government to undertake to draw up unilaterally a program designed to place Europe on its feet economically. This is the business of the Europeans. The initiative, I think, must come from Europe. The role of this country should consist of friendly aid in the drafting of a European program and of later support of such a program so far as it may be practical for us to do so. The program should be a joint one, agreed to by a number, if not all European nations.

An essential part of any successful action on the part of the United States is an understanding on the part of the people of America of the character of the problem and the remedies to be applied. ...

Source: George C. Marshall, "European Initiative Essential to Economic Recovery," *Department of State Bulletin* 16, no. 415 (1947): 1159–60.

DOCUMENT 6
Senator Joseph McCarthy's Lincoln Day Speech
Wheeling, West Virginia, February 9, 1950

Invited by the Republican Women's Club of Wheeling, West Virginia, to give the Annual Lincoln's Day Speech, Senator Joseph R. McCarthy (R-WI) took the opportunity to announce that communists had infiltrated the United States government. In his attack on the State Department, McCarthy launched what became known as McCarthyism, which—based on false, fabricated, misleading, and/or unsubstantiated accusations—prevailed for several years, and along with other congressional probes into alleged communist infiltration of key American institutions, silenced the critics of McCarthyism that included moderates, artists, intellectuals, educators, and anyone in public life supposedly sympathetic to communist ideas and influence. In 1954 McCarthy was censured by the Senate for his behavior and reckless accusations.

... Five years after a world war has been won, men's hearts should anticipate a long peace, and men's minds should be free from the heavy weight that comes with war. But this is not such a period—for this is not a period of peace. This is a time of the "cold war." This is a time when all the world is split into two vast, increasingly hostile armed camps—a time of great armaments race. ...

Six years ago, at the time of the first conference to map out the peace—Dumbarton Oaks—there was within the Soviet orbit 180,000,000 people. Lined up on the anti-totalitarian side there were in the world at that time roughly 1,625,000,000 people. Today, only 6 years later, there are 800,000,000 people under the absolute domination of Soviet Russia—an increase of over 400 percent. On our side, the figure has shrunk to around 500,000,000. In other words, in less than 6 years the odds have changed from 9 to 1 in our favor to 8 to 5 against us. This indicates the swiftness of the tempo of Communist victories and American defeats in the cold war. As one of our outstanding historical figures once said, "When a great democracy is destroyed, it will not be because of enemies from without, but rather because of enemies from within ..."

The reason why we find ourselves in a position of impotency is not because our only powerful potential enemy has sent men to invade our shores, but rather because of the traitorous actions of those who have been treated so well by this Nation. It has not been the less fortunate or members of minority groups who have been selling this Nation out, but rather those who have had all the benefits that the wealthiest nation on earth has had to offer—the finest homes, the finest college education, and the finest jobs in Government [that] we can give.

This is glaringly true in the State Department. There the bright young men who are born with silver spoons in their mouths are the ones who have been the worst. ...

Now I know it is very easy for anyone to condemn a particular bureau or department in general terms. Therefore, I would like to cite one rather unusual case—the case of a man who has done much to shape our foreign policy.

When Chiang Kai-shek was fighting our war, the State Department had in China a young man named John S. Service. His task, obviously, was not to work for the communization of China. Strangely, however, he sent official reports back to the State Department urging that we torpedo our ally Chiang Kai-shek and stating, in effect, that communism was the best hope [for] China.

Later, this man—John Service—was picked up by the Federal Bureau of Investigation for turning over to the Communists secret State Department information. Strangely, however, he was never prosecuted. However, Joseph Grew, the Under Secretary of State, who insisted on his prosecution, was forced to resign. Two days after Grew's successor, Dean Acheson, took over as Under Secretary of State, this man—John Service—who had been picked up by the FBI and who had previously urged that communism was the best hope [for] China, was not only reinstated in the State Department but promoted. And finally, under Acheson, placed in charge of all placements and promotions.

Today . . . this man Service is on his way to represent the State Department and Acheson in Calcutta—by far and away the most important listening post in the Far East. . . .

This . . . gives you somewhat of a picture of the type of individuals who have been helping to shape our foreign policy. In my opinion the State Department, which is one of the most important government departments, is thoroughly infested with Communists.

I have in my hand 57 [reportedly, McCarthy initially stated that there were more than 200 communists in the State Department] cases of individuals who would appear to be either card carrying members or certainly loyal to the Communist Party, but who nevertheless are still helping to shape our foreign policy. . . .

This brings us down to the case of one Alger Hiss who is more important not as an individual any more, but rather because he is so representative of a group in the State Department. . . .

If time permitted, it might be well to go into detail about the fact that Hiss was Roosevelt's chief advisor at Yalta when Roosevelt was admittedly in ill health and tired physically and mentally. . . .

According to the then Secretary of State Stettinius, here are some of the things that Hiss helped to decide at Yalta. (1) The establishment of a European High Commission; (2) the treatment of Germany—this you will recall was the conference at which it was decided that we would occupy Berlin with Russia occupying an area completely circling the city, which, as you know, resulted in the Berlin airlift which cost 31 American lives; (3) the Polish question. . . (6) Iran; (7) China—here's where we gave away Manchuria; (8) Turkish Straits question; (9) international trusteeships; (10) Korea. . . .

As you hear this story of high treason, I know that you are saying to yourself, "Well, why doesn't the Congress do something about it?" Actually . . . one of the important reasons for the graft, the corruption, the dishonesty, the disloyalty, the treason in high Government positions —one of the most important reasons why this continues is a lack of moral uprising on the part of the 140,000,000 American people. In the light of history, however, this is not hard to explain.

It is the result of an emotional hangover and a temporary moral lapse which follows every war . . . However, the morals of our people have not been destroyed. They still exist. This cloak of numbness and apathy has only needed a spark to rekindle them. Happily, this spark has finally been supplied.

When this pompous diplomat [Acheson] in striped pants, with a phony British accent, proclaimed to the American people that Christ on the Mount endorsed communism, high treason, and betrayal of a sacred trust, the blasphemy was so great that it awakened the dormant indignation of the American people . . .

Source: Congressional Record, Senate, 81st Congress 2nd Session, February 20, 1950, 1954–57.

DOCUMENT 7
National Security Council Report 68
United States Objectives and Programs for National Security, April 14, 1950

In response to the continuing deterioration of relations between the United States and its allies and the Soviet Union, the need for improved coordination between the White House and Departments of State and Defense was evident. On January 31, 1950, President Harry Truman directed that the State and Defense Departments consider all aspects of a strategy on American objectives on peace and war and submit a report. A National Security Council (NSC) group was organized with Paul Nitze as chair. Dean Acheson also served on the study group. The result was NSC-68, which served as the basis of American foreign policy for two decades. It reflected the American sense of history and its role in the post– World War II era, and it led to American actions in Latin America, Europe, and Southeast Asia.

I. Background of the Present Crisis

Within the past thirty-five years the world has experienced two global wars of tremendous violence. It has witnessed two revolutions—the Russian and the Chinese—of extreme scope and intensity. It has also seen the collapse of five empires—the Ottoman, the Austro-Hungarian, German, Italian, and Japanese—and the drastic decline of two major imperial systems, the British and the French. During the span of one generation, the international distribution of power has been fundamentally altered. For several centuries it had proved impossible for any one nation to gain such preponderant strength that a coalition of other nations could not in time face it with greater strength. The international scene was marked by recurring periods of violence and war, but a system of sovereign and independent states was maintained, over which no state was able to achieve hegemony.

Two complex sets of factors have now basically altered this historic distribution of power. First, the defeat of Germany and Japan and the decline of the British and French Empires have interacted with the development of the United States and the Soviet Union in such a way that power increasingly gravitated to these two centers. Second, the Soviet Union, unlike previous aspirants to hegemony, is animated by a new fanatic faith, antithetical to our own, and seeks to impose its absolute authority over the rest of the world. Conflict has, therefore, become endemic and is waged, on the part of the Soviet Union, by violent or non-violent methods in accordance with the dictates of expediency. With the development of increasingly terrifying weapons of mass destruction, every individual faces the ever-present possibility of annihilation should the conflict enter the phase of total war.

On the one hand, the people of the world yearn for relief from the anxiety arising from the risk of atomic war. On the other hand, any substantial further extension of the area under the domination of the Kremlin would raise the possibility that no coalition adequate to confront the Kremlin with greater strength could be assembled. It is in this context that this Republic and its citizens in the ascendancy of their strength stand in their deepest peril. . . .

II. Fundamental Purpose of the United States

. . . In essence, the fundamental purpose is to assure the integrity and vitality of our free society, which is founded upon the dignity and worth of the individual.

Three realities emerge as a consequence of this purpose: our determination to maintain the essential elements of individual freedom . . . our determination to create conditions under which our free and democratic system can live and prosper; and our determination to fight if necessary to defend our way of life . . .

III. Fundamental Design of the Kremlin

The fundamental design of those who control the Soviet Union and the international communist movement is to retain and solidify their absolute power, first in the Soviet Union and second in the areas now under their control. . . .

The design, therefore, calls for the complete subversion or forcible destruction of the machinery of government and structure of society in the countries of the non-Soviet world and their replacement by an apparatus and structure subservient to and controlled from the Kremlin. To that end Soviet efforts are now directed toward the domination of the Eurasian land mass. The United States, as the principal center of power in the non-Soviet world and the bulwark of opposition to Soviet expansion, is the principal enemy whose integrity and vitality must be subverted or destroyed by one means or another if the Kremlin is to achieve its fundamental design.

IV. The Underlying Conflict in the Realm of ideas and Values between the U.S. Purpose and the Kremlin Design
A. NATURE OF CONFLICT

The Kremlin regards the United States as the only major threat to the conflict between idea of slavery under the grim oligarchy of the Kremlin, which has come to a crisis with the polarization of power described in

Section I, and the exclusive possession of atomic weapons by the two protagonists. The idea of freedom, moreover, is peculiarly and intolerably subversive of the idea of slavery. But the converse is not true. The implacable purpose of the slave state to eliminate the challenge of freedom has placed the two great powers at opposite poles. It is this fact which gives the present polarization of power the quality of crisis.

The free society values the individual as an end in himself, requiring of him only that measure of self-discipline and self-restraint which make the rights of each individual compatible with the rights of every other individual. The freedom of the individual has as its counterpart, therefore, the negative responsibility of the individual not to exercise his freedom in ways inconsistent with the freedom of other individuals and the positive responsibility to make constructive use of his freedom in the building of a just society.

From this idea of freedom with responsibility derives the marvelous diversity, the deep tolerance, [and] the lawfulness of the free society. This is the explanation of the strength of free men. It constitutes the integrity and the vitality of a free and democratic system. The free society attempts to create and maintain an environment in which every individual has the opportunity to realize his creative powers. It also explains why the free society tolerates those within it who would use their freedom to destroy it. By the same token, in relations between nations, the prime reliance of the free society is on the strength and appeal of its idea, and it feels no compulsion sooner or later to bring all societies into conformity with it . . .

B. OBJECTIVES

The objectives of a free society are determined by its fundamental values and by the necessity for maintaining the material environment in which they flourish. Logically and in fact, therefore, the Kremlin's challenge to the United States is directed not only to our values but to our physical capacity to protect their environment. It is a challenge which encompasses both peace and war and our objectives in peace and war must take account of it.

1. Thus we must make ourselves strong, both in the way in which we affirm our values in the conduct of our national life, and in the development of our military and economic strength.

2. We must lead in building a successfully functioning political and economic system in the free world. It is only by practical affirmation, abroad as well as at home, of our essential values, that we can preserve our own integrity, in which lies the real frustration of the Kremlin design.

3. But beyond thus affirming our values our policy and actions must be such as to foster a fundamental change in the nature of the Soviet system, a change toward which the frustration of the design is the first and perhaps the most important step. Clearly it will not only be less costly but more effective if this change occurs to a maximum extent as a result of internal forces in Soviet society . . .

There is no reason, in the event of war, for us to alter our overall objectives. They do not include unconditional surrender, the subjugation of the Russian peoples or a Russia shorn of its economic potential. Such a course would irrevocably unite the Russian people behind the regime which enslaves them. Rather these objectives contemplate Soviet acceptance of the specific and limited conditions requisite to an international environment in which free institutions can flourish, and in which the Russian peoples will have a new chance to work out their own destiny. If we can make the Russian people our allies in the enterprise we will obviously have made our task easier and victory more certain.

C. MEANS

The free society is limited in its choice of means to achieve its ends. Compulsion is the negation of freedom, except when it is used to enforce the rights common to all. The resort to force, internally or externally, is therefore a last resort for a free society. The act is permissible only when one individual or groups of individuals within it threaten the basic rights of other individuals or when another society seeks to impose its will upon it . . .

The Kremlin is able to select whatever means are expedient in seeking to carry out its fundamental design . . . We have no such freedom of choice, and least of all in the use of force . . . The idea of slavery can only be overcome by the timely and persistent demonstration of the superiority of the idea of freedom. . . .

Practical and ideological considerations therefore both impel us to the conclusion that we have no choice but to demonstrate the superiority of the idea of freedom by its constructive application, and to attempt to change the world situation by means short of war in such a way as to frustrate the Kremlin design and hasten the decay of the Soviet system.

For us the role of military power is to serve the national purpose by deterring an attack upon us while we seek by other means to create an environment in which our free society can flourish, and by fighting, if necessary, to defend the integrity and vitality of our free society and to defeat any aggressor . . .

But if war comes, what is the role of force? Unless we so use it that the Russian people can perceive that our effort is directed against the regime and its power for aggression, and not against their own interests, we will unite the regime and the people in the kind of last ditch fight in which no underlying problems are solved, new ones are created, and where our basic principles are obscured and compromised. If we do not in the application of force demonstrate the nature of our objectives we will, in fact, have compromised from the outset our fundamental purpose. In the words of the *Federalist* (No. 28) "The means to be employed must be proportioned to the extent of the mischief." The mischief may be a global war or it may be a Soviet campaign for limited objectives. In either case we should take no avoidable initiative which would cause it to become a war of annihilation, and if we have the forces to defeat a Soviet drive for limited objectives it may well be to our interest not to let it become a global war. Our aim in applying force must be to compel the acceptance of terms consistent with our objectives, and our capabilities for the application of force should, therefore, within the limits of what we can sustain over the long pull, be congruent to the range of tasks which we may encounter. . . .

Conclusions

The foregoing analysis indicates that the probable fission bomb capability and possible thermonuclear bomb capability of the Soviet Union have greatly intensified the Soviet threat to the security of the United States. This threat is . . . more immediate than had previously been estimated. In particular, the United States now faces the contingency that within the next four or five years the Soviet Union will possess the military capability of delivering a surprise atomic attack of such weight that the United States must have substantially increased general air, ground, and sea strength, atomic capabilities, and air and civilian defenses to deter war and to provide reasonable assurance, in the event of war, that it could survive the initial blow and go on to the eventual attainment of its objectives. In return, this contingency requires the intensification of our efforts in the fields of intelligence and research and development.

Allowing for the immediacy of the danger, the following statement of Soviet threats, contained in NSC 20/4, remains valid:

14. The gravest threat to the security of the United States within the foreseeable future stems from the hostile designs and formidable power of the USSR, and from the nature of the Soviet system.

15. The political, economic, and psychological warfare which the USSR is now waging has dangerous potentialities for weakening the relative world position of the United States and disrupting its traditional institutions by means short of war, unless sufficient resistance is encountered in the policies of this and other non-communist countries.

16. The risk of war with the USSR is sufficient to warrant, in common prudence, timely and adequate preparation by the United States.

a. Even though present estimates indicate that the Soviet leaders probably do not intend deliberate armed action involving the United States at this time, the possibility of such deliberate resort to war cannot be ruled out.

b. Now and for the foreseeable future there is a continuing danger that war will arise either through Soviet miscalculation of the determination of the United States to use all the means at its command to safeguard its security, through Soviet misinterpretation of our intentions, or through U.S. miscalculation of Soviet reactions to measures which we might take.

17. Soviet domination of the potential power of Eurasia, whether achieved by armed aggression or by political and subversive means, would be strategically and politically unacceptable to the United States.

18. The capability of the United States either in peace or in the event of war to cope with threats to its security or to gain its objectives would be severely weakened by internal development, important among which are:

a. Serious espionage, subversion and sabotage, particularly by concerted and well-directed communist activity.

b. Prolonged or exaggerated economic instability.

c. Internal political and social disunity.

d. Inadequate or excessive armament or foreign aid expenditures.

e. An excessive or wasteful usage of our resources in time of peace.

f. Lessening of U.S. prestige and influence through vacillation of appeasement or lack of skill and imagination in the conduct of its foreign policy or by shirking world responsibilities.

g. Development of a false sense of security through a deceptive change in Soviet tactics . . .

The analysis also confirms that our objectives with respect to the Soviet Union, in time of peace as well as in time of war, as stated in NSC 20/4 (para. 19), are still valid, as are the aims and measures stated therein (paras. 20 and 21). Our current security programs and strategic plans are based upon these objectives, aims, and measures:

a. To reduce the power and influence of the USSR to limits which no longer constitute a threat to the peace, national independence, and stability of the world family of nations.

b. To bring about a basic change in the conduct of international relations by the government in power in Russia, to conform with the purposes and principles set forth in the UN Charter.

In pursuing these objectives, due care must be taken to avoid permanently impairing our economy and the fundamental values and institutions inherent in our way of life.

We should endeavor to achieve our general objectives by methods short of war through the pursuit of the following aims:

a. To encourage and promote the gradual retraction of undue Russian power and influence from the present perimeter areas around traditional Russian boundaries and the emergence of the satellite countries as entities independent of the USSR.

b. To encourage the development among the Russian peoples of attitudes which may help to modify current Soviet behavior and permit a revival of the national life of groups evidencing the ability and determination to achieve and maintain national independence.

c. To eradicate the myth by which people remote from Soviet military influence are held in a position of subservience to Moscow and to cause the world at large to see and understand the true nature of the USSR and the Soviet-directed world communist party, and to adopt a logical and realistic attitude toward them.

d. To create situations which will compel the Soviet Government to recognize the practical undesirability of acting on the basis of its present concepts and the necessity of behaving in accordance with precepts of international conduct, as set forth in the purposes and principles of the UN Charter.

Attainment of these aims requires that the United States:

a. Develop a level of military readiness which can be maintained as long as necessary as a deterrent to Soviet aggression, as indispensable support to our political attitude toward the USSR, as a source of encouragement to nations resisting Soviet political aggression, and as an adequate basis for immediate military commitments and for rapid mobilization should war prove unavoidable.

b. Assure the internal security of the United States against dangers of sabotage, subversion, and espionage.

c. Maximize our economic potential, including the strengthening of our peacetime economy and the establishment of essential reserves readily available in the event of war.

d. Strengthen the orientation toward the United States of the non-Soviet nations; and help such of those nations as are able and willing to make an important contribution to U.S. security, to increase their economic and political stability and their military capability.

e. Place the maximum strain on the Soviet structure of power and particularly on the relationships between Moscow and the satellite countries.

f. Keep the U.S. public fully informed and cognizant of the threats to our national security so that it will be prepared to support the measures which we must accordingly adopt . . .

Our position as the center of power in the free world places a heavy responsibility upon the United States for leadership. We must organize and enlist the energies and resources of the free world in a positive program for peace which will frustrate the Kremlin design for world domination by creating a situation in the free world to which the Kremlin will be compelled to adjust . . .

In summary, we must, by means of a rapid and sustained build-up of the political, economic, and military strength of the free world, and by means of an affirmative program intended to wrest the initiative from the Soviet Union, confront it with convincing evidence of the determination and ability of the free world to frustrate the Kremlin design of a world dominated by its will . . .

The whole success of the proposed program hangs ultimately on recognition by this Government, the American people, and all free peoples, that the cold war is in fact a real war in which the survival of the free world is at stake . . .

Recommendations

That the President:

a. Approve the foregoing Conclusions.

b. Direct the National Security Council, under the continuing direction of the President, and with the participation of other Departments and Agencies as appropriate, to coordinate and insure the implementation of the Conclusions herein on an urgent and continuing basis for as long as necessary to achieve our objectives . . .

Source: U.S. Department of State, "NSC 68: United States Objectives and Programs for National Security," in *Foreign Relations of the United States, 1950: National Security Affairs; Foreign Economic Policy,* edited by S. Everett Gleason, Fredrick Aandahl, and William Slany. Vol. 1. Washington, DC: U.S. Government Printing Office, 1976, 234–92.

DOCUMENT 8
"Declaration of Conscience"
Senator Margaret Chase Smith, June 1, 1950

Alarmed by the persistence of and mounting support for Senator Joseph McCarthy's unsubstantiated attacks on the State Department and the accompanying intolerance and anti-intellectualism in American politics, Senator Margaret Chase Smith (R-ME), with the support of other Republican Senators, advanced a "Declaration of Conscience" that was as an assault on McCarthy

*and his sensational and dangerous methods. Chase's rebuke of McCarthyism was
a serious challenge from a member of McCarthy's own party. It had limited immediate impact and did not deter McCarthy from his reckless behavior, but it did signal a break from a silence of complicity that allowed McCarthy and his supporters
to go unchallenged in the public square.*

Mr. President, I would like to speak briefly and simply about a serious
national condition. It is a national feeling of fear and frustration that could
result in national suicide and the end of everything that we Americans hold
dear. It is a condition that comes from the lack of effective leadership in
either the legislative branch or the executive branch of our Government.

That leadership is so lacking that serious and responsible proposals are
being made that national advisory commissions be appointed to provide
such critically needed leadership. . . .

The United States Senate has long enjoyed worldwide respect as the
greatest deliberative body in the world. But recently that deliberative character has too often been debased to the level of a forum of hate and character assassination sheltered by the shield of congressional immunity.

It is ironical that we Senators can debate in the Senate directly or indi-
rectly, by any form of words impute to any American, who is not a Senator,
any conduct or motive unworthy or unbecoming an American—and without that non-Senator American having any legal redress against it—yet if
we say the same thing in the Senate about our colleagues we can be
stopped on the grounds of being out of order.

It is strange that we can verbally attack anyone else without restraint
and with full protection and yet we hold ourselves above the same type
of criticism here on the Senate floor. Surely the United States Senate is
big enough to take self-criticism and self-appraisal. Surely we should
be able to take the same kind of character attacks that we "dish out" to
outsiders. . . .

I think that it is high time that we remembered that we have sworn to
uphold and defend the Constitution. I think that it is high time that we
remembered that the Constitution, as amended, speaks not only of the
freedom of speech, but also of trial by jury instead of trial by accusation.

Whether it be a criminal prosecution in court or a character prosecution
in the Senate, there is little practical distinction when the life of a person
has been ruined.

Those of us who shout the loudest about Americanism in making character assassinations are all too frequently those who, by our own words and acts, ignore some of the basic principles of Americanism—the right to criticize; the right to hold unpopular beliefs; the right to protest; [and] the right of independent thought.

The exercise of these rights should not cost one single American citizen his reputation or his right to a livelihood nor should he be in danger of losing his reputation or livelihood merely because he happens to know someone who holds unpopular beliefs. Who of us doesn't? Otherwise none of us could call our souls our own. Otherwise thought control would have set in.

The American people are sick and tired of being afraid to speak their minds lest they be politically smeared as "Communists" or "Fascists" by their opponents. Freedom of speech is not what it used to be in America. It has been so abused by some that it is not exercised by others . . .

Today our country is being psychologically divided by the confusion and the suspicions that are bred in the United States Senate to spread like cancerous tentacles of "know nothing, suspect everything" attitudes . . .

The Democratic administration has greatly lost the confidence of the American people by its complacency to the threat of communism here at home and the leak of vital secrets to Russia through key officials of the Democratic administration. There are enough proved cases to make this point without diluting our criticism with unproved charges . . .

Yet to displace it with a Republican regime embracing a philosophy that lacks political integrity or intellectual honesty would prove equally disastrous to this Nation. The Nation sorely needs a Republican victory. But I don't want to see the Republican Party ride to political victory on the four horsemen of calumny—fear, ignorance, bigotry and smear . . .

As a United States Senator, I am not proud of the way in which the Senate has been made a publicity platform for irresponsible sensationalism. I am not proud of the reckless abandon in which unproved charges have been hurled from this side of the aisle. I am not proud of the obviously staged, undignified countercharges that have been attempted in retaliation from the other side of the aisle.

I don't like the way the Senate has been made a rendezvous for vilification, for selfish political gain at the sacrifice of individual reputations and national unity. I am not proud of the way we smear outsiders from the floor of the Senate and hide behind the cloak of congressional immunity and still place ourselves beyond criticism on the floor of the Senate.

As an American, I am shocked at the way Republicans and Democrats alike are playing directly into the Communist design of "confuse, divide and conquer." As an American, I don't want a Democratic administration "whitewash" or "cover-up" any more than I want a Republican smear or witch-hunt.

As an American, I condemn a Republican "Fascist" just as much as I condemn a Democrat "Communist." I condemn a Democrat "Fascist" just as much as I condemn a Republican "Communist." They are equally dangerous to you and me and to our country. As an American, I want to see our Nation recapture the strength and unity it once had when we fought the enemy instead of ourselves.

It is with these thoughts I have drafted what I call a Declaration of Conscience . . .

1. We are Republicans. But we are Americans first. It is as Americans that we express our concern with the growing confusion that threatens the security and stability of our country. Democrats and Republicans alike have contributed to that confusion.

2. The Democratic administration has initially created the confusion by its lack of effective leadership, by its contradictory grave warnings and optimistic assurances, by its complacency to the threat of communism here at home, by its over sensitiveness to rightful criticism, by its petty bitterness against its critics.

3. Certain elements of the Republican Party have materially added to this confusion in the hopes of riding the Republican party to victory through the selfish political exploitation of fear, bigotry, ignorance, and intolerance. There are enough mistakes of the Democrats for Republicans to criticize constructively without resorting to political smears.

4. To this extent, Democrats and Republicans alike have unwittingly, but undeniably, played directly into the Communist design of "confuse, divide and conquer."

5. It is high time that we stopped thinking politically as Republicans and Democrats about elections and started thinking patriotically as Americans about national security based on individual freedom. It is high time that we all stopped being tools and victims of totalitarian techniques—techniques

that, if continued here unchecked, will surely end what we have come to cherish as the American way of life.

Source: Congressional Record, Senate, 81st Congress, 2nd Session, 7894–95.

DOCUMENT 9
Speech on Massive Retaliation
Secretary of State John Foster Dulles, January 12, 1954

Within a few months after an armistice concluded the combat in the Korean War, Secretary of State John Foster Dulles, in an address to the Council on Foreign Relations in New York, announced that the United States would avoid regional conflicts in its struggle with communism. He stated that the United States would respond with massive (nuclear) retaliation against its enemies (the Soviet Union and China) if necessary. This threat continued through the end of the Eisenhower presidency in January 1961, though in practice the government continued to use covert operations and conventional military means to "contain communism." Eisenhower and Dulles were concerned with the mounting costs of maintaining and deploying extensive conventional forces throughout the world and the impact of those costs on the American economy.

. . . First of all, let us recognize that many of the preceding foreign policies were good. Aid to Greece and Turkey had checked the Communist drive to the Mediterranean. The European Recovery Program [Marshall Plan] had helped the peoples of Western Europe to pull out of the postwar morass. The Western powers were steadfast in Berlin and overcame the blockade with their airlift. As a loyal member of the United Nations, we had reacted with force to repel the Communist attack in Korea. When that effort exposed our military weakness, we rebuilt rapidly our military establishment. We also sought a quick build up of armed strength in Western Europe.

These were the acts of a nation which saw the danger of Soviet communism; which realized that its own safety was tied up with that of others; which was capable of responding boldly and promptly to emergencies. These are precious values to be acclaimed . . .

But we need to recall that what we did was in the main emergency action, imposed on us by our enemies. . . . We live in a world where emergencies are always possible, and our survival may depend upon our capacity to meet emergencies. Let us pray that we shall always have that capacity. But, having said that, it is necessary also to say that emergency measures—however good for the emergency—do not necessarily make good permanent policies. Emergency measures are costly; they are superficial; and they imply that the enemy has the initiative. They cannot be depended on to serve our long-time interests. . . .

It is not sound military strategy permanently to commit U.S. land forces to Asia to a degree that leaves us no strategic reserves. It is not sound economics, or good foreign policy to support permanently other countries, for in the long run, that creates as much ill will as good will. Also, it is not sound to become permanently committed to military expenditures so vast that they lead to "practical bankruptcy."

Change was imperative to assure the stamina needed for permanent security. But it was equally imperative that change should be accompanied by understanding of our true purposes. Sudden and spectacular change had to be avoided. Otherwise, there might have been a panic among our friends and miscalculated aggression by our enemies. We can, I believe, make a good report in these respects. We need allies and collective security. Our purpose is to make these relations more effective, less costly. This can be done by placing more reliance on deterrent power and less dependence on local defensive power. . . . We want, for ourselves and the other free nations, a maximum deterrent at a bearable cost.

Local defense will always be important. But there is no local defense which alone will contain the mighty land power of the Communist world. Local defenses must be reinforced by the further deterrent of massive retaliatory power. A potential aggressor must know that he cannot always prescribe battle conditions that suit him. Otherwise, for example, a potential aggressor, who is glutted with manpower, might be tempted to attack in confidence that resistance would be confined to manpower. He might be tempted to attack in places where his superiority was decisive.

The way to deter aggression is for the free community to be willing and able to respond vigorously at places and with means of its own choosing. So long as our basic policy concepts were unclear, our military leaders could not be selective in building our military power. If an enemy could pick his time and place and method of warfare—and if our policy was to remain the traditional one of meeting aggression by direct and local opposition—then we needed to be ready to fight in the Arctic and in the Tropics; in Asia, the Near East, and in Europe; by sea, by land, and by air; with old weapons and with new weapons ...

But before military planning could be changed, the President and his advisers, as represented by the National Security Council, had to take some basic policy decisions. This has been done. The basic decision was to depend primarily upon a great capacity to retaliate, instantly, by means and at places of our choosing ... As a result, it is now possible to get, and share, more basic security at less cost ...

Source: John Foster Dulles, "The Evolution of Foreign Policy," *Department of State Bulletin* 30, no. 761 (1954): 107–10.

DOCUMENT 10
President Dwight D. Eisenhower's Farewell Address
January 17, 1961

Three days before the transfer of presidential power to John F. Kennedy, President Dwight D. Eisenhower made a farewell address on television and radio. In this speech he referred to the Cold War and warned that American culture and values could be adversely affected by the new military-industrial complex that had become a permanent element in American society with the advent of the Cold War. Eisenhower's insights on this issue have continued to attract the interest and the praise of many Cold War scholars, though in practice the military-industrial complex continued to grow during and because of the Cold War.

... This evening I come to you with a message of leave-taking and farewell, and to share a few final thoughts with you, my countrymen.

Like every other citizen, I wish the new President, and all who will labor with him, Godspeed. I pray that the coming years will be blessed with peace and prosperity for all.

Our people expect their President and the Congress to find essential agreement on issues of great moment, the wise resolution of which will better shape the future of the Nation.

My own relations with the Congress, which began on a remote and tenuous basis when, long ago, a member of the Senate appointed me to West Point, have since ranged to the intimate during the war and immediate post-war period, and, finally, to the mutually interdependent during these past eight years.

In this final relationship, the Congress and the Administration have, on most vital issues, cooperated well, to serve the national good rather than mere partisanship, and so have assured that the business of the Nation should go forward. . . .

Throughout America's adventure in free government, our basic purposes have been to keep the peace; to foster progress in human achievement, and to enhance liberty, dignity and integrity among people and among nations. To strive for less would be unworthy of a free and religious people. Any failure traceable to arrogance, or our lack of comprehension or readiness to sacrifice would inflict upon us grievous hurt both at home and abroad.

Progress toward these noble goals is persistently threatened by the conflict now engulfing the world. It commands our whole attention, absorbs our very beings. We face a hostile ideology—global in scope, atheistic in character, ruthless in purpose, and insidious in method. Unhappily the danger it poses promises to be of indefinite duration. To meet it successfully, there is called for, not so much the emotional and transitory sacrifices of crisis, but rather those which enable us to carry forward steadily, surely, and without complaint, the burdens of a prolonged and complex struggle—with liberty at stake. Only thus shall we remain, despite every provocation, on our charted course toward permanent peace and human betterment.

Crises there will continue to be. In meeting them, whether foreign or domestic, great or small, there is a recurring temptation to feel that some spectacular and costly action could become the miraculous solution to all current difficulties. A huge increase in newer elements of our defense; development of unrealistic programs to cure every ill in agriculture; a dramatic expansion in basic and applied research—these and many other possibilities, each possibly promising in itself, may be suggested as the only way to the road we which to travel.

But each proposal must be weighed in the light of a broader consideration: the need to maintain balance in and among national programs—balance between the private and the public economy, balance between cost and hoped for advantage—balance between the clearly necessary and the comfortably desirable; balance between our essential requirements as a nation and the duties imposed by the nation upon the individual; balance between action of the moment and the national welfare of the future.

Good judgment seeks balance and progress; lack of it eventually finds imbalance and frustration. . . .

A vital element in keeping the peace is our military establishment. Our arms must be mighty, ready for instant action, so that no potential aggressor may be tempted to risk his own destruction.

Our military organization today bears little relation to that known by any of my predecessors in peace time, or indeed by the fighting men of World War II or Korea.

Until the latest of our world conflicts, the United States had no armaments industry. American makers of plowshares could, with time and as required, make swords as well. But now we can no longer risk emergency improvisation of national defense; we have been compelled to create a permanent armaments industry of vast proportions. Added to this, three and a half million men and women are directly engaged in the defense establishment. We annually spend on military security more than the net income of all United State corporations.

This conjunction of an immense military establishment and a large arms industry is new in the American experience. The total influence—economic, political, even spiritual—is felt in every city, every state house, every office of the Federal government. We recognize the imperative need for this development. Yet we must not fail to comprehend its grave implications. Our toil, resources and livelihood are all involved; so is the very structure of our society.

In the councils of government, we must guard against the acquisition of unwarranted influence, whether sought or unsought, by the military-industrial complex. The potential for the disastrous rise of misplaced power exists and will persist.

We must never let the weight of this combination endanger our liberties or democratic processes. We should take nothing for granted, only an alert and knowledgeable citizenry can compel the proper meshing of huge industrial and military machinery of defense with our peaceful methods and goals, so that security and liberty may prosper together.

Akin to, and largely responsible for the sweeping changes in our industrial-military posture, has been the technological revolution during recent decades.

In this revolution, research has become central; it also becomes more formalized, complex, and costly. A steadily increasing share is conducted for, by, or at the direction of, the Federal government.

Today, the solitary inventor, tinkering in his shop, has been over shadowed by task forces of scientists in laboratories and testing fields. In the same fashion, the free university, historically the fountainhead of free ideas and scientific discovery, has experienced a revolution in the conduct of research. Partly because of the huge costs involved, a government contract becomes virtually a substitute for intellectual curiosity. For every old blackboard there are now hundreds of new electronic computers.

The prospect of domination of the nation's scholars by Federal employment, project allocations, and the power of money is ever present and is gravely to be regarded.

Yet, in holding scientific research and discovery in respect, as we should, we must also be alert to the equal and opposite danger that public policy could itself become the captive of a scientific-technological elite ... Disarmament, with mutual honor and confidence, is a continuing imperative. Together we must learn how to compose [sic] difference, not with arms, but with intellect and decent purpose. Because this need is so sharp and apparent I confess that I lay down my official responsibilities in this field with a definite sense of disappointment. As one who has witnessed the horror and the lingering sadness of war—as one who knows that another war could utterly destroy this civilization which has been so slowly and painfully built over thousands of years—I wish I could say tonight that a lasting peace is in sight.

Happily, I can say that war has been avoided. Steady progress toward our ultimate goal has been made. But, so much remains to be done. As a private citizen, I shall never cease to do what little I can to help the world advance along that road. ...

Source: Dwight D. Eisenhower, *Public Papers of the Presidents of the United States: Dwight D. Eisenhower, 1960–1961.* Washington, DC: U.S. Government Printing Office, 1961, 1035–40.

DOCUMENT 11
Address to the Nation by President John F. Kennedy on the Cuban Missile Crisis
October 22, 1962

Perhaps the most dangerous crisis of the Cold War between the United States and the Soviet Union was the Cuban missile crisis of October 1962. Americans discovered that the Soviet Union was in the process of deploying intermediate-range ballistic missiles with nuclear capability in Cuba. If installed and made operational, the missiles could reach targets in the United States, and the mere presence of such a threat so close to American shores could impact the balance of power. On October 22, 1962, President John F. Kennedy addressed the American people and advised them of the precarious situation and the government's reaction to this threat. Tensions ran high, and many expected a nuclear war. But such a war was avoided through diligent and quiet negotiations with the Soviet Union.

Good Evening, My Fellow Citizens:

This government, as promised, has maintained the closest surveillance of the Soviet military buildup on the island of Cuba. Within the past week, unmistakable evidence has established the fact that a series of offensive missile sites is now in preparation on that imprisoned island. The purpose of these bases can be none other than to provide a nuclear strike capability against the Western Hemisphere.

Upon receiving the first preliminary hard information of this nature last Tuesday morning at 9 a.m., I directed that our surveillance be stepped up. And having now confirmed and completed our evaluation of the evidence and our decision on a course of action, this government feels obliged to report this new crisis to you in fullest detail.

The characteristics of these new missile sites indicate two distinct types of installations. Several of them include medium range ballistic missiles, capable of carrying a nuclear warhead for a distance of more than 1,000 nautical miles. Each of these missiles, in short, is capable of striking Washington, D.C., the Panama Canal, Cape Canaveral, Mexico City, or any other city in the southeastern part of the United States, in Central America or in the Caribbean area.

Additional sites not yet completed appear to be designed for intermediate range ballistic missiles—capable of traveling more than twice as far—and thus capable of striking most of the major cities in the Western Hemisphere, ranging as far north as Hudson Bay, Canada, and as far south as Lima, Peru. In addition, jet bombers capable of carrying nuclear weapons are now being uncrated and assembled in Cuba while the necessary air bases are being prepared.

This urgent transformation of Cuba into an important strategic base— by the presence of these large, long-range, and clearly offensive weapons of sudden mass destruction—constitutes an explicit threat to the peace and security of all Americas, in flagrant and deliberate defiance of the Rio Pact of 1947, the traditions of this nation and hemisphere, the joint resolution of the 87th Congress, the Charter of the United Nations, and my own public warnings to the Soviets on September 4 and 13. This action also contradicts the repeated assurances of Soviet spokesmen, both publicly and privately delivered, that the arms buildup in Cuba would retain its original defensive character, and that the Soviet Union had no need or desire to station strategic missiles on the territory of any other nation . . .

But this secret, swift and extraordinary buildup of communist missiles . . . is a deliberately provocative and unjustified change in the status quo which cannot be accepted by this country, if our courage and our commitments are ever to be trusted again by either friend or foe . . .

Acting, therefore, in the defense of our own security and of the entire Western Hemisphere, and under the authority entrusted to me by the Constitution as endorsed by the resolution of the Congress, I have directed that the following initial steps be taken immediately:

First: To halt this offensive buildup, a strict quarantine on all offensive military equipment under shipment to Cuba is being initiated. All ships of any kind bound for Cuba from whatever nation and port will, if found to contain cargoes of offensive weapons, be turned back. This quarantine will be extended, if needed, to other types of cargo and carriers. We are not at this time, however, denying the necessities of life as the Soviets attempted to do in their Berlin blockade of 1948.

Second: I have directed the continued and increased close surveillance of Cuba and its military buildup. The foreign ministers of the OAS [Organization of American States], in their communiqué of October 6, rejected secrecy on such matters in this hemisphere. Should these offensive military preparations continue, thus increasing the threat to the hemisphere, further action will be justified. I have directed the Armed Forces to prepare for any eventualities; and I trust that in the interest of both the Cuban people and the Soviet technicians at the sites, the hazards to all concerned of continuing the threat will be recognized.

Third: It shall be the policy of this nation to regard any nuclear missile launched from Cuba against any nation in the Western Hemisphere as an attack on the United States, requiring a full retaliatory response upon the Soviet Union.

Fourth: As a necessary military precaution, I have reinforced our base at Guantanamo, evacuated today the dependents of our personnel there, and ordered additional military units to be on a standby alert status.

Fifth: We are calling tonight for an immediate meeting of the Organization of American States, to consider this threat to hemispheric security and to invoke articles 6 and 8 of the Rio Treaty in support of all necessary action. The United Nations Charter allows for regional security arrangements—and the nations of this hemisphere decided long ago against the military presence of outside powers. Our other allies around the world have also been alerted.

Sixth: Under the Charter of the United Nations, we are asking tonight that an emergency meeting of the Security Council be convoked without delay to take action against this latest Soviet threat to world peace. Our resolution will call for the prompt dismantling and withdrawal of all offensive weapons in Cuba, under the supervision of U.N. observers, before the quarantine can be lifted.

Seventh and finally: I call upon Chairman Khrushchev to halt and eliminate this clandestine, reckless, and provocative threat to world peace and to stable relations between our two nations. I call upon him further to abandon this course of world domination, and to join in an historic effort to end the perilous arms race and to transform the history of man. He has an opportunity now to move the world back from the abyss of destruction—by returning to his government's own words that it had no need to station missiles outside its own territory, and withdrawing these weapons from Cuba—by refraining from any action which will widen or deepen the present crisis—and then by participating in a search for peaceful and permanent solutions . . .

My fellow citizens: let no one doubt that this is a difficult and dangerous effort on which we have set out. No one can foresee precisely what course it will take or what costs or casualties will be incurred. Many months in which both our patience and our will will be tested—months in which many threats and denunciations will keep us aware of our dangers. But the greatest danger of all would be to do nothing . . .

Our goal is not the victory of might, but the vindication of right—not peace at the expense of freedom, but both peace and freedom, here in this hemisphere, and we hope, around the world. God willing, that goal will be achieved . . .

Source: John F. Kennedy, *Public Papers of the Presidents of the United States: John F. Kennedy, 1962.* Washington, DC: U.S. Government Printing Office, 1963, 806–9.

DOCUMENT 12
President John F. Kennedy's *"Ich bin ein Berliner"* Speech
June 26, 1963

While on a trip to West Germany, President John F. Kennedy visited West Berlin on June 26, 1963, to demonstrate continuing American support for the city and its inhabitants, which was a flashpoint of East-West tensions. While the speech received an enthusiastic reception from Berliners and Americans alike, it confused the Soviets, who had thought that the United States was moving toward a more conciliatory position during the months prior to the speech. Later on the same day Kennedy adopted a much less harsh tone in a speech at the Free University of Berlin, which created further confusion among the Soviets.

I am proud to come to this city as the guest of your distinguished Mayor, who has symbolized throughout the world the fighting spirit of West Berlin. And I am proud to visit the Federal Republic with your distinguished Chancellor who for so many years has committed Germany to democracy and freedom and progress, and to come here in the company of my fellow American, General Clay, who has been in this city during its great moments of crisis and will come again if ever needed

Two thousand years ago the proudest boast was *"civis Romanus sum."* Today, in the world of freedom, the proudest boast is *"Ich bin ein Berliner."* . . .

There are many people in the world who really don't understand, or say they don't, what is the great issue between the free world and the Communist world. Let them come to Berlin. There are some who say that communism is the wave of the future. Let them come to Berlin. And there are some who say in Europe and elsewhere we can work with the Communists. Let them come to Berlin. And there are even a few who say that it is true that communism is an evil system, but it permits us to make economic progress. *Lass' sie nach Berlin kommen.* Let them come to Berlin.

Freedom has many difficulties and democracy is not perfect, but we have never had to put a wall up to keep our people in, to prevent them from leaving us. I want to say, on behalf of my countrymen, who live many miles away on the other side of the Atlantic, who are far distant from you, that they take the greatest pride that they have been able to share with you, even from a distance, the story of the last 18 years . . . While the wall is the most obvious and vivid demonstration of the failures of the Communist system, for all the world to see, we take no satisfaction in it, for it is, as your Mayor has said, an offense not only against history but an offense against humanity, separating families, dividing husbands and wives and brothers and sisters, and dividing a people who wish to be joined together.

What is true of this city is true of Germany—real, lasting peace in Europe can never be assured as long as one German out of four is denied the elementary right of free men, and that is to make a free choice. . . .

Freedom is indivisible, and when one man is enslaved, all are not free. When all are free, then we can look forward to that day when this city will be joined as one and this country and this great Continent of Europe in a peaceful and hopeful globe. When that day finally comes, as it will, the people of West Berlin can take sober satisfaction in the fact that they were in the front lines for almost two decades.

All free men, wherever they may live, are citizens of Berlin, and, therefore, as a free man, I take pride in the words "*Ich bin ein Berliner.*"

Source: John F. Kennedy, *Public Papers of the Presidents of the United States: John F. Kennedy, Containing the Public Messages, Speeches, and Statements of the President, January 1 to November 22, 1963.* Washington, DC: U.S. Government Printing Office, 1964, 524–25.

DOCUMENT 13
President Lyndon B. Johnson's Address at The Johns Hopkins University, "Peace without Conquest"
April 7, 1965

During 1964 the United States expanded its presence in South Vietnam. President Lyndon B. Johnson used the Gulf of Tonkin incident to justify an increase in troop and equipment levels in South Vietnam. At The Johns Hopkins University in Baltimore, Maryland, Johnson articulated his foreign policy in

Southeast Asia, specifically the crisis in South Vietnam. These remarks were a
prelude to a massive American military build-up in South Vietnam and an aban-
donment of the Eisenhower's administration policy of avoiding regional conflicts.
Johnson argued that American action in South Vietnam was not based on con-
quest but rather was warranted because the United States was defending basic
human freedoms. He also suggested that if the United States did not assist South
Vietnam, the rest of Southeast Asia would fall to the communists—the domino
theory. This shift in policy proved to be a defining moment in Johnson's
presidency.

. . . Tonight Americans and Asians are dying for a world where each people may choose its own path to change.

This is the principle for which our ancestors fought in the valleys of
Pennsylvania. It is the principle for which our sons fight tonight in the
jungles of Viet-Nam. Viet-Nam is far away from this quiet campus. We
have no territory there, nor do we seek any. The war is dirty and brutal
and difficult. And some 400 young men, born into an America that is
bursting with opportunity and promise, have ended their lives on Viet-
Nam's steaming soil. . . .

We fight because we must fight if we are to live in a world where every
country can shape its own destiny. And only in such a world will our own
freedom be finally secure . . .

The world as it is in Asia is not a serene or peaceful place. The first reality is that North Viet-Nam has attacked the independent nation of South
Viet-Nam. Its object is total conquest.

Of course, some of the people of South Viet-Nam are participating in
attack on their own government. But trained men and supplies, orders
and arms, flow in a constant stream from north to south. . . .

The confused nature of this conflict cannot mask the fact that it is the
new face of an old enemy.

Over this war—and all Asia—is another reality: the deepening shadow
of Communist China. The rulers in Hanoi are urged on by Peking . . . The
contest in Viet-Nam is part of a wider pattern of aggressive purposes . . .

We are there because we have a promise to keep. Since 1954 every
American President has offered support to the people of South Viet-
Nam. We have helped to build, and we have helped to defend. Thus, over

many years, we have made a national pledge to help South Viet-Nam defend its independence.

And I intend to keep that promise.

To dishonor that pledge, to abandon this small and brave nation to its enemies, and to the terror that must follow, would be an unforgivable wrong.

We are also there to strengthen world order. Around the globe, from Berlin to Thailand, are people whose well being rests, in part, on the belief that they can count on us if they are attacked. To leave Viet-Nam to its fate would shake the confidence of all these people in the value of an American commitment and in the value of America's word. The result would be increased unrest and instability, and even wider war. . . .

There are those who wonder why we have a responsibility there. Well, we have it there for the same reason that we have a responsibility for the defense of Europe. World War II was fought in both Europe and Asia, and when it ended we found ourselves with continued responsibility for the defense of freedom.

Our objective is the independence of South Viet-Nam, and its freedom from attack. We want nothing for ourselves—only that the people of South Viet-Nam be allowed to guide their own country in their own way.

We will do everything necessary to reach that objective . . .

We hope that peace will come swiftly. But that is in the hands of others besides ourselves. And we must be prepared for a long continued conflict. It will require patience as well as bravery, the will to endure as well as the will to resist. ; . . .

Stability and peace do not come easily in such a land. Neither independence nor human dignity will ever be won, though, by arms alone. It also requires the work of peace . . .

The first step is for the countries of southeast Asia to associate themselves in a greatly expanded cooperative effort for development. We would hope that North Viet-Nam would take its place in the common effort just as soon as peaceful cooperation is possible . . .

For our part I will ask the Congress to join in a billion dollar American investment in this effort as soon as it is underway.

And I would hope that all other industrialized countries, including the Soviet Union, will join in this effort to replace despair with hope, and terror with progress.

The task is nothing less than to enrich the hopes and the existence of more than a hundred million people. And there is much to be done. . . .

[W]e will always oppose the effort of one nation to conquer another nation.

We will do this because our own security is at stake.

But there is more to it than that. For our generation has a dream. It is a very old dream. But we have the power and now we have the opportunity to make that dream come true.

For centuries nations have struggled among each other. But we dream of a world where disputes are settled by law and reason. And we will try to make it so. . . .

Source: Lyndon Baines Johnson, *Public Papers of the Presidents of the United States: Lyndon B. Johnson, 1965.* Vol. I. Washington, DC: U.S. Government Printing Office, 1966, 394–99.

DOCUMENT 14
Détente with the Soviet Union
June 28, 1968

Prior to the election of President Richard M. Nixon in November 1968, the United States initiated a policy to ease tensions with the Soviet Union. Labeled "détente" by the Nixon administration, it dominated U.S.-Soviet relations during the late 1960s and into the 1970s. It was characterized by treaties to reduce nuclear armaments, but it did not normalize relations between the powers, as was evident in the crisis associated with the Yom Kippur War in October 1973. The document provided here outlines NATO's anticipated outcome for a détente initiative.

The NATO foreign ministers, at the spring ministerial session of the North Atlantic Council, convened for the first time in Iceland, issued a "signal" to the USSR to encourage it to prepare for future discussions on the possibility of mutual force reductions in Europe, evidenced concern over increased Soviet activities in the Mediterranean, and declared their solidarity on the issue of access to Berlin. They thus concentrated on the twin goals of insuring collective defense and promoting détente, which were outlined in last December's Report on the Future Tasks of the Alliance (the Harmel Report) . . .

East-West Relations. In their general review of the international situation, several ministers touched on the elusive nature of détente, referring especially to continued evidence of the rigid posture of the Soviet Union towards the West. Following consideration of a review of East-West relations since 1966, prepared by the permanent Council as part of the follow-up to the Harmel Report, there was a prolonged debate on how to achieve a proper balance in communiqué references to détente. It was finally agreed—as is usually the case in NATO discussions of this subject—that the ministers would publicly reaffirm their intention to continue efforts to promote détente, while warning that opportunities for rapid progress should not be overrated. The ministers also restated their intention to continue the examination and review of European security problems and to prepare for the time when "fruitful discussions" of these questions might be possible with the East, as originally called for in the Harmel Report.

Several members welcomed the recent UN General Assembly endorsement of the NPT, but no attempt was made at the meeting to reach agreement on a statement regarding the treaty for inclusion in the communiqué.

Mutual Force Reductions. In their major détente-oriented action, all ministers confirmed the decision of the permanent Council to give priority to the study, also undertaken as a Harmel Report follow-up, of the possibility of balanced and mutual force reductions by East and West. This provided the opportunity for the Fourteen to attempt to counter domestic pressures for defense cuts by reaffirming recent statements by NATO's Defense Planning Committee that the overall military capacity of the Alliance should not be reduced except as part of mutual force reductions. Belgian defense cuts announced last December and public debate about possible defense reductions in Germany had aroused concern that unilateral slashes by several NATO members might occur and that this could lead to a general downward spiral of national commitments to and hardware allocations for the common defense. Thus, the hope of heading off any unilateral cuts, by stressing the need for reciprocity, and the desire to reduce domestic budget-cutting pressures, by showing the public that NATO was as forthcoming on arms control as could prudently be afforded, were prime factors in renewing allied activity in the field of mutual East-West force reductions, even though no member government expected Moscow to be receptive to the idea at an early date.

Ministers of the Fourteen [member states] adopted a declaration on this subject which was made public as an attachment to the ministerial communiqué, thus serving notice that it was up to the Soviet Union and other Eastern European countries also to begin preparations for possible future discussions. While accepting the general statements in the declaration regarding hopes for progress in the field of arms control and, more specifically, the desirability of an East-West agreement on mutual force reductions, France disassociated itself from those portions which specified the principles to be followed in continuing the NATO study and which reaffirmed the need to maintain the overall military capacity of the Alliance in the meantime. The French did, however, affirm publicly their intention to continue to participate in this NATO study.

Mediterranean Security. Mindful of the fact that a year has passed since a major expansion of Soviet naval presence in the Mediterranean began, most members were anxious to give some evidence of the Alliance's awareness that this Soviet activity could pose an additional threat to its members' security. The most that could be agreed upon publicly by all fifteen members was their approval of a Harmel follow-up report dealing with "the situation in the Mediterranean" and their readiness to extend consultations on this subject within NATO as circumstances required. France would not concur in any reference to a Soviet threat as such and disputed the need for specific recommendations by the ministers. It thus disassociated itself from a further communiqué paragraph which expressed allied concern over the recent expansion of Soviet activity in the area and which noted that early consideration would be given to measures designed to safeguard the security interests of NATO members there, including increased surveillance activities. Previous discussion within the permanent Council had made apparent considerable apprehension that any specific measures undertaken might seem unduly provocative to the Soviets or to the Arab nations. Ministers of the Fourteen did agree, however, that activation of a NATO maritime air surveillance command for the Mediterranean should be expedited. They also instructed the permanent representatives to consider other possible measures, including an expansion of allied military exercises in the area and the formation of a standby multi-national naval force to be available on call. These latter actions were not made public. . . .

Berlin. The NATO ministers also focused their attention on the recent East German attempts to encroach on the political and psychological position of West Berlin. All fifteen ministers approved and publicly associated themselves with the expressed determination of the US, the UK and France to maintain freedom of access to that city. The ministerial communiqué called attention to Soviet responsibility for any action which hampered or endangered free access to Berlin and urged that such actions, which it called "a deliberate attempt to jeopardize détente," be discontinued. The statement adopted was based on a draft proposed by the West Germans; even though Foreign Minister Brandt had been prepared, in case of French opposition, to accept a Four-Power declaration on Berlin appended to the NATO communiqué, approval by all NATO members was achieved.

Conclusions. The NATO ministerial session just concluded was relatively undramatic, as the principal items on the agenda, viz., the three follow-up reports relating to aspects of the Harmel Study, were approved and the recommendations accepted with few changes from the drafts presented by the permanent representatives, who had succeeded in making unusually thorough and effective preparations. Likewise, the French reservations on these drafts had already been spelled out in full. The position of France in NATO has thus remained consistent for over a year. It is a rather reluctant ally. It seeks continued participation in the political and many military discussions, consultations, and studies of the Alliance, and it will often join in statements of general position. However, it disassociates itself from almost all concrete actions or calls for action, and from moves that imply a coordination of future policy, lest any of this imply a subordination of French policy to the US or to others. . . .

Source: Foreign Relations of the United States, 1964–1968: Volume XIII. Western Europe Region, U.S. Department of State, Document 316.

DOCUMENT 15
Joint Communiqué of the United States of America and the People's Republic of China
The Shanghai Communiqué
February 27, 1972

*During the late 1960s relations between the Soviet Union and the People's Repub-
lic of China deteriorated to such an extent that they were involved in armed conflicts on their border. Fearing an American-condoned Soviet attack on Chinese
nuclear facilities, Mao Zedong moved toward a rapprochement with the United
States. The American government, led by President Richard M. Nixon, responded
favorably to the Chinese overtures, and Secretary of State Henry
Kissinger made secret trips to China in 1971 that led to a state visit by Nixon
between February 21 and February 28, 1972. As the Nixon visit closed the
Chinese and Americans jointly issued the Shanghai Communiqué. It did not restore
formal diplomatic relations between the two nations, but it did provide a path and
means for normalization. It also provided an example of the principle of triangulation
that Nixon and Kissinger were developing in dealing with Cold War concerns.*

... During the visit, extensive, earnest, and frank discussions were held
between President Nixon and Premier Chou En-lai on the normalization
of relations between the United States of America and the People's
Republic of China, as well as on other matters of interest to both sides.
In addition, Secretary of State William Rogers and Foreign Minister Chi
P'eng-fei held talks in the same spirit.

President Nixon and his party visited Peking and viewed cultural,
industrial and agricultural sites, and they also toured Hangchow and
Shanghai where, continuing discussions with Chinese leaders, they viewed
similar places of interest.

The leaders of the People's Republic of China and the United States of
America found it beneficial to have this opportunity, after so many years
without contact, to present candidly to one another their views on a variety of issues. They reviewed the international situation in which important
changes and great upheavals are taking place and expounded their respective positions and attitudes.

The U.S. side stated: Peace in Asia and peace in the world requires
efforts both to reduce immediate tensions and to eliminate the basic causes
of conflict. The United States will work for a just and secure peace: just,
because it fulfills the aspirations of peoples and nations for freedom and
progress; secure, because it removes the danger of foreign aggression. The
United States supports individual freedom and social progress for all the
peoples of the world, free of outside pressure or intervention. The United

States believes that the effort to reduce tensions is served by improving communication between countries that have different ideologies so as to lessen the risks of confrontation through accident, miscalculation or misunderstanding. Countries should treat each other with mutual respect and be willing to compete peacefully, letting performance be the ultimate judge. No country should claim infallibility and each country should be prepared to re-examine its own attitudes for the common good. The United States stressed that the peoples of Indochina should be allowed to determine their destiny without outside intervention; its constant primary objective has been a negotiated solution; the eight-point proposal put forward by the Republic of Vietnam and the United States on January 27, 1972 represents a basis for the attainment of that objective; in the absence of a negotiated settlement the United States envisages the ultimate withdrawal of all U.S. forces from the region consistent with the aim of self-determination for each country of Indochina. The United States will maintain its close ties with and support for the Republic of Korea; the United States will support efforts of the Republic of Korea to seek a relaxation of tension and increased communication in the Korean peninsula. The United States places the highest value on its friendly relations with Japan; it will continue to develop the existing close bonds. Consistent with the United Nations Security Council Resolution of December 21, 1971, the United States favors the continuation of the ceasefire between India and Pakistan and the withdrawal of all military forces to within their own territories and to their own sides of the ceasefire line in Jammu and Kashmir; the United States supports the right of the peoples of South Asia to shape their own future in peace, free of military threat, and without having the area become the subject of great power rivalry.

The Chinese side stated: Wherever there is oppression, there is resistance. Countries want independence, nations want liberation and the people want revolution—this has become the irresistible trend of history. All nations, big or small, should be equal; big nations should not bully the small and strong nations should not bully the weak. China will never be a superpower and it opposes hegemony and power politics of any kind. The Chinese side stated that it firmly supports the struggles of all the oppressed people and nations for freedom and liberation and that the people of all countries have the right to choose their social systems according to their own wishes and the right to safeguard the independence, sovereignty and territorial integrity of their own countries and oppose foreign aggression, interference, control and subversion. All foreign troops should be withdrawn to their own countries.

The Chinese side expressed its firm support to the peoples of Vietnam, Laos, and Cambodia in their efforts for the attainment of their goal and its firm support to the seven-point proposal of the Provisional Revolutionary Government of the Republic of South Vietnam and the elaboration of February this year on the two key problems in the proposal, and to the Joint Declaration of the Summit Conference of the Indochinese Peoples. It firmly supports the eight-point program for the peaceful unification of Korea put forward by the Government of the Democratic People's Republic of Korea on April 12, 1971, and the stand for the abolition of the "U.N. Commission for the Unification and Rehabilitation of Korea." It firmly opposes the revival and outward expansion of Japanese militarism and firmly supports the Japanese people's desire to build an independent, democratic, peaceful and neutral Japan. It firmly maintains that India and Pakistan should, in accordance with the United Nations resolutions on the India-Pakistan question, immediately withdraw all their forces to their respective territories and to their own sides of the ceasefire line in Jammu and Kashmir and firmly supports the Pakistan Government and people in their struggle to preserve their independence and sovereignty and the people of Jammu and Kashmir in their struggle for the right of self-determination.

There are essential differences between China and the United States in their social systems and foreign policies. However, the two sides agreed that countries, regardless of their social systems, should conduct their relations on the principles of respect for the sovereignty and territorial integrity of all states, nonaggression against other states, noninterference in the internal affairs of other states, equality and mutual benefit, and peaceful coexistence. International disputes should be settled on this basis, without resorting to the use or threat of force. The United States and the People's Republic of China are prepared to apply these principles to their mutual relations.

With these principles of international relations in mind the two sides stated that:

- progress toward the normalization of relations between China and the United States is in the interests of all countries;

- both wish to reduce the danger of international military conflict;
- neither should seek hegemony in the Asia-Pacific region and each is opposed to efforts by any other country or group of countries to establish such hegemony; and
- neither is prepared to negotiate on behalf of any third party or to enter into agreements or understandings with the other directed at other states.

Both sides are of the view that it would be against the interests of the peoples of the world for any major country to collude with another against other countries, or for major countries to divide up the world into spheres of interest.

The two sides reviewed the long-standing serious disputes between China and the United States. The Chinese side reaffirmed its position: The Taiwan question is the crucial question obstructing the normalization of relations between China and the United States; the Government of the People's Republic of China is the sole legal government of China; Taiwan is a province of China which has long been returned to the motherland; the liberation of Taiwan is China's internal affair in which no other country has the right to interfere; and all U.S. forces and military installations must be withdrawn from Taiwan. The Chinese Government firmly opposes any activities which aim at the creation of "one China, one Taiwan," "one China, two governments," "two Chinas," and "independent Taiwan" or advocate that "the status of Taiwan remains to be determined."

The U.S. side declared: The United States acknowledges that all Chinese on either side of the Taiwan Strait maintain there is but one China and that Taiwan is a part of China. The United States Government does not challenge that position. It reaffirms its interest in a peaceful settlement of the Taiwan question by the Chinese themselves. With this prospect in mind, it affirms the ultimate objective of the withdrawal of all U.S. forces and military installations from Taiwan. In the meantime, it will progressively reduce its forces and military installations on Taiwan as the tension in the area diminishes.

The two sides agreed that it is desirable to broaden the understanding between the two peoples. To this end, they discussed specific areas in such fields as science, technology, culture, sports and journalism, in which people-to-people contacts and exchanges would be mutually beneficial. Each side undertakes to facilitate the further development of such contacts and exchanges.

Both sides view bilateral trade as another area from which mutual benefit can be derived, and agreed that economic relations based on equality and mutual benefit are in the interest of the people of the two countries. They agree to facilitate the progressive development of trade between their two countries.

The two sides agreed that they will stay in contact through various channels, including the sending of a senior U.S. representative to Peking from time to time for concrete consultations to further the normalization of relations between the two countries and continue to exchange views on issues of common interest.

The two sides expressed the hope that the gains achieved during this visit would open up new prospects for the relations between the two countries. They believe that the normalization of relations between the two countries is not only in the interest of the Chinese and American peoples but also contributes to the relaxation of tension in Asia and the world.

Source: "Text of Joint Communiqué, Issued at Shanghai, February 27 [1972]," *Department of State Bulletin*, 66, no. 435 (1972): 435–38.

DOCUMENT 16
President Jimmy Carter's Remarks at the Signing of the Peace Treaties between Egypt and Israel
March 26, 1979

The most notable and enduring foreign policy achievements of the Carter administration were the peace treaties signed between Egyptian President Anwar El Sadat and Israeli Prime Minister Menachem Begin. After the initial Camp David Accords, President Jimmy Carter continued to moderate the finalization of the peace treaties between the two leading powers of the Middle East. Settling the status of Israel among its neighbors and building working understandings with Middle Eastern nations was an important element in American Cold War policy, given the strategic importance of the region in terms of oil resources and transportation routes.

During the past 30 years, Israel and Egypt have waged war. But for the past 16 months, these same two great nations have waged peace. Today we celebrate a victory—not of a bloody military campaign but of an inspiring peace campaign. Two leaders who will loom large in the history of nations—President Anwar al-Sadat and Prime Minister Menahem Begin—have conducted this campaign with all the courage, tenacity, brilliance, and inspiration of any generals who have ever led men and machines onto the field of battle.

At the end of this campaign, the soil of the two lands is not drenched with young blood. The country sides of both lands are free from the litter and the carnage of a wasteful war. Mothers in Egypt and Israel are not weeping today for their children fallen in senseless battle. The dedication and determination of these two world statesmen have borne fruit. Peace has come to Israel and to Egypt. . . .

We have won at last the first step of peace, a first step on a long and difficult road. We must not minimize the obstacles which still lie ahead. Differences still separate the signatories to this treaty from one another, and also from some of their neighbors who fear what they have just done. To overcome these differences, to dispel these fears, we must rededicate ourselves to the goal of a broader peace with justice for all who have lived in a state of conflict in the Middle East.

We have no illusions—we have hopes, dreams, and prayers, yes, but no illusions. There now remains the rest of the Arab world, whose support and whose cooperation in the peace process is needed and honestly sought. I am convinced that other Arab people need and want peace. But some of their leaders are not yet willing to honor these needs and desires for peace. We must now demonstrate the advantages of peace and expand its benefits to encompass all those who have suffered so much in the Middle East.

Obviously, time and understanding will be necessary for people, hitherto enemies, to become neighbors in the best sense of the word.

Just because a paper is signed, all the problems will not automatically go away. Future days will require the best from us to give reality to these lofty aspirations.

Let those who would shatter peace, who would callously spill more blood, be aware that we three and all others who may join us will vigorously wage peace.

So let history record that deep and ancient antagonism can be settled without bloodshed and without staggering waste of precious lives, without rapacious destruction of the land.

It has been said, and I quote: "Peace has one thing in common with its enemy, with the fiend it battles, with war; peace is active, not passive; peace is doing, not waiting; peace is aggressive—attacking; peace plans its strategy and encircles the enemy; peace marshals its forces and storms the gates; peace gathers its weapons and pierces the defense; peace, like war, is waged."

It is true that we cannot enforce trust and cooperation between nations, but we can use all our strength to see that nations do not again go to war.

All our religious doctrines give us hope. In the Koran we read: "But if the enemy incline towards peace, do thou also incline towards peace, and trust in God; for He is the One that heareth and knoweth all things."

And the prophet Isaiah said: "Nations shall beat their swords into plow-shares and their spears into pruning-hooks: nation shall not lift up sword against nation, neither shall they learn war any more."

So let us now lay aside war. Let us now reward all the children of Abraham who hunger for a comprehensive peace in the Middle East. Let us now enjoy the adventure of becoming fully human, fully neighbors, even brothers and sisters. We pray God, we pray God together, that these dreams will come true. I believe they will.

Source: U.S. Department of State, *Department of State Bulletin* 79, no. 2025 (April 1979): 39–40.

DOCUMENT 17
President Ronald Reagan's Remarks at the Annual Convention of the National Association of Evangelicals, "The Evil Empire" Speech, Orlando, Florida
March 8, 1983

During his first term President Ronald Reagan was involved in a renewed arms race with the Soviet Union. At the same time the United States was interested in reducing the threat of a nuclear war. In this speech Reagan denounced any uni-lateral American reduction in nuclear weapons and argued that the Soviets contin-ued to constitute a serious threat to the United States and its values. He also tied American strength abroad to its moral integrity at home—an old theme in American thinking about America's place in the world—and condemned the Soviet Union as an "evil empire."

... During my first press conference as President, in answer to a direct question, I pointed out that, as good Marxist-Leninists, the Soviet leaders have openly and publicly declared that the only morality they recognize is that which will further their cause, which is world revolution. I think I should point out I was only quoting Lenin, their guiding spirit, who said in 1920 that they repudiate all morality that proceeds from supernatural ideas—that's their name for religion—or ideas that are outside class conceptions. Morality is entirely subordinate to the interests of class war. And everything is moral that is necessary for the annihilation of the old, exploiting social order and for uniting the proletariat.

Well, I think the refusal of many influential people to accept this elementary fact of Soviet doctrine illustrates an historical reluctance to see totalitarian powers for what they are. We saw this phenomenon in the 1930's. We see it too often today.

This doesn't mean we should isolate ourselves and refuse to seek an understanding with them. I intend to do everything I can to persuade them of our peaceful intent, to remind them that it was the West that refused to use its nuclear monopoly in the forties and fifties for territorial gain and which now proposes [a] 50-percent cut in strategic ballistic missiles and the elimination of an entire class of land-based, intermediate-range nuclear missiles.

At the same time, however, they must be made to understand we will never compromise our principles and standards. We will never give away our freedom. We will never abandon our belief in God. And we will never stop searching for a genuine peace. But we can assure none of these things America stands for through the so-called nuclear freeze solutions proposed by some.

The truth is that a freeze now would be a very dangerous fraud, for that is merely the illusion of peace. The reality is that we must find peace through strength. . . .

A freeze would reward the Soviet Union for its enormous and unparalleled military buildup. It would prevent the essential and long overdue modernization of United States and allied defenses and would leave our aging forces increasingly vulnerable. And an honest freeze would require extensive prior negotiations on the systems and numbers to be limited and on the measures to ensure effective verification and compliance. And the kind of a freeze that has been suggested would be virtually impossible to verify. Such a major effort would divert us completely from our current negotiations on achieving substantial reductions. . . .

[L]et us pray for the salvation of all of those who live in that totalitarian darkness — pray they will discover the joy of knowing God. But until they do, let us be aware that while they preach the supremacy of the state, declare its omnipotence over individual man, and predict its eventual domination of all peoples on the Earth, they are the focus of evil in the modern world. . . .

Well, because these "quiet men" do not "raise their voices," because they sometimes speak in soothing tones of brotherhood and peace, because, like other dictators before them, they're always making "their final territorial demand," some would have us accept them at their word and accommodate ourselves to their aggressive impulses. But if history teaches anything, it teaches that simple-minded appeasement or wishful thinking about our adversaries is folly. It means the betrayal of our past, the squandering of our freedom.

So, I urge you to speak out against those who would place the United States in a position of military and moral inferiority. . . . [I]n your discussions of the nuclear freeze proposals, I urge you to beware the temptation of pride—the temptation of blithely declaring yourselves above it all and label both sides equally at fault, to ignore the facts of history and the aggressive impulses of an evil empire, to simply call the arms race a giant misunderstanding and thereby remove yourself from the struggle between right and wrong and good and evil. . . .

While America's military strength is important, let me add here that I've always maintained that the struggle now going on for the world will never be decided by bombs or rockets, by armies or military might. The real crisis we face today is a spiritual one; at root, it is a test of moral will and faith.

Whittaker Chambers, the man whose own religious conversion made him a witness to one of the terrible traumas of our time, the Hiss-Chambers case, wrote that the crisis of the Western World exists to the degree in which the West is indifferent to God, the degree to which it collaborates in communism's attempt to make man stand alone without God. And then he said, for Marxism-Leninism is actually the second oldest faith, first proclaimed in the Garden of Eden with the words of temptation, "Ye shall be as gods."

The Western World can answer this challenge, he wrote, "but only provided that its faith in God and the freedom He enjoins is as great as communism's faith in Man."

I believe we shall rise to the challenge. I believe that communism is another sad, bizarre chapter in human history whose last pages even now are being written. I believe this because the source of our strength in the quest for human freedom is not material, but spiritual. And because it knows no limitation, it must terrify and ultimately triumph over those who would enslave their fellow man. For in the words of Isaiah: "He giveth power to the faint; and to them that have no might He increased strength. . . . But they that wait upon the Lord shall renew their strength; they shall mount up with wings as eagles; they shall run, and not be weary. . . ."

Source: Ronald Reagan, *Public Papers of the Presidents of the United States: Ronald Reagan, 1983,* Vol. 1. Washington, DC: U.S. Government Printing Office, 1984, 359–64.

DOCUMENT 18
President Ronald W. Reagan's
"Tear Down This Wall" Speech, Berlin
June 12, 1987

On June 12, 1987, President Ronald Reagan spoke before 45,000 Berliners at the Brandenburg Gate. In his speech he challenged Soviet leader Mikhail Gorbachev to demonstrate his new policy of openness by dismantling the Berlin Wall that had been erected in 1961. Reagan wanted to sustain the pressure on the Soviets and to support Gorbachev in his internal struggles with the hardline members of the Soviet "old guard."

In the 1950s, Khrushchev predicted: "We will bury you." But in the West today, we see a free world that has achieved a level of prosperity and well-being unprecedented in all human history. In the Communist world, we see failure, technological backwardness, declining standards of health, even want of the most basic kind—too little food. Even today, the Soviet Union still cannot feed itself. After these four decades, then, there stands before the entire world one great and inescapable conclusion: Freedom leads to prosperity. Freedom replaces the ancient hatreds among the nations with comity and peace. Freedom is the victor.

And now the Soviets themselves may, in a limited way, be coming to understand the importance of freedom. We hear much from Moscow about a new policy of reform and openness. Some political prisoners have been released. Certain foreign news broadcasts are no longer being jammed. Some economic enterprises have been permitted to operate with greater freedom from state control.

Are these the beginnings of profound changes in the Soviet state? Or are they token gestures, intended to raise false hopes in the West, or to strengthen the Soviet system without changing it? We welcome change and openness; for we believe that freedom and security go together, that the advance of human liberty can only strengthen the cause of world peace. There is one sign the Soviets can make that would be unmistakable, that would advance dramatically the cause of freedom and peace.

General Secretary Gorbachev, if you seek peace, if you seek prosperity for the Soviet Union and Eastern Europe, if you seek liberalization: Come here to this gate! Mr. Gorbachev, open this gate! Mr. Gorbachev, tear down this wall!'"

[. . .]

Source: Ronald Reagan, *Public Papers of the Presidents of the United States, Ronald Reagan, 1987*, Vol. 1 Washington, DC: U.S. Government Printing Office, 1989, 634–38.

DOCUMENT 19
Intermediate-Range Nuclear Forces Treaty
December 8, 1987

In 1986 President Ronald Reagan proposed a ban on all ballistic missiles while retaining his Strategic Defense Initiative (SDI). Negotiations with the Soviet Union led to the Reykjavik Summit (Iceland) between Reagan and First Secretary Mikhail Gorbachev of the Soviet Union on October 11–12, 1986. However, the two parties failed to reach an agreement at the summit. Discussions continued through the next year that resulted in the Intermediate-Range Nuclear Forces Treaty between the United States and the Soviet Union, which was signed on December 8, 1987, during Gorbachev's visit to Washington, DC.

[. . . .]

Article IV

1. Each Party shall eliminate all its intermediate-range missiles and launchers of such missiles, and all support structures and support

equipment of the categories listed in the Memorandum of Understanding associated with such missiles and launchers, so that no later than three years after entry into force of this Treaty and thereafter no such missiles, launchers, support structures or support equipment shall be possessed by either Party.

2. To implement paragraph 1 of this Article, upon entry into force of this Treaty, both Parties shall begin and continue throughout the duration of each phase, the reduction of all types of their deployed and non-deployed intermediate-range missiles and deployed and non-deployed launchers of such missiles and support structures and support equipment associated with such missiles and launchers in accordance with the provisions of this Treaty. These reductions shall be implemented in two phases so that:

4. (a) by the end of the first phase, that is, no later than 29 months after entry into force of this Treaty:

(i) the number of deployed launchers of intermediate-range missiles for each Party shall not exceed the number of launchers that are capable of carrying or containing at one time missiles considered by the Parties to carry 171 warheads; (ii) the number of deployed intermediate-range missiles for each Party shall not exceed the number of such missiles considered by the Parties to carry 180 warheads; (iii) the aggregate number of deployed and non-deployed launchers of intermediate-range missiles for each Party shall not exceed the number of launchers that are capable of carrying or containing at one time missiles considered by the Parties to carry 200 warheads; (iv) the aggregate number of deployed and non-deployed intermediate-range missiles for each Party shall not exceed the number of such missiles considered by the Parties to carry 200 warheads; and (v) the ratio of the aggregate number of deployed and non-deployed intermediate-range GLBMs of existing types for each Party to the aggregate number of deployed and non-deployed intermediate-range missiles of existing types possessed by that Party shall not exceed the ratio of such intermediate-range GLBMs to such intermediate-range missiles for that Party as of November 1, 1987, as set forth in the Memorandum of Understanding; and

(b) by the end of the second phase, that is, no later than three years after entry into force of this Treaty, all intermediate-range missiles of each Party, launchers of such missiles and all support structures and support equipment of the categories listed in the Memorandum of Understanding associated with such missiles and launchers, shall be eliminated.

Article XII

1. For the purpose of ensuring verification of compliance with the provisions of this Treaty, each Party shall use national technical means of verification at its disposal in a manner consistent with generally recognized principles of international law.

2. Neither Party shall:

(a) interfere with national technical means of verification of the other Party operating in accordance with paragraph 1 of this Article; or (b) use concealment measures which impede verification of compliance with the provisions of this Treaty by national technical means of verification carried out in accordance with paragraph 1 of this Article. This obligation does not apply to cover or concealment practices, within a deployment area, associated with normal training, maintenance and operations, including the use of environmental shelters to protect missiles and launchers.

3. To enhance observation by national technical means of verification, each Party shall have the right until a Treaty between the Parties reducing and limiting strategic offensive arms enters into force, but in any event for no more than three years after entry into force of this Treaty, to request the implementation of cooperative measures at deployment bases for road-mobile GLBMs with a range capability in excess of 5500 kilometers, which are not former missile operating bases eliminated pursuant to paragraph 8 of Article X of this Treaty. The Party making such a request shall inform the other Party of the deployment base at which cooperative measures shall be implemented. The Party whose base is to be observed shall carry out the following cooperative measures:

(a) no later than six hours after such a request, the Party shall have opened the roofs of all fixed structures for launchers located at the base, removed completely all missiles on launchers from such fixed structures for launchers and displayed such missiles on launchers in the open without using concealment measures; and (b) the Party shall leave the roofs open and the missiles on launchers in place until twelve hours have elapsed from the time of the receipt of a request for such an observation.

Each Party shall have the right to make six such requests per calendar year. Only one deployment base shall be subject to these cooperative measures at any one time.

Source: "Treaty between the United States of America and the Union of Soviet Socialist Republics on the Elimination of Their Intermediate-Range and Shorter-Range Missiles," December 8, 1987, Senate Treaty Document 100-11, 100th Congress, 2nd session.

DOCUMENT 20
President George H. W. Bush's State of the Union Address
January 28, 1992

President George H. W. Bush addressed a joint session of the Congress to deliver his State of the Union Address on January 28, 1992, a little more than a month after the dissolution of the Soviet Union. In this address Bush reported on the victory in the Cold War and launched a new agenda with reduced American military expenditures for the United States and a program to address domestic needs. At the same time Bush was adamant that the United States would not disarm, nor would it withdraw from its responsibilities in the world.

... I mean to speak tonight of big things, of big changes and the promises they hold, and of some big problems and how, together, we can solve them and move our country forward as the undisputed leader of the age.

We gather tonight at a dramatic and deeply promising time in our history and in the history of man on Earth. For in the past 12 months, the world has known changes of almost Biblical proportions. And even now, months after the failed coup that doomed a failed system, I'm not sure we've absorbed the full impact, the full import of what happened. But communism died this year.

Even as President, with the most fascinating possible vantage point, there were times when I was so busy managing progress and helping to lead change that I didn't always show the joy that was in my heart. But the biggest thing that has happened in the world in my life, in our lives, is this: By the grace of God, America won the cold war.

I mean to speak this evening of the changes that can take place in our country, now that we can stop making the sacrifices we had to make when we had an avowed enemy that was a superpower. Now we can look homeward even more and move to set right what needs to be set right.

I will speak of those things. But let me tell you something I've been thinking these past few months. It's a kind of roll call of honor. For the cold war didn't end; it was won. And I think of those who won it, in places like Korea and Vietnam. And some of them didn't come back. Back then they were heroes, but this year they were victors.

The long roll call, all the G.I. Joes and Janes, all the ones who fought faithfully for freedom, who hit the ground and sucked the dust and knew their share of horror. This may seem frivolous, and I don't mean it so, but it's moving to me how the world saw them. The world saw not only their special valor but their special style: their rambunctious, optimistic bravery, their do-or-die unity unhampered by class or race or region. What a group we've put forth, for generations now, from the ones who wrote "Kilroy was here"' on the walls of the German stalags to those who left signs in the Iraqi desert that said, "I saw Elvis." ' What a group of kids we've sent out into the world.

And there's another to be singled out, though it may seem inelegant, and I mean a mass of people called the American taxpayer. No one ever thinks to thank the people who pay a country's bill or an alliance's bill. But for half a century now, the American people have shouldered the burden and paid taxes that were higher than they would have been to support a defense that was bigger than it would have been if imperial communism had never existed. But it did; doesn't anymore. And here's a fact I wouldn't mind the world acknowledging: The American taxpayer bore the brunt of the burden and deserves a hunk of the glory.

So now, for the first time in 35 years, our strategic bombers stand down. No longer are they on 'round-the-clock alert. Tomorrow our children will go to school and study history and how plants grow. And they won't have, as my children did, air raid drills in which they crawl under their desks and cover their heads in case of nuclear war. My grandchildren don't have to do that and won't have the bad dreams children had once, in decades past. There are still threats. But the long, drawn-out dread is over. . . .

Much good can come from the prudent use of power. And much good can come of this: A world once divided into two armed camps now recognizes one sole and preeminent power, the United States of America. And they regard this with no dread. For the world trusts us with power, and the world is right. They trust us to be fair and restrained. They trust us to be on the side of decency. They trust us to do what's right. . . .

Two years ago, I began planning cuts in military spending that reflected the changes of the new era. But now, this year, with imperial communism gone, that process can be accelerated. Tonight I can tell you of dramatic changes in our strategic nuclear force. These are actions we are taking on our own because they are the right thing to do. After completing 20 planes for which we have begun procurement, we will shut down further production of the B-2 bombers. We will cancel the small ICBM program. We will cease production of new warheads for our sea-based ballistic missiles. We will stop all new production of the Peacekeeper missile. And we will not purchase any more advanced cruise missiles.

This weekend I will meet at Camp David with Boris Yeltsin of the Russian Federation. I've informed President Yeltsin that if the Commonwealth, the former Soviet Union, will eliminate all land-based multiple-warhead ballistic missiles, I will do the following: We will eliminate all Peacekeeper missiles. We will reduce the number of warheads on Minuteman missiles to one and reduce the number of warheads on our sea-based missiles by about one-third. And we will convert a substantial portion of our strategic bombers to primarily conventional use. President Yeltsin's early response has been very positive, and I expect our talks at Camp David to be fruitful.

I want you to know that for half a century, American Presidents have longed to make such decisions and say such words. But even in the midst of celebration, we must keep caution as a friend. For the world is still a dangerous place. Only the dead have seen the end of conflict. And though yesterday's challenges are behind us, tomorrow's are being born.

The Secretary of Defense recommended these cuts after consultation with the Joint Chiefs of Staff. And I make them with confidence. But do not misunderstand me. The reductions I have approved will save us an additional billion over the next 5 years. By 1997, we will have cut defense by 30 percent since I took office. These cuts are deep, and you must know my resolve: This deep, and no deeper. To do less would be insensible to progress, but to do more would be ignorant of history. We must not go back to the days of "the hollow army." ' We cannot repeat the mistakes made twice in this century when armistice was followed by recklessness and defense was purged as if the world were permanently safe.

I remind you this evening that I have asked for your support in funding a program to protect our country from limited nuclear missile attack. We must have this protection because too many people in too many countries have access to nuclear arms. And I urge you again to pass the Strategic Defense Initiative, SDI.

There are those who say that now we can turn away from the world, that we have no special role, no special place. But we are the United States of America, the leader of the West that has become the leader of the world. And as long as I am President, I will continue to lead in support of freedom everywhere, not out of arrogance, not out of altruism, but for the safety and security of our children. This is a fact: Strength in the pursuit of peace is no vice; isolationism in the pursuit of security is no virtue. . . .

And so, we move on together, a rising nation, the once and future miracle that is still, this night, the hope of the world. Thank you. God bless you, and God bless our beloved country. . . .

Source: "Address before a Joint Session of the Congress on the State of the Union," George H. W. Bush, January 28, 1992, *Public Papers of the President, George Bush: Vol. 1. 1992–93,* Washington, DC: U.S. Government Printing Office, 1993, 156–58.

ANNOTATED BIBLIOGRAPHY

ONLINE MATERIALS

Primary Sources

All of the relevant presidential libraries and museums provide online access to important primary sources on the Cold War. Note that the University of Texas is the online site for the Ford and Reagan Libraries and Museums.

Franklin D. Roosevelt Presidential Library and Museum, Hyde Park, New York, http://www.fdrlibrary.marist.edu/archies/collections.html

Harry S. Truman Presidential Library and Museum, Independence, Missouri, http://www.trumanlibrary.org

Dwight David Eisenhower Presidential Library and Museum, Abilene, Kansas, http://www.eisenhower.archives.gov

John F. Kennedy Presidential Library and Museum, Columbia Point, Boston, Massachusetts, http://www.jfklibrary.org/Search. In particular, students may want to refer to CloudsOverCuba.com (available through this source), an interactive site that provides a wide range of primary documents.

Lyndon Baines Johnson Library and Museum, Austin, Texas, http://www.lbjlibrary.org/collections

Richard M. Nixon Presidential Library and Museum, Yorba Linda, California, http://nixon.archives.gov/

Gerald R. Ford Presidential Library and Museum, Grand Rapids, Michigan, http://www.ford.utexas.edu/library/docs.asp

Jimmy Carter Library and Museum, Atlanta, Georgia, http://www.jimmy carterlibrary.gov/library/

Ronald Reagan Presidential Foundation and Library, Ventura, California, http://www.reagan.utexas.edu/archives/research.html

George H. W. Bush Presidential Library and Museum, College Station, Texas, http://www.bushlibrary.tamu.edu/research/research.php

Additional primary sources may be located at:

"Documents Relating to American Foreign Policy, the Cold War," Mount Holyoke College, South Hadley, Massachusetts, http://www.mtholyoke.edu/acad/intrel/coldwar.htm; a comprehensive collection of documents arranged chronologically for easy access.

Harvard Project on Cold War Studies, Davis Center for Russian and Eurasian Studies, Harvard University, http://www.fas.harvard.edu/~hpcws/index.2.htm; an outstanding collection of relevant documents and links that should be useful to all students studying this topic.

Lillian Goldman Law Library, Yale University, "The Avalon Project," http://avalon.law.yale.edu/; an outstanding collection of documents, many relating to America and the Cold War.

National Archives of the United Kingdom, "The Cold War," http://www.nationalarchives.gov.uk/education/coldwar/default.htm; an excellent resource that includes many documents relating to questions and issues related to the United States and the Cold War.

National Security Archive, George Washington University, "The Cuban Missile Crisis, 1962," http://www.gwu.edu/~nsarchiv/nsa/cuba_mis_cri; reliable and useful resource on the crisis.

Pollak Library, California State University, Fullerton, "Primary Sources: The Cold War," http://www.guides.library.fullerton,edu/docslinks/primarycoldwar.htm; includes documents on American foreign policy during the Cold War as well as domestic sources on the House Committee on Un-American Activities, internal security, subversive activities, sedition, and political crimes and offenses.

"Stalin Digital Archive," Yale University, http://www.stalindigitalarchive.com; this extensive collection of documents and other primary sources is available through purchase or subscription starting in 2012; check with your library to determine if it is or will be available.

Vassar College, "Vietnam Archive," http://www.vietnam.vassar.edu/abstracts/index.html; Includes 20 useful documents or excerpts from documents.

Other Online Sources

There are thousands of online sites/hits related to this topic. Care must be exercised in using online sources. Students are advised to use the search engines that are provided by their libraries and schools. Among the more reputable search engines are: EBSCO, FirstSearch, JSTOR, Lexis/Nexis, CIAO, and Project Muse. Generally speaking, sites ending in **org, gov,** or **edu** are preferable to those ending in **com**. A few of the reputable sites that may be of interest include:

Cold War International History Project, George Washington University, http://www.seas.gwu.edu.nsarchive/cwhip; includes both primary and secondary sources.

Ehrman, John, "The Alger Hiss Case: A Half-Century of Controversy," Center For the Study of Intelligence, Central Intelligence Agency, http://www.cia.gov/library/center-for-the-study-of-intelligence/kent~csi/docs/v44i5a01p.htm; a useful site for the Hiss case.

"McCarthy," University of Colorado, http://www.colorado.edu/AmStudies/lewis/2010/mccarthy.htm; an excellent resource with links to many primary and secondary sources; developed by Chris H. Lewis, Ph.D., University of Colorado, Boulder.

"Red Scare," http://www.spartacus.schoolnet.co.uk/USArredscare.htm; includes excerpts from primary and secondary sources and a narrative on the first Red Scare.

"Venona Project," National Security Agency, http://nsa.gov:8080/docs/venona/venona.html; excellent source on Soviet espionage efforts in the United States.

PRINT MATERIALS

Primary Sources

Books

Acheson, Dean. *Present at the Creation: My Years in the State Department.* New York: Norton, 1969. Includes extensive materials on the Cold War and the implementation of the containment policy.

Bernstein, Barton J., and Allen J. Matuscow (eds.). *The Truman Administration: A Documentary History.* New York: Harper Colophon, 1966. Includes relevant primary sources on the Cold War.

Blight, James G., and Janet M. Lang. *The Armageddon Letters: Kennedy, Khrushchev, Castro in the Cuban Missile Crisis.* New York: Rowman and Littlefield, 2012. Using primary sources in the text, Blight and Lang have attempted to re-create the crisis of October 1962; note that depending upon how this work is used, it may be considered as either a primary or secondary source.

Bohlen, Charles E. *Witness to History, 1929–1969.* New York: W. W. Norton, 1973. Bohlen, who served as U.S. ambassador to the Soviet Union and in many other roles related to the Cold War, produced a useful autobiography.

Bohlen, Charles E. *The Transformation of American Foreign Policy.* New York: W. W. Norton, 1969. An important assessment by a key participant in the development of American Cold War policy.

Branyan, Robert L., and L. H. Larsen (eds.). *The Eisenhower Administration, 1953–1961: A Documentary History.* New York: Random House, 1971. An excellent collection of primary sources, including many on the Cold War.

Carland, John M., and Edward C. Keefer (eds.). *Foreign Relations of the United States, 1969–1976: Volume IX. Vietnam, October 1972–January 1973.* Washington, DC: U.S. Government Printing Office, 2010. A key volume in this series that reflects Nixon's evolving policy on Vietnam.

Caughey, John Hart. *The Marshall Mission to China, 1945–1947: The Letters and Diary of Colonel John Hart Caughley.* Edited by Roger B. Jeans. Lanham, MD: Rowman and Littlefield, 2011. Memoir by Marshall's executive officer during his mission to China; provides a new perspective.

Chambers, Whittaker. *Witness.* New York: Random House, 1952. An extremely important and widely read Cold War memoir of a former communist who testified against Alger Hiss and others.

Chang, Laurence, and Peter Kornbluh (eds.). *Cuban Missile Crisis, 1962: A National Security Archive Documents Reader*. Rev. ed. New York: New Press, 1999. A valuable collection of primary sources, including correspondence between Kennedy and Khrushchev, and Khrushchev and Castro.

Clifford, Clark in collaboration with Richard Holbrooke. *Counsel to the President: A Memoir*. New York: Random House, 1991. By a key Washington insider, this memoir is useful on the first decades of the Cold War.

Draper, Hal. *Berkeley: The New Student Revolt*. Charleston, SC: CreateSpace, 2010. Includes eyewitness accounts of the student revolts associated with the free speech movement at the University of California, Berkeley.

Dulles, Allen W. *The Marshall Plan*. London: Berg, 1993. Originally written by Dulles during 1947 and 1948, this valuable manuscript was not discovered until the early 1990s and then published in 1993.

Dulles, John Foster. *War, Peace, and Change*. New York: Harper and Row, 1939. Dulles's denunciation of fascism and his advocacy for international organizations are hallmarks of this book.

Dulles, John Foster. *War or Peace*. New York: Macmillan, 1950. In this work Dulles calls for liberation of Soviet-controlled peoples rather than containment against the expansion of communism.

Eisenhower, Dwight D. *The White House Years: Mandate for Change, 1953–1956*. New York: Doubleday, 1963. Eisenhower's memoir that provides his views on the Cold War and McCarthyism.

Elsey, George McKee. *An Unplanned Life: A Memoir*. Columbia: University of Missouri Press, 2005. Important recollections by one of the authors of the Marshall Plan.

Flank, Lenny. *At the Edge of the Abyss: A Declassified Documentary History of the Cuban Missile Crisis*. St. Petersburg, FL: Red and Black Publishers, 2010. Includes declassified American and Soviet sources on the two weeks that were the focus of the crisis.

Geselbracht, Ray, and David C. Acheson (eds.). *Affection and Trust: The Personal Correspondence of Harry S. Truman and Dean Acheson, 1953–1971*. New York: Knopf, 2010. A fascinating volume of letters that reflects the ideas of two Cold War warriors after they departed from office.

Hanhimi, Jussi M., and Odd Arne Westad (eds.). *The Cold War: A History in Documents and Eyewitness Accounts*. New York: Oxford University Press, 2004. Includes official and unofficial documents that are very useful.

Hargis, Billy James. *Communist America: Must It Be?* 2nd ed. Tulsa, OK: Christian Crusade, 1960. Advances the arch-conservative views of one of America's most popular Christian leaders during the 1960s.

Hunt, Michael H. (ed.). *A Vietnam War Reader: A Documentary History from American and Vietnamese Perspectives.* Chapel Hill: University of North Carolina Press, 2010. A valuable resource for all students interested in the Vietnam War.

Jensen, Kenneth M. *Origins of the Cold War: The Novikov, Kennan, and Roberts "Long Telegrams" of 1946.* Rev. ed. Washington, DC: U.S. Institute of Peace, 1993. This work marks the first publication of Nikolai Novikov's (Soviet ambassador to the United States) telegram to the Soviet Foreign Office in September 1946.

Judge, Edward H., and John W. Langdon. *The Cold War: A Global History with Documents.* 2nd ed. Upper Saddle River, NJ: Prentice Hall, 2010. With more than 100 primary documents, this introduction to the Cold War is useful to students.

Keefer, Edward C., and David C. Geyer (eds.). *Soviet-American Relations: The Détente Years, 1969–1972.* Washington, DC: U.S. Department of State, 2007. Both Soviet and American documents are presented in parallel; also provides full coverage of the first Moscow Summit between Nixon and Brezhnev.

Kennan, George F. *Measures Short of War: The George F. Kennan Lectures at the National War College, 1946–47.* Edited by G. D. Harlow and G. C. Maerz. Washington, DC: National Defense University Press, 1991. These lectures provide insights into Kennan's thoughts on American strategy regarding the Soviet Union.

Kennan, George F. *Around the Cragged Hill: A Personal and Political Philosophy.* New York: W. W. Norton, 1994. Kennan's reflections on a long life, in particular, his thoughts on America and its place in the world.

Kennan, George F. *Memoirs, 1925–1950.* New York: Pantheon, 1983. Excellent source for Kennan's life and thoughts during his years of service as a Soviet expert and diplomat.

Kennan, George F. *Sketches from a Life.* New York: W. W. Norton, 2000. Extended memoirs of Kennan's career and experiences spanning more than 70 years.

Kennan, George F. *At a Century's Ending: Reflections, 1982–1995.* New York: W. W. Norton, 1989. Additional volume of the Kennan memoirs.

Kennan, George F., and John Lukacs. *George F. Kennan and the Origins of Containment, 1944–1946: The Kennan-Lukacs Correspondence*. Columbia: University of Missouri Press, 1997. An important collection of letters that reflect Kennan's thoughts on the Soviet Union and the beginnings of the containment policy.

Kennan, George F., and John Lukacs. *Through the History of the Cold War: The Correspondence of George F. Kennan and John Lukacs*. Philadelphia: University of Pennsylvania Press, 2010. Includes correspondence spanning five decades, much of which concerned the Cold War.

Kennedy, Robert. *Thirteen Days: A Memoir of the Cuban Missile Crisis*. New ed. New York: W. W. Norton, 1999. A valuable account of the Kennedy White House's decisions and processes by the president's brother, who was a primary participant.

Kissinger, Henry. *On China*. New York: Penguin, 2011. Both a primary source (in parts) and a history, this new study by Kissinger provides insights into that historical thinking that served as the basis for his policies and decisions.

Kissinger, Henry. *White House Years*. Reprint. New York: Simon and Schuster, 2011. An important memoir that covers Kissinger's four years as assistant to President Nixon for national security affairs and secretary of state (1969–1973).

Kissinger, Henry. *Years of Upheaval*. Reprint. New York: Simon and Schuster, 2011. This second volume of Kissinger's memoirs focuses on his tenure as secretary of state under Nixon (1972–1974).

Kissinger, Henry. *Years of Renewal*. New York: Simon and Schuster, 2000. The final volume of Kissinger's memoirs is concerned with Kissinger's life and thoughts after the Nixon era.

Kutler, Stanley. *Abuse of Power: The New Nixon Tapes*. New York: Touchstone, 1998. Provides extensive excerpts from the official transcript of Nixon's White House tapes.

Lynd, Staughton, and Thomas Hayden. *The Other Side*. New York: Signet/ New American Library, 1967. An account of the authors' trip to North Vietnam in 1965.

Marshall, George C. *The Papers of George Catlett Marshall: "The Whole World Hangs in the Balance," January 8, 1947–September 30, 1949: Vol. 6*. Edited by Larry I. Bland, Sharon Ritenour Stevens, Daniel D. Holt, and Mark A. Stoler. Baltimore: The Johns Hopkins University Press, 2012. Covers

Marshall's career as secretary of state and the beginning of the Cold War—the Truman Doctrine, Marshall Plan, Berlin blockade, origins of NATO, and so on.

May, Ernest R. *American Cold War Strategy: Interpreting NSC 68*. New York: Bedford/St. Martin's, 1993. Includes the complete text of NSC-68, which was written in 1950, and a broad range of commentaries.

May, Ernest R., and Philip D. Zelikow (eds.). *The Kennedy Tapes: Inside the White House during the Cuban Missile Crisis*. New York: W. W. Norton, 2002. Based on released tapes from the John F. Kennedy Presidential Library and Museum.

McCarthy, Eugene with a foreword by Christopher Hitchens. *1968: War and Democracy*. Petersham, MA: Lone Oak Press, 2000. Significant recollections and reflections on McCarthy's campaign in 1968.

McGovern, George. *Grassroots: The Autobiography of George McGovern*. New York: Random House, 1977. An important memoir by the Democratic candidate for president in 1972 and a leading anti–Vietnam War advocate.

McNamara. Robert, James Blight, Robert Brigham, Thomas Biersteker, and Herbert Schandler, *Argument without End: In Search of Answers to the Vietnam Tragedy*. New York: Public Affairs, 1999. Former Defense Secretary Robert McNamara's recollections and assessment of American policy in Vietnam.

Mikoyan, Sergo. *The Soviet Cuban Missile Crisis: Castro, Mikoyan, Kennedy, Khrushchev, and the Missiles of November*. Edited by Svetlana Savranskaya. Stanford, CA: Stanford University Press, 2012. A narrative by Mikoyan's son, who served as his secretary during the Cuban crisis; argues that the crisis for Moscow continued into November because of the strained relationship between Moscow and Havana.

Miller, Arthur. *Timebends: A Life*. New York: Penguin, 1995. A very important memoir by one of the leading American dramatists during the Cold War.

Nitze, Paul H. *Tension between Opposites: Reflections on the Practice and Theory of Politics*. New York: Charles Scribner's, 1993. Provides valuable firsthand insights into the politics and diplomacy of the Cold War.

Nitze, Paul H. *Securing the Seas: The Soviet Naval Challenge and Western Alliance Options: An Atlantic Council Policy Study*. Boulder, CO: Westview Press, 1979. Includes Nitze's concerns on the expansion of the Soviet military and the dangers to the West.

Nitze, Paul H., Ann M. Smith, and Steven L. Rearden. *From Hiroshima to Glasnost: At the Center of Decision*. New York: Grove Weidenfeld, 1989. Nitze's memoir of his decades in the American government during the Cold War.

Nixon, Richard M. *RN: The Memoirs of Richard Nixon*. 2 vols. New York: Warner Books, 1979. Nixon's memoirs on his public life as a congressman, senator, vice president, and president.

Savranskaya, Sventlana, Thomas Blanton, and Vladislav Zubok (eds.). *Masterpieces of History: The Peaceful End of the Cold War in Europe, 1989*. National Security Archive Cold War Readers Series. New York and Budapest: Central European University Press, 2010. Provides 122 primary sources on the revolutions of 1989.

Schrecker, Ellen W. (ed.). *The Age of McCarthyism: A Brief History with Documents*. Boston: Bedford/St. Martin's, 1994. Includes primary documents on the rise, fall, and impact of McCarthyism.

Sheen, Fulton J. *Treasure in Clay: The Autobiography of Fulton J. Sheen*. New York: Image, 1982. Valuable work that includes extensive commentary of Sheen's media work during the Cold War.

Solzhenitsyn, Alekandr. *Détente, Democracy, and Dictatorship*. 3rd ed. Piscataway, NJ: Transaction Publishers, 2009. Includes Solzhenitsyn's addresses in Washington, DC (1975) and at Harvard University (1978), and his final interview (2007).

Southern, Terry. *Now Dig This: The Unspeakable Writings of Terry Southern, 1950–1995*. New York: Grove Press, 2002. This remarkable book provides extensive insights into the life, thought, and work of Southern, who was a significant author, screenwriter, and satirist during the Cold War.

Steury, Donald P. *On the Front Lines of the Cold War: Documents on the Intelligence War in Berlin, 1946–1961*. N.P.: Military Bookshop, 2011. Includes new documents from both the American and Soviet archives.

Thatcher, Margaret. *The Downing Street Years*. New York: HarperCollins, 1993. The memoirs of the prime minister, including valuable information on the collapse of the Soviet Union and the end of the Cold War.

Topping, Seymour. *On The Front Lines of the Cold War: An American Correspondent's Journal from the Chinese Civil War to the Cuban Missile Crisis and Vietnam*. Baton Rouge: Louisiana State University Press, 2010. An important memoir by a correspondent who witnessed firsthand the emergence and early development of the Cold War.

Winkler, Allan M. *The Cold War: A History in Documents*. 2nd ed. New York and Oxford: Oxford University Press, 2011. Includes excerpts from a wide range of documents.

Articles

Churchill, Winston S. "The Sinews of Peace." In *Sources of World History*, edited by Mark A. Kislansky. New York: HarperCollins, 1995. An accurate transcript of Churchill's famous speech delivered at Westminster College, Fulton, Missouri, in 1946.

Lattimore, Owen. "American Responsibilities in the Far East." *Virginia Quarterly Review*, 16 (Spring 1940): 161–74. An important article by a perceptive contemporary China expert.

Miller, Arthur. "Why I Wrote 'The Crucible.'" *New Yorker*, 72 (October 21, 1996): 158ff. A very important statement by a pre-eminent playwright who opposed the anti-intellectualism and other dangers of McCarthyism.

Tydings, Millard E. "McCarthyism: How It All Began." *Reporter*, 7 (August 19, 1952): 11–15. Tydings, who lost his Senate seat because of McCarthyism, presents his views on the rise of McCarthy and his methodology.

Secondary Sources

Books

Ackerman, Kenneth. *Young J. Edgar: Hoover, the Red Scare, and the Assault on Civil Liberties*. Cambridge, MA: Carroll and Graf, 2007. A valuable study of Hoover's motives and actions during the first Red Scare and their impact on civil rights.

Adler, Selig. *The Isolationist Impulse, Its Twentieth Century Reaction*. New York: Collier, 1961. While dated, this is one of the most outstanding studies that connects American isolationism with postwar politics and foreign policy.

Agarossi, Elena, and Victor Zaslavsky. Stalin and Togliatti: Italy and the Origins of the Cold War. Cold War International History Project. Stanford, CA: Stanford University Press, 2011. A translation of an updated edition that focuses on the dependency of the Italian Communist Party on the Soviet Union during the postwar period.

Aikman, David. *Billy Graham: His Life and Influence*. New York: Thomas Nelson, 2010. A valuable biographical study by a renowned journalist.

Ali, S. Mahmud. *US-China Cold War Collaboration, 1971–1989*. Routledge Studies in the Modern History of Asia, no. 31. London and New York: Routledge, 2005. A well-documented and useful study of the many layers and facets of American-Chinese relations during the last decades of the Cold War.

Alperovitz, Gar. *The Decision to Use the Atomic Bomb*. New York: Vintage, 1996. Argues that the United States did not need to use the atomic bomb against Japan; using it shaped the Cold War and post-1945 American policies.

Anderson, Carol. *Eyes off the Prize: The United Nations and the African-American Struggle for Human Rights, 1944–1955*. New York: Cambridge University Press, 2003. An acclaimed study that examines the values, policies, and history of the United Nations and their impact on the civil rights movement in the United States during the first decade of the Cold War.

Andrew, Christopher. *For the President's Eyes Only: Secret Intelligence and the American Presidency from Washington to Bush*. New York: Harper Perennial, 1996. Includes useful information on the processes used to gather and assess intelligence during the Cuban missile crisis.

Applebaum, Anne. *Iron Curtain: The Crushing of Eastern Europe, 1944–1956*. London: Allen Lane/Penguin Press, 2012. An astute and seminal study of the Soviet Union's imposition of totalitarianism in Eastern Europe.

Aronsen, Lawrence. *The Origins of the Cold War in Comparative Perspective: American, British, and Canadian Relations with the Soviet Union, 1941–48*.New York: Macmillan, 1988. A seminal analysis on the deterioration of relations that led to the outbreak of the Cold War.

Asselin, Pierre. *A Bitter Peace: Washington, Hanoi, and the Making of the Paris Agreement*. Chapel Hill: University of North Carolina Press, 2007. A valuable and absorbing study of the negotiations that led to the Paris Peace Accord.

Ausland, John C. *Kennedy, Khrushchev and the Berlin-Cuba Crisis, 1961–64*. Oslo, Norway: Ashehoug, 1996. An account by an American insider with a foreword by Paul Nitze.

Bacon, Jon Lance. *Flannery O'Connor and Cold War Culture*. Cambridge: Press Syndicate of the University of Cambridge, 1994. A significant study that should be consulted by students working on literature and the Cold War.

Barnouin, Barbara, and Changgen Yu. *Zhou Enlai: A Political Life*. Hong Kong: Chinese University Press, 2007. An important biography based on a wide range of primary sources.

Barrass, Gordon. *The Great Cold War: A Journey through the Hall of Mirrors.* Stanford, CA: Stanford Security Studies, 2009. A provocative new study on how each side in the Cold War interpreted the other's motives, intentions, and actions.

Beisner, Robert L. *Dean Acheson: A Life in the Cold War.* Oxford and New York: Oxford University Press, 2006. An excellent biography of an early Cold War warrior.

Berhow, Mark. *US Strategic and Defensive Missile Systems, 1950–2004.* Oxford: Osprey, 2005. A military history that focuses on American fixed-launch-site missile systems during the Cold War and after.

Bernhard, Nancy E. *U.S. Television News and Cold War Propaganda, 1947–1960.* New York: Cambridge University Press, 1999. A valuable study of American television journalism during the Cold War.

Bigsby, Christopher. *Arthur Miller.* Cambridge, MA: Harvard University Press, 2010. The most comprehensive and scholarly biography of Miller published to date.

Bischof, Gunter, Stefan Karner, and Peter Ruggenthaler (eds.). *The Prague Spring and the Warsaw Pact Invasion of Czechoslavakia in 1968.* Lanham, MD: Lexington Books/Rowman and Littlefield, 2010. A collection of scholarly essays by academics who have accessed recently available documents.

Black, Conrad. *Richard M. Nixon: A Life in Full.* New York: Public Affairs, 2007. A detailed and well-documented comprehensive biography.

Blight, James G., and J. M. Long. *The Fog of War: Eleven Lessons from the Life of Robert S. McNamara.* Lanham, MD: Rowman and Littlefield, 2005. A provocative work based on astute historical analysis.

Bogus, Carl T. *Buckley: William F. Buckley, Jr. and the Rise of American Conservatism.* New York: Bloomsbury Press, 2011. A scholarly biography of one of the most prominent American conservatives during the second half of the twentieth century.

Bon Tempo, Carl J. *Americans at the Gate: The United States and Refugees during the Cold War.* Politics and Society in Twentieth-Century America Series. Princeton, NJ: Princeton University Press, 2008. A worthwhile study on American policies related to Cold War refugees, from the postwar refugee program to the Refugee Act of 1980 and the Reagan administration's refugee policies.

Borstelmann, Thomas. *The Cold War and the Color Line: American Race Relations in the Global Arena*. Cambridge, MA: Harvard University Press, 2003. An excellent analysis of the impact of racism in Cold War America and the transformation of race relations in the United States.

Bostdorff, Denise M. *Proclaiming the Truman Doctrine: The Cold War Call to Arms*. College Station: Texas A&M University Press, 2008. An in-depth analysis on the origins, development, and consequences of Truman's address to Congress on March 12, 1947, in which he proposed the Truman Doctrine.

Boyer, Paul. *By the Bomb's Early Light: American Thought and Culture at the Dawn of the Atomic Age*. Chapel Hill: University of North Carolina Press, 1994 (Originally published in 1985). A seminal study that examines the cultural consequences of American life with the atomic bomb.

Boyle, Peter G. *American Soviet Relations: From the Russian Revolution to the Fall of Communism*. New York: Routledge, 1993. A reliable study that covers the period from 1917 to 1991.

Brands, H. W. *The Devil We Knew: Americans and the Cold War*. New York: Oxford University Press, 1994. A scholarly and readable study of Cold War America in which impressions and perceptions on the Cold War were frequently contrived or baseless.

Brezinski, Zbigniew. *Strategic Vision: America and the Crisis of Global Power*. New York: Basic Books, 2012. A well-argued assessment of the post–Cold War world and America's role in it.

Brinkley, Douglas. *Dean Acheson: The Cold War Years, 1953–1971*. New Haven, CT: Yale University Press, 1992. A well-written and well-documented biography of Acheson after he served as secretary of state.

Brinkley, Douglas. *Cronkite*. New York: Harper, 2012. An acclaimed biography of Walter Cronkite, the CBS TV news anchor who was considered the pre-eminent public source of information in the United States during the 1960s and 1970s; he emerged as a critic of the Vietnam war.

Brogi, Alessandro. *Confronting America: The Cold War between the United States and the Communists in France and Italy*. The New Cold War Series. Chapel Hill: University of North Carolina Press, 2011. A comprehensive study with special value on the period from 1944 to 1956.

Brower, Charles F. (ed.). *George C. Marshall: Servant of the American Nation*. The World of the Roosevelts Series. New York: Palgrave Macmillan, 2011. A collection of useful essays on the many aspects of Marshall's career.

Bullock, Alan. *Ernest Bevin: Foreign Secretary, 1945–1951*. Oxford: Oxford University Press, 1985. Outstanding and unsurpassed study of the British foreign secretary during the early years of the Cold War.

Busch, Andrew E. *Truman's Triumphs: The 1948 Election and the Making of Postwar America*. Lawrence: University Press of Kansas, 2012. Busch's study includes useful insights on Truman's foreign policy.

Callahan, David. *Dangerous Capabilities: Paul Nitze and the Cold War*. New York: HarperCollins, 1990. A severe indictment of Nitze and his recommendations and actions during the Cold War.

Campbell, John. *The Iron Lady: Margaret Thatcher, from Grocer's Daughter to Prime Minister*. New York: Penguin, 2011. A comprehensive and reliable biography.

Carruthers, Susan L. *Cold War Captives: Imprisonment, Escape, and Brainwashing*. Berkeley and Los Angeles: University of California Press, 2009. An acclaimed study of the psychological, social, and political implications of the imprisonment and liberation of American and enemy prisoners during the Cold War.

Caute, David. *The Great Fear: The Anticommunist Purge under Truman and Eisenhower*. New York: Simon and Schuster, 1979. Still a standard source on the impact of McCarthyism on American life.

Clark, Katerina. *Moscow: the Fourth Rome; Stalinism, Cosmopolitanism and the Evolution of Soviet Culture, 1931–41*. Cambridge, MA: Harvard University Press, 2011. Provides valuable insights on the transformation of Soviet culture during the prewar decade.

Clarke, Thurston. *The Last Campaign: Robert F. Kennedy and 82 Days That Inspired America*. New York: Henry Holt, 2009. An excellent study of Robert Kennedy's presidential campaign in 1968.

Coleman, David G. *The Fourteenth Day: JFK and the Aftermath of the Cuban Missile Crisis: The Secret White House Tapes*. New York: W. W. Norton, 2012. Based on recently released tapes, this study of the Kennedy presidency presents a fresh interpretation of the difficulties Kennedy experienced after the crisis.

Collier, Peter. *Political Woman: The Big Little Life of Jean Kirkpatrick*. New York: Encounter Books, 2012. A biography of Kirkpatrick, who served as the American ambassador to the United Nations during the Reagan administration and was a primary author and advocate of the Reagan Doctrine.

Congdon, Lee. *George Kennan: A Writing Life*. 2nd ed. Wilmington, DE: Intercollegiate Studies Institute, 2008. An excellent study of the complex intellect and personality of George Kennan.

Costigliola, Frank. *Roosevelt's Lost Alliances: How Personal Politics Helped Start the Cold War*. Princeton, NJ: Princeton University Press, 2011. Argues that Roosevelt's personal diplomacy and Truman's reliance on his Soviet experts contributed to the outbreak of the Cold War; very good bibliography.

Cottam, Richard W. *Iran and the United States: A Cold War Case Study*. Pitt Series in Policy and Institutional Studies. Pittsburgh, PA: University of Pittsburgh Press, 1988. A thorough and useful study of American intervention in Iran and the Iranian reaction.

Cowley, Robert (ed.). *The Cold War: A Military History*. New York: Random House, 2005. A collection of 26 valuable essays by prominent scholars, including Thomas Fleming, Victor Hansen, and Stephen Ambrose; perhaps the best single volume on the military history of the Cold War.

Craig, Campbell, and Fredrik Logevall. *America's Cold War: The Politics of Insecurity*. Cambridge, MA: Belknap Press of Harvard University Press, 2009. This well-documented study includes valuable chapters called "The Demise of Free Security," "The Nuclear Rubicon," and "Nixon's World."

Craig, Campbell, and Sergey S. Radchenko. *The Atomic Bomb and the Origins of the Cold War*. New Haven, CT: Yale University Press, 2008. Suggests that the technology of the atomic bomb was a primary cause for the outbreak of the Cold War.

Cray, Ed. *General of the Army: George C. Marshall, Soldier and Statesman*. New York: Cooper Square Press, 2000. A reliable biography that includes information on Marshall's role in the outbreak of the Cold War.

Crockett, Richard. *The United States and the Cold War, 1941–53*. Brighton, UK: British Association for American Studies, 1989. A useful introduction to America's role during the early years of the Cold War.

Cull, Nicholas J. *The Cold War and the United States Information Agency: American Propaganda and Public Diplomacy, 1945–1989*. Cambridge and New York: Cambridge University Press, 2008. A comprehensive examination of the origins and effectiveness of the U.S. Information Agency during the Cold War.

Cummings, Richard H. *Cold War Radio: The Dangerous History of American Broadcasting in Europe, 1950–1989*. Jefferson, NC: McFarland, 2009. Provides information on the efforts of the Soviet Union and its allies to limit the impact of American broadcasting during the Cold War, including murders of writers and violence against others associated with Radio Free Europe.

Dallek, Robert. *The Lost Peace: Leadership in a Time of Horror and Hope, 1945–1953.* New York: HarperPerennial, 2010. Dallek looks at the multiple mistakes that world leaders made and the problems that ensued, including the Cold War.

Dallek, Robert. *Nixon and Kissinger: Partners in Power.* New York: Harpers, 2007. A scholarly and provocative study of Nixon and Kissinger and their relationship during the White House years.

Dallek, Robert. *An Unfinished Life: John F. Kennedy, 1917–1963.* New York: Little, Brown, 2003. A provocative biography that sheds new light on Kennedy's Cold War policies and decisions.

Dallek, Robert. *Harry S. Truman.* American Presidents Series, edited by Arthur M. Schlesinger, Jr. and Sean Wilentz. New York: Times Books, 2008. A solid introductory biography.

David-Fox, Michael. *Showcasing the Great Experiment: Cultural Diplomacy and Western Visits to the Soviet Union, 1921–1941.* New York and Oxford: Oxford University Press, 2011. A provocative study of Soviet efforts to gain sympathetic supporters in the United States and elsewhere during the interwar period.

Davis, Donald E., and Eugene P. Trani. *The First Cold War: The Legacy of Woodrow Wilson in U.S.-Soviet Relations.* Columbia: University of Missouri Press, 2002. Indicates that Wilson knew little about Russia, and his recognition of the provisional government followed by his repudiation of the Bolsheviks led to confusion on American policy.

Dedman, Martin. *The Origins and Development of the European Union 1945–2008: A History of European Integration.* 2nd ed. Oxford: Routledge, 2009. An outstanding study that provides information on the connections between American Cold War policies and the movement toward economic and political integration.

Del Pero, Mario. *The Eccentric Realist: Henry Kissinger and the Shaping of American Foreign Policy.* Ithaca, NY: Cornell University Press, 2009. An acclaimed study of the life and impact of Henry Kissinger.

Dijk, Ruud van, William G. Gray, Svetlana Savranskaya, Jeremi Suri, and Qiang Zhai (eds.). *Encyclopedia of the Cold War.* 2 vols. New York: Routledge, 2008. A reliable reference work.

Divine, Robert A. *Eisenhower and the Cold War*. New York: Oxford University Press, 1981. A brief but useful study of the Cold War during the Eisenhower era.

Dobbs, Michael. *One Minute to Midnight: Kennedy, Khrushchev, and Castro on the Brink of Nuclear War*. Reprint. New York: Vintage, 2009. A well-written account of the Cuban missile crisis.

Dobbs, Michael. *Six Months in 1945: FDR, Stalin, Churchill, and Truman; From World War to Cold War*. New York: Knopf Doubleday, 2012. An important recent study that is based on solid research—useful to students and general readers.

Dobbs, Michael. *Down with Big Brother: The Fall of the Soviet Empire*. New York: Vintage, 1998. A leading journalist's account and analysis of the collapse of the Soviet Union.

Dockrill, Saki Ruth. *The End of the Cold War Era: The Transformation of the Global Security Order*. Historical Endings Series. New York: Bloomsbury, 2005. An analysis of the end of the Cold War and its impact on Europe, superpower relations, and the Third World.

Dudziak, Mary L. *Cold War Civil Rights, Race and the Image of American Democracy*. New ed. Princeton, NJ: Princeton University Press, 2011. An important study on the intersection of the Cold War with American law, history, and political science.

Edwards, Lee. *William F. Buckley, Jr.: The Maker of a Movement*. Wilmington, DE: ISI Books, 2010. An acclaimed biography of one of America's leading conservatives during the Cold War.

Elsteins, Modris. *Walking since Daybreak: A Story of Eastern Europe, World War II, and the Heart of Our Century*. New York: Mariner Books, 2000. An enduring account of the impact of World War II and the Cold War on the Baltic states.

Engel, Jeffrey A. (ed.). *The Fall of the Berlin Wall: The Revolutionary Legacy of 1989*. New York: Oxford University Press, 2011. Includes important essays by renowned scholars such as Jeffrey Engel, Melvyn Leffler, Chen Jian, James Sheehan, William Taubman, and Svetlana Savranskaya.

Engelhardt, Tom. *The End of Victory Culture: Cold War America and the Disillusioning of a Generation*. New York: Basic Books, 1995. A penetrating and valuable analysis of the impact of the Cold War on American society.

Engerman, David C. *Know Your Enemy: The Rise and Fall of America's Soviet Experts*. New York: Oxford University Press, 2009. An analysis of the emergence and decline of Soviet studies in the United States and the inter-connections of academia and think tanks with American politics.

Evans, M. Stanton. *Blacklisted by History: The Untold Story of Senator Joe McCarthy and his Fight against America's Enemies*. New York: Crown Forum, 2007. A defense of McCarthy and his efforts to uncover the extent of the communist threat within the United States and its government.

Evans, M. Stanton., and Herbert Romerstein. *Stalin's Secret Agents: The Subversion of Roosevelt's Government*. New York: Threshold/Simon and Schuster, 2012. An important new study on the extensive Soviet intelligence operations within Roosevelt's administration.

Farabaugh, Patrick. *Carl McIntire's Crusade against the Fairness Doctrine: Fundamentalist Preacher and Radio Commentator Challenges Federal Communications and its Fairness Rules*. Saarbrücken, Germany: VDM Verlag Dr. Müller, 2010. Farabaugh suggests that McIntire's battle with the Federal Communications Commission (FCC) has not been appreciated as a key struggle in the history of the American media.

Farish, Matthew. *The Contours of America's Cold War*. Minneapolis: University of Minnesota Press, 2010. A recent study that focuses on the impact of the Cold War on thinking about the utilization of geography in a nuclear age.

Ferrell, Robert H. *Harry S. Truman and the Cold War Revisionists*. Columbia: University of Missouri Press, 2006. Ferrell argues that the revisionist interpretation on Truman and the Cold War is based on an inadequate understanding of the era and historical facts.

Frankel, Max. *High Noon in the Cold War: Kennedy, Khrushchev, and the Cuban Missile Crisis*. New York: Presidio Press, 2004. Well-written study focuses on the leaders and how they confronted the crisis.

Fried, Richard M. *The Russians Are Coming! The Russians Are Coming! Pageantry and Patriotism in Cold War America*. New York: Oxford University Press, 1998. A very useful study on the impact of the Cold War on American culture.

Friedman, Leon, and William F. Levantrossa (eds.). *Cold War Patriot and Statesman: Richard M. Nixon*. Westport, CT: Greenwood, 1993. An excellent collection of articles on Nixon's policies and actions related to the Cold War.

Fousek, John. *To Lead the Free World: American Nationalism and the Cultural Roots of the Cold War*. Chapel Hill: University of North Carolina Press, 2000.

Fousek argues that Americans supported the Cold War against the Soviet Union because of national values, not on behalf of Western civilization or capitalism.

Fursenko, Aleksandr. *One Hell of a Gamble: Khrushchev, Castro, and Kennedy, 1958–1964: The Secret History of the Cuban Missile Crisis*. New York: W. W. Norton, 1998. Based on Soviet documents, this book provides valuable information on the crisis, especially from the Soviet strategic perspective.

Gaddis, John Lewis. *George F. Kennan: An American Life*. New York: Penguin, 2011. The most significant study of Kennan by the leading American historian of the Cold War.

Gaddis, John Lewis. *Strategies of Containment: A Critical Appraisal of American National Security Policy during the Cold War*. Rev. ed. New York: Oxford University Press, 2005. Gaddis argues that Reagan completed the process of containment and in doing so brought the Cold War to an end.

Gaddis, John Lewis. *The Cold War: A New History*. New York: Penguin, 2006. The best introduction to the history of the Cold War.

Gaddis, John Lewis. *The United States and the End of the Cold War: Implications, Reconsiderations, Provocations*. New York: Oxford University Press, 1992. A study on prospects for a post–Cold War America and the new Russian confederation.

Gaddis, John Lewis. *The United States and the Origins of the Cold War, 1941–1947*. Contemporary American History Series. New York: Columbia University Press, 2000. Originally published in 1972, this edition provides an important new introduction; available as an eBook (ACLS Humanities E-Book.)

Gaddis, John Lewis. *Russia, the Soviet Union, and the United States: An Interpretative History*. New York: John Wiley and Sons, 1978. A reflective essay on the evolution of the Soviet-American relationship.

Garthoff, Raymond L. *Détente and Confrontation: American-Soviet Relations from Nixon to Reagan*. Rev. ed. Washington, DC: Brookings Institution Press, 1994. An important study that focuses on essential determinants of American and Soviet policies.

Gavin, Francis J. *Nuclear Statecraft: History and Strategy in America's Atomic Age*. Cornell Studies in Security Affairs. Ithaca, NY: Cornell University Press, 2012. Using recently declassified documents and keen analytical skills, Gavin has produced the best book on the impact of atomic weapons on the Cold War.

Gavin, Francis J. (ed.). *The Cold War*. 2 vols. Chicago: Fitzroy Dearborn Publishers, 2001. A useful set that consists of reprints of articles from the *New York Times*.

Genter, Robert. *Late Modernism: Art, Culture, and Politics in Cold War America*. The Arts and Intellectual Life of Modern America Series. Philadelphia: University of Pennsylvania Press, 2010. An important study on the impact of the Cold War on American artists and thinkers in an age of mass culture; Genter contends that the 1950s marked the high point of modernism in American culture.

George, Alice L. *Awaiting Armageddon: How Americans Faced the Cuban Missile Crisis*. Chapel Hill: University of North Carolina Press, 2006. An important study on how Americans reacted to the crisis and prepared for nuclear war.

Gibson, David R. *Talk at the Brink: Deliberation and Decision during the Cuban Missile Crisis*. Princeton, NJ: Princeton University Press, 2012. A new study focused on the decision-making process and based on audio recordings of the meetings that were held in the White House during the crisis.

Gimbel, John. *The Origins of the Marshall Plan*. Stanford, CA: Stanford University Press, 1976. A reliable and useful study of the European economic crisis that resulted in the Marshall Plan.

Glain, Stephen. *State vs. Defense: The Battle to Define America's Empire*. New York: Crown, 2011. A useful study on the competing views and strategies advanced by the leaders of the State and Defense Departments; throughout the Cold War, the militarists prevailed.

Goddeeris, Idesbald (ed.). *Solidarity with Solidarity: Western European Trade Unions and the Polish Crisis, 1980–1982*. Lanham, MD: Lexington Books/Rowman and Littlefield, 2010. An acclaimed study edited by the authority on the Solidarity movement; includes 13 essays by prominent European experts.

Gottfried, Martin. *Arthur Miller: His Life and Work*. New York: Da Capo Press, 2004. A perceptive and valuable study of Arthur Miller.

Graebner, Norman A., Richard Dean Burns, and Joseph M. Siracusa. *Reagan, Bush, Gorbachev: Revisiting the End of the Cold War*. Westport, CT: Praeger Security International, 2008. An important study on the impact of American and Soviet leaders during the last decade of the Cold War.

Griffith, Robert, and Athan Theoharis (eds.). *The Specter: Original Essays on the Cold War and the Origins of McCarthyism*. New York: New Viewpoints/

Franklin Watts, 1974. Consists of 12 scholarly essays by authorities on the subject.

Harbutt, Fraser J. *The Cold War Era*. Malden, MA: Blackwell, 2002. A survey that provides information on politics, foreign relations, and American social history during the Cold War.

Harbutt, Fraser J. *The Iron Curtain: Churchill, America, and the Origins of the Cold War*. New York: Oxford University Press, 1986. A worthwhile study of Churchill's impact on postwar diplomacy and the outbreak of the Cold War.

Harper, John L. *The Cold War*. Oxford Histories Series. New York: Oxford University Press, 2011. A good introduction to the Cold War.

Hartman, Andrew. *Education and the Cold War: The Battle for the American School*. New York: Palgrave Macmillan, 2008. A study on the impact of the Cold War on American educational thought and practices; includes a very interesting introduction.

Haslam, Jonathan. *Russia's Cold War: From the October Revolution to the Fall of the Wall*. New Haven, CT: Yale University Press, 2011. Focuses on the Soviet side of the struggle from 1917 to 1989.

Haynes, John Earl. *Red Scare or Red Menace? American Communism and Anticommunism in the Cold War Era*. Chicago: Ivan R. Dee, 1996. A classic study by a prominent authority on the Cold War.

Haynes, John Earl, and Harvey Klehr. *Venona: Decoding Soviet Espionage in America*. New Haven, CT: Yale University Press, 1999. The essential source on the topic and an intriguing read.

Haynes, John Earl, and Harvey Klehr. *In Denial: Historians, Communism, and Espionage*. Encounter Books, 2005. A brilliant attack on American revisionist historians who denied the extensive Soviet spy network in the United States.

Haynes, John Earl, and Harvey Klehr. *Early Cold War Spies: The Espionage Trials That Shaped American Politics*. Cambridge Essential Histories. New York: Cambridge University Press, 2006. Includes valuable information on Hiss-Chambers, Rosenberg, and other cases.

Haynes, John Earl, Harvey Klehr, and Alexander Vassiliev. *The Rise and Fall of the KGB in America*. New Haven, CT: Yale University Press, 2009. The most comprehensive study of Soviet spy activities in the United States before and after the outbreak of the Cold War.

Hendershot, Heather. *What's Fair on the Air? Cold War Right Wing Broadcasting and the Public Interest.* Chicago: University of Chicago Press, 2011. An important contribution to the history of American media during the Cold War.

Henriksen, Margot E. *Dr. Strangelove's America: Society and Culture in the Atomic Age.* Berkeley: University of California Press, 1997. Another worthwhile study of the Cold War's impact on American society.

Herken, Gregg. *The Winning Weapon: The Atomic Bomb in the Cold War, 1945–1950.* New York: Knopf, 1980. Examines the role of nuclear weapons in the Cold War.

Herzog, Jonathan P. *The Spiritual-Industrial Complex: America's Religious Battle against Communism in the Early Cold War.* New York: Oxford University Press, 2011. Advances an interpretation that American leaders and people viewed communism as a religion during the early years of the Cold War and countered it with faith-based zeal and institutional support.

Hewison, Robert. *In Anger: Culture in the Cold War, 1945–60.* London: Weidenfeld and Nicolson, 1981. A still useful study that considers the cultural impact of the Cold War.

Hey, Nigel. *The Star Wars Enigma: Behind the Scenes of the Cold War Race for Missile Defense.* Dulles, VA: Potomac Books, 2007. This work traces the origins, early development, and impact of the Strategic Defense Initiative (SDI).

Hoffman, David. *The Dead Hand: The Untold Story of the Cold War Arms Race and Its Dangerous Legacy.* New York: Anchor, 2010. A renowned scholarly work based on primary documents and interviews; Pulitzer Prize winner.

Hogan, Michael J. *A Cross of Iron: Harry S. Truman and the Origins of the National Security State, 1945–1954.* New York: Cambridge University Press, 1998. A very important work on the transformation of the American state and society during the early years of the Cold War.

Holmes, David L. *The Faiths of Postwar Presidents: From Truman to Obama.* George H. Shriver Lecture Series in Religion in American History. Athens: University of Georgia Press, 2012. Provides insights on the values and thoughts of American presidents during the Cold War.

Hunt, Michael H. *Lyndon Johnson's War: America's Cold War Crusade in Vietnam, 1945–1968.* New York: Hill and Wang, 1997. A very good introduction to American involvement in Southeast Asia that led to the Vietnam War.

Hurst, Steven. *Cold War U.S. Foreign Policy: Key Perspectives*. Edinburgh: Edinburgh University Press, 2005. The rationale, formulation, implementation, and consequences of American policies are covered in this volume.

Ikenberry, G. John. *Liberal Leviathan: The Origins, Crisis, and Transformation of the American World Order*. Princeton Studies in International History and Politics. Princeton, NJ: Princeton University Press, 2012. Examines the impact of the United States on global politics during the Cold War and the challenges to its authority.

Immerman, Richard H. *John Foster Dulles: Piety, Pragmatism, and Power in U.S. Foreign Policy*. Lanham, MD: Rowman and Littlefield, 1998. A scholarly study of driving forces behind Dulles's tenure as secretary of state.

Immerman, Richard H. (ed.). *John Foster Dulles and the Diplomacy of the Cold War*. Princeton, NJ: Princeton University Press, 1992. A valuable collection of articles on Dulles and the Cold War.

Immerman, Richard H. *Empire for Liberty: A History of American Imperialism from Benjamin Franklin to Paul Wolfowitz*. Princeton, NJ: Princeton University Press, 2012. An important work that includes valuable insights on the Cold War and its place in American imperial history.

Isaacson, Walter. *The Wise Men: Six Friends and the World They Made*. New York: Simon and Schuster, 1997. Includes an insightful and readable portrait of George Kennan.

Isaacson, Walter. *Kissinger: A Biography*. New York: Simon and Schuster, 1992. Still a very useful study that was based in large part on more than 150 interviews.

Jeffers, H. Paul, and Alan Alexrod. *Marshall: Lessons in Leadership*. Great Generals Series. Reprint. New York: Palgrave Macmillan, 2011. An excellent recent biography that includes information on Marshall's views on the Soviet Union during and after World War II.

Jensen, Kenneth M. *Origins of the Cold War: The Novikov, Kennan, and Roberts "Long Telegrams" of 1946*. 2nd ed. Washington, DC: U.S. Institute of Peace Press, 1994. An analysis of the Soviet ambassador's assessment of Kennan's views on U.S.-Soviet relations.

Jian, Chen. *Mao's China and the Cold War*. New Cold War History Series. Chapel Hill: University of North Carolina Press, 2000. A reliable history of China's role in the Cold War from the late 1940s through the mid-1970s.

Johnson, A. Ross. *Radio Free Europe and Radio Liberty: The CIA Years and Beyond*. Cold War International History Project. Stanford, CA: Stanford University

Press, 2010. Johnson, a senior scholar at the Woodrow Wilson Center, has produced the best study on this aspect of Cold War history.

Johnson, A. Ross, and R. Eugene Parta (eds.). *Cold War Broadcasting: Impact on the Soviet Union and Eastern Europe*. Budapest and New York: Central European University Press, 2010. A valuable collection of scholarly essays that evaluate the success of American broadcasting efforts directed at the citizens of the Soviet Union and its Eastern European allies.

Johnson, Robert D. *Congress and the Cold War*. New York: Cambridge University Press, 2006. Traces the emergence of a bipartisan foreign policy within Congress and considers the independent positions taken by Wayne Morse, Stuart Symington, and others.

Judt, Tony. *Postwar: A History of Europe Since 1945*. New York: Penguin, 2006. An outstanding survey of European history since World War II that provides insightful commentary on the impact of the Cold War and the role of the United States in Western European affairs.

Judt, Tony. *Reappraisals: Reflections on the Forgotten Twentieth Century*. New York: Penguin, 2008. Judt argues that we are detached from our recent past and that the results are catastrophic.

Judt, Tony, with Timothy Snyder. *Thinking the Twentieth Century*. New York: Penguin, 2012. Includes valuable reflections on the significance of the Cold War.

Kagan, Robert. *The World America Made*. New York: Alfred A. Knopf, 2012. An important study of the post–Cold War world by a pre-eminent scholar.

Kempe, Frederick. *Berlin 1961: Kennedy, Khrushchev, and the Most Dangerous Place on Earth*. New York: Berkeley Trade, 2012. A good introduction to the Berlin crisis.

Kennan, George F. *The Decision to Intervene: Soviet-American Relations, 1917–1920, Vol. II*. Princeton, NJ: Princeton University Press, 1989. Kennan provides an excellent review of the crisis that gripped Russia after the Bolshevik Revolution and Wilson's decision to send American troops to Northern Russia and Siberia.

Kennan, George F. *Russia Leaves the War: Soviet-American Relations, 1917–1920, Vol. I*. Princeton, NJ: Princeton University Press, 1989. A valuable study of Soviet-American relations during 1917 and 1918.

Kennan, George F. *Soviet Foreign Policy, 1917–1941*. Malabar, FL: R. E. Krieger, 1979. Provides valuable information on what motivated Soviet leaders in the formulation of foreign policy, its implementation, and consequences.

Kennedy-Pipe, Caroline. *The Origins of the Cold War*. Basingstoke, UK: Palgrave-Macmillan, 2007. A useful study of the decline of Soviet-American relations and the early failures to work toward resolutions of the developing struggle.

Kessler, Lauren. *Clever Girl: Elizabeth Bentley, the Spy Who Ushered in the McCarthy Era*. New York: Harper, 2003. A solid and readable biography of Bentley.

Kessler-Harris, Alice. *A Difficult Woman: The Challenging Life and Times of Lillian Hellman*. London: Bloomsbury, 2012. An important scholarly study that includes extensive information on Hellman's impact on Cold War culture.

Ketchum, James S. *Chemical Warfare Secrets Almost Forgotten: A Personal Story of Medical Testing of Army Volunteers*. 2nd ed. Santa Rosa, CA: ChemBook, 2006. An account of medical experimentation on Americans motivated by the Cold War; parts of this book may be considered a primary source.

Khalidi, Rashid. *Resurrecting Empire: Western Footprints and America's Perilous Path in the Middle East*. Boston: Beacon Press, 2005. A powerful critique of American policy in the Middle East since the end of World War II.

Khalidi, Rashid. *Sowing Crisis: The Cold War and American Dominance in the Middle East*. Boston: Beacon Press, 2010. Acclaimed study on the negative impact of American and Soviet involvement in the Middle East.

Kofsky, Frank. *Harry S. Truman and the War Scare of 1948: A Successful Campaign to Deceive a Nation*. New York: St. Martin's, 1993. A well-argued critique of Truman and his aides' performance during the early years of the Cold War.

Koistinen, Paul A. C. *State of War: The Political Economy of American Warfare, 1945–2011*. Modern War Studies. Lawrence: University Press of Kansas, 2012. A useful analysis of the political economy of the United States during the Cold War.

Kotkin, Stephen. *Armageddon Averted: Soviet Collapse, 1970–2000*. Updated ed. New York: Oxford University Press, 2008. An astute analysis of the breakup of the Soviet Union, where reforms led to dissolution.

Kramer, Hilton. *The Twilight of the Intellectuals: Culture and Politics in the Era of the Cold War*. Chicago: Ivan R. Dee, 2000. A useful study on the impact of ideology on public intellectuals.

Krenn, Michael L. (ed.). *Race and U.S. Foreign Policy during the Cold War*. Race and U.S. Foreign Policy from the Colonial Period to the Present, no. 4. New York: Garland, 1998. An important collection of essays on the intersection of American values, social history, and foreign policy during the Cold War.

Kutler, Stanley I. *The American Inquisition: Justice and Injustice in the Cold War*. New York: Hill and Wang, 1982. Still a very good source on the impact of the Cold War on internal security, loyalty programs, and justice.

Kutler, Stanley I. *The Wars of Watergate: The Last Crisis of Richard Nixon*. New York: W. W. Norton, 1992. Kutler's scholarly study of the fall of Richard Nixon is still one of the best works on the subject.

Kuznick, Peter J., and James Gilbert (eds.). *Rethinking Cold War Culture*. Washington, DC: Smithsonian Institution Press, 2001. A collection of essays by prominent scholars such as Stephen J. Whitfield, Alan Brinkley, Leo Ribuffo, and Ann Markusen.

Kwon, Heonik. *The Other Cold War*. Columbia Studies in International and Global History. New York: Columbia University Press, 2010. An important sociological examination of many long-neglected issues related to the Cold War, including the division between labor and culture in the study of the Cold War and other social and ethnographic concerns.

LaFeber, Walter. *America, Russia, and the Cold War, 1945–2006*. Updated 10th ed. Boston: McGraw-Hill, 2008. A standard work with a very good bibliography.

Lahr, Angela M. *Millennial Dreams and Apocalyptic Nightmares: The Cold War Origins of Political Evangelicalism*. New York: Oxford University Press, 2007. Lahr argues that the Religious Right had its origins during the early years of the Cold War; Billy Graham and others awakened evangelicals to the need for political action.

Larres, Klaus, and Ann Lane (eds.). *The Cold War: The Essential Readings*. Blackwell Essential Readings in History. Oxford and Malden, MA: Blackwell, 2001. An excellent historiographical collection of essays by prominent scholars on the Cold War, including Melvyn Leffler, John L. Gaddis, H. W. Brands, and Klaus Larres.

Ledbetter, James. *Unwarranted Influence: Dwight D. Eisenhower and the Military-Industrial Complex*. New Haven, CT: Yale University Press, 2011. Provides valuable insights on the impact of the Cold War on the military-industrial complex in the United States.

Leffler, Melvyn P. *For the Soul of Mankind: The United States, the Soviet Union, and the Cold War*. New York: Hill and Wang, 2008. Leffler argues that there were several opportunities to end the Cold War, but it was not until Gorbachev, and to a lesser extent Reagan and Bush, that leaders removed themselves from the ideological constraints of the past that the conflict was terminated.

Leffler, Melvyn P. *The Specter of Communism: The United States and the Origins of the Cold War, 1917–1953*. New York: Hill and Wang, 1994. An important and worthwhile survey of Soviet-American relations from the Revolution to the death of Stalin; focused on American politics and anxieties.

Leffler, Melvyn P. *A Preponderance of Power: National Security, the Truman Administration, and the Cold War*. Stanford, CA: Stanford University Press, 1992. An excellent study of converging forces and attitudes that contributed to the outbreak of the Cold War.

Leffler, Melvyn P., and Odd Avre Westad (eds.). *Cambridge History of the Cold War*, 3 vols. Cambridge: Cambridge University Press, 2010. Excellent scholarship consisting of scores of essays in three volumes: "Origins," "Crises and Détente," and "Endings."

Leshuk, Leonard. *US Intelligence Perceptions of Soviet Power, 1921–1946*. Lanham, MD: Routledge, 2002. An important scholarly work on the reality of Soviet power versus the American perception.

Levering, Ralph B. *The Cold War: A Post–Cold War History*. 2nd ed. Wheeling, IL: Harlan Davidson, 2005. An outstanding survey that includes information from the Soviet archives.

Levering, Ralph B., Vladimir O. Perchatnov, Verena Botzenhart-Viehe, and C. Earl Edmondson. *Debating the Origins of the Cold War: American and Russian Perspectives*. Debating Twentieth-Century America Series. New York: Rowman and Littlefield, 2002. In two extensive essays the authors demonstrate the extensive gap between American and Soviet understandings of the origins of the Cold War.

Levin, N. Gordon, Jr. *Woodrow Wilson and World Politics: America's Response to War and Revolution*. New York: Oxford University Press, 1970. This winner of the 1970 Bancroft Prize from the American Historical Association provides an astute analysis of Wilson's foreign policy from 1917 to 1919.

Litwak, Robert S. *Détente and the Nixon Doctrine: American Foreign Policy and the Pursuit of Stability, 1969–1976*. New York: Cambridge University Press, 1986. Currently the definitive history of the Nixon Doctrine on American security priorities.

Logevall, Fredrik. *Embers of War: The Fall of an Empire and the Making of America's Vietnam*. New York: Random House, 2012. Examines the defeat of the French and the assumption and expansion of the struggle by the United States—a valuable book.

Lucas, Edward. *Deception, Spies, Lies, and How Russia Dupes the West*. London: Bloomsbury, 2012. Provides valuable insights on Soviet/Russian policies and practices during and after the Cold War.

Lukacs, John. *George Kennan: A Study of Character*. New Haven, CT: Yale University Press, 2009. An insightful analysis of Kennan by the historian John Lukacs, friend and correspondent.

Lukacs, John. *A New History of the Cold War*. New York: Anchor, 1966. A revised study by a significant and controversial historian.

Lukes, Igor. *On the Edge of the Cold War: American Diplomats and Spies in Postwar Prague*. New York: Oxford University Press, 2012. A well-documented and readable study of the American-Soviet struggle for influence in Prague after World War II.

Maddox, Robert J. *The New Left and the Origins of the Cold War*. Princeton, NJ: Princeton University Press, 1973. Considers the options and paths taken by American leftists during the early decades of the Cold War.

Maddox, Robert J. *From War to Cold War: The Education of Harry S. Truman*. Boulder, CO: Westview Press, 1988. The transformation of Truman into a Cold War warrior.

Mann, James. *The Rebellion of Ronald Reagan: A History of the End of the Cold War*. New York: Viking, 2009. Advances an interpretation of Reagan as a focused president who followed his strategy for ending the Cold War.

Manso, Peter. *Mailer: His Life and Times*. New York: Washington Square Press, 2008. Reprint. The authorized biography of Norman Mailer.

Mastny, Vojtech. *Russia's Road to the Cold War: Diplomacy, Warfare, and the Politics of Communism, 1941–1945*. New York: Columbia University Press, 1979. A valuable study that traces the Russian path to the Cold War through its role in World War II.

Matlock, Jack. *Reagan and Gorbachev: How the Cold War Ended*. New York: Random House, 2004. A valuable account by the former U.S. ambassador to the Soviet Union.

May, Elaine Tyler. *Homeward Bound: American Families in the Cold War Era*. New York: Basic Books, 2008 (Originally published in 1988). A classic work addressing the interconnections between the Cold War and American family and personal life.

Mayers, David. *George Kennan and the Dilemmas of US Foreign Policy*. New York: Oxford University Press, 1990. A worthwhile study of Kennan's life and his impact on Soviet-American diplomacy and relations.

Maynard, Christopher. *Out of the Shadow: George H. W. Bush and the End of the Cold War*. Foreign Relations and the Presidency Series. College Station: Texas A&M University Press, 2008. Rather than considering the Bush presidency as an extension of Reagan's, Maynard argues that Bush approached the Soviet Union differently, and his policies contributed significantly to the collapse of the Soviet Union.

McAlister, Melani. *Epic Encounters: Culture, Media, and U.S. Interests in the Middle East since 1945*. Rev. ed. Berkeley: University of California Press, 2005. An important study that focuses on American cultural impressions of the Middle East and its geopolitical significance.

McCauley, Martin. *Russia, America, and the Cold War, 1949–1991*. Seminar Studies in History. Harlow, England and New York: Pearson/Longman, 2008. A useful work that covers the period from the first Berlin crisis to the collapse of the Soviet Union; good bibliography.

McCauley, Martin. *The Origins of the Cold War, 1941–1949*. Seminar Studies in History. London and New York: Pearson/Longman, 2003. A useful study of Soviet/American relations during and after World War II.

McClenahan, William M. Jr., and William H. Becker. *Eisenhower and the Cold War Economy*. Baltimore: The Johns Hopkins University Press, 2011. A seminal study that focuses on Eisenhower's concerns and policies related to developing the domestic economy while at the same time fighting the Cold War.

McCullough, David. *Truman*. New York: Simon and Schuster, 1992. A readable and generally sympathetic biography.

Medhurst, Martin J. *Cold War Rhetoric: Strategy, Metaphor, and Ideology*. Rev. ed. East Lansing: Michigan State University Press, 1997. A provocative scholarly work on the language and context of Cold War argumentation.

Medland, William J. *The Cuban Missile Crisis of 1962: Needless or Necessary?* Westport, CT: Praeger, 1988. Includes a review of the historiography on the crisis and advances some new thoughts on its meaning and outcomes.

Medovoi, Leerom. *Rebels: Youth and the Cold War Origins of Identity*. Durham, NC: Duke University Press, 2005. A fascinating thesis in which rebellious

American youths (both real and imagined) and their advocates are representative of the freedom-seeking nations of the Third World during the early decades of the Cold War.

Miller, William Lee. *Two Americans: Truman, Eisenhower and a Dangerous World*. New York: Knopf Doubleday, 2012. Acclaimed dual biography that includes valuable insights on America during the early years of the Cold War.

Mills, Nicolaus. *Winning the Peace: The Marshall Plan and America's Coming of Age as a Superpower*. New York: Wiley, 2008. A readable and well-researched study on the intricacies associated with establishing the Marshall Plan.

Milward, Alan S. *The Reconstruction of Western Europe, 1945–1951*. Berkeley: University of California Press, 1984. Includes significant information on the Marshall Plan.

Miroff, Bruce. *The Liberals' Moment: The McGovern Insurgency and the Identity Crisis of the Democratic Party*. Lawrence: University Press of Kansas, 2007. Provides valuable insights on the liberal view of the Cold War in 1972.

Munton, David, and David A Welch. *The Cuban Missile Crisis: A Concise History*. 2nd ed. New York: Oxford University Press, 2011. A solid work that incorporates the most recent scholarship and source materials.

Nash, George (ed.). *Freedom Betrayed: Herbert Hoover's Secret History of the Second World War and Its Aftermath*. Stanford, CA: Hoover Institution Press, 2011. Published almost 50 years after his death, Hoover's analysis of Roosevelt's foreign policy and the origins of the Cold War need to be considered by students of the Cold War.

Nelson, Deborah. *Pursuing Privacy in Cold War America*. New York: Columbia University Press, 2002. An intriguing cultural history of the idea and practice of privacy during the Cold War; the rights of writers, readers, and individuals are addressed.

Neville, John F. *The Press, the Rosenbergs, and the Cold War*. Westport, CT: Praeger, 1995. A valuable study of the Rosenberg case and the press during the McCarthy era; very good bibliography.

Newton, Jim. *Eisenhower: The White House Years*. New York: Doubleday, 2011. A well-researched and well-written biography that credits Eisenhower with a political acumen that other scholars neglect.

Nguyen, Lien-Hang T. *Hanoi's War: An International History of the War for Peace in Vietnam*. The New Cold War History. Chapel Hill: University of North

Carolina Press, 2012. Examines the war in an international context during the Cold War.

Nichols, David A. *Eisenhower 1956: The President's Year of Crisis; Suez and the Brink of War*. New York: Simon and Schuster, 2011. Using declassified documents, Nichols analyzes Eisenhower's most challenging year as president.

Noer, Thomas J. *Cold War and Black Liberation: The United States and White Rule in Africa, 1949–1968*. Columbia: University of Missouri Press, 1985. A provocative and worthwhile study of American foreign relations with white-controlled regimes in Africa during two difficult decades of the Cold War.

Nogee, Joseph L. *Peace Impossible, War Unlikely: The Cold War between the United States and the Soviet Union*. Glenview, IL: Scott, Foresman, Little, 1988. An interesting volume that reflects an intellectual's attitude near the end of the Cold War.

Nuti, Leopoldo (ed.). *The Crisis of Détente in Europe: From Helsinki to Gorbachev, 1975–1985*. New York: Routledge, 2008. In this collection of essays on human rights, armament deployment, and economic issues, the hardening of East-West relations is examined.

Oates, Stephen B. *Let the Trumpet Sound: A Life of Martin Luther King, Jr.* New York: Harper Perennial, 1994. A valuable biography that includes information on King's views on the Cold War.

O'Clery, Conor. *Moscow, December 25, 1991: The Last Day of the Soviet Union*. New York: Public Affairs, 2011. A well-written and acclaimed study of the final days of the Soviet Union.

Offner, Arnold A. *Another Such Victory: President Truman and the Cold War, 1945–1953*. Stanford Nuclear Age Series. Stanford, CA: Stanford University Press, 2002. An important work that in part blames Truman for the Cold War; he was too provincial and inexperienced to understand and manage the global forces that emerged after the end of World War II.

Olmsted, Kathryn S. *Red Spy Queen: A Biography of Elizabeth Bentley*. Chapel Hill: University of North Carolina Press, 2002. A scholarly biography of the Soviet spy whose defection was an important element in the development of the Red Scare.

Oshinsky, David M. *A Conspiracy So Immense: The World of Joe McCarthy*. New York: Free Press, 1983. An excellent study of McCarthy and his impact.

Ovendale, Ritchie. *The English-Speaking Alliance: Britain, the United States, the Dominions, and the Cold War, 1945–1951*. London: G. Allen and Unwin, 1985. A provocative study on the early years of the Cold War.

Pach, Chester J. *Arming the Free World: The Origins of the United States Military Assistance Program*. Chapel Hill: University of North Carolina Press, 2010. The definitive study on the emergence of military assistance as an essential component of American foreign policy during the Cold War.

Pantsov, Alexander, and Steven I. Levine. *Mao: The Real Story*. New York: Simon and Schuster, 2012. A valuable biography based in part on recently released Russian documents.

Paterson, Thomas G. *Cold War Critics: Alternatives to American Foreign Policy in the Truman Years*. Chicago: Quadrangle Books, 1971. A valuable study of dissenters to Truman's Cold War policies.

Paterson, Thomas G. *Soviet-American Confrontation: Postwar Reconstruction and the Origins of the Cold War*. Baltimore: The Johns Hopkins University Press, 1973. A seminal study by a reputable American academic.

Perlmutter, Amos. *FDR and Stalin: A Not So Grand Alliance, 1943–1945*. Columbia: University of Missouri Press, 1993. Critical of Roosevelt's personal foreign policy and his appeasement of Soviet demands.

Platt, Tony, and Flora Biancatana (eds.). *Tropical Gulag: The Construction of Cold War Images of Cuba in the United States*. San Francisco: Global Options, 1987. An interesting study on the reality and the impression of life in Cuba during the Cold War.

Powaski, Ronald E. *The Cold War: The United States and the Soviet Union, 1917–1991*. New York: Oxford University Press, 1997. A valuable interpretation on the origins of the Cold War that suggests the conflict's seeds were centuries old.

Powers, Richard Gid. *Not without Honor: The History of American Anticommunism*. New York: Free Press, 1996. A reliable and comprehensive study that should be useful to most students.

Powers, Richard Gid. *Secrecy and Power: The Life of J. Edgar Hoover*. New York: Free Press, 1988. An acclaimed biography that should be useful to students working on any research project related to Hoover.

Prados, John. *How the Cold War Ended: Debating and Doing History*. Issues in the History of American Foreign Relations Series. Dulles, VA: Potomac Books, 2010. Prados presents alternative views on the close of the Cold War; this work also includes a useful guide on historical method and analysis.

Puddington, Arch. *Broadcasting Freedom: The Cold War Triumph of Radio Free Europe and Radio Liberty*. Lexington: University Press of Kentucky, 2003. A well-written and well-documented study that should be useful to students researching communications and propaganda during the Cold War.

Quirk, Robert E. *Fidel Castro*. New York: W. W. Norton, 1995. A massive biography by a recognized scholar.

Rabe, Stephen G. *The Killing Zone: The United States Wages Cold War in Latin America*. New York: Oxford University Press, 2012. Provides information on the Kennan Corollary, Guatemala, and the Kennedy and Johnson Doctrines.

Radosh, Ronald, and Joyce Milton. *The Rosenberg File: A Search for the Truth*. New York: Holt, Rinehart, Winston, 1984. A thorough study with detailed information not found elsewhere.

Ratnesar, Romesh. *Tear Down This Wall: A City, A President, and the Speech That Ended the Cold War*. New York: Simon and Schuster, 2009. Very sympathetic to Reagan and his role in ending the Cold War.

Reeves, Thomas C. *The Life and Times of Joe McCarthy*. New York: Stein and Day, 1982. Still the best biography of McCarthy.

Reeves, Thomas C. *America's Bishop: The Life and Times of Fulton J. Sheen*. New York: Encounter Books, 2001. An acclaimed work of scholarship; the best available work on Sheen.

Reynolds, David. *From World War to Cold War: Churchill, Roosevelt, and the International History of the 1940s*. New York: Oxford University Press, 2007. An outstanding study by a preeminent historian on the outbreak of the Cold War.

Reynolds, David. *In Command of History: Churchill Fighting and Writing the Second World War*. New York: Random House, 2005. Includes valuable insights on Churchill's views on the Cold War and his impact on the culture of Cold War America.

Rhoads, Gladys Titzck. *McIntire: Defender of Faith and Freedom*. Maitland, FL: Xulon Press, 2012. A sympathetic biography but still useful in the context of McIntire's struggle with the Federal Communications Commission.

Richmond, Yale. *Cultural Exchange and the Cold War: Raising the Iron Curtain*. University Park: Pennsylvania State University Press, 2003. Provides information and analysis on a wide range of Soviet-American cultural exchanges during the Cold War, from the Moscow Youth Festival, scholarly exchanges, and nongovernmental organization (NGO) exchanges to exhibitions and the performing arts.

Roberts, Priscilla Mary. *Cuban Missile Crisis: The Essential Reference Guide*. Santa Barbara, CA: ABC-CLIO, 2012. A reliable reference tool with an excellent bibliography.

Roll, David L. *The Hopkins Touch: Harry Hopkins and the Forging of the Alliance to Defeat Hitler*. New York: Oxford University Press, 2013. Acclaimed biography of FDR's aide, includes extensive information on American-Soviet relations during the war.

Rose, Lisle A. *The Cold War Comes to Main Street: America in 1950*. Lawrence: University Press of Kansas, 1999. A study of the impact of the early Cold War on American culture.

Rosenfeld, Seth. *Subversives: The FBI's War on Student Radicals and Reagan's Rise to Power*. New York: Farrar, Straus, and Giroux, 2012. A fascinating account of the Berkeley free speech movement and the three individuals who dominated the crisis: Mario Savio, Clark Kerr, and Ronald Reagan.

Ross, Steven J. *Hollywood Left and Right: How Movie Stars Shaped American Politics*. New York: Oxford University Press, 2011. An acclaimed scholarly study of the impact of many artists on American politics before, during, and after the Cold War.

Rubin, Andrew N. *Archives of Authority: Empire, Culture, and the Cold War*. Princeton, NJ: Princeton University Press, 2012. Focuses on American support for the arts during the Cold War and the transfer of Western cultural leadership from Britain to the United States.

Ruddy, T. Michael. *The Cautious Diplomat: Charles E. Bohlen and the Soviet Union, 1929–1969*. Kent, OH: Kent State University Press, 1987. An excellent scholarly analysis of Bohlen as diplomat and as Soviet specialist.

Russell, Jesse, and Ronald Cohn (eds.). *Tom Hayden*. Stoughton, WI: Books on Demand, 2012. A useful collection of essays and speeches by Hayden.

Sandbrook, Dominic. *Eugene McCarthy: The Rise and Fall of Postwar American Liberalism*. New York: Anchor, 2005. An analysis of McCarthy's impact on liberalism during the 1960s and 1970s.

Saunders, Frances Stonor. *Who Paid the Piper: The CIA and the Cultural Cold War*. London: Granta Books, 2000. A valuable study on the use and abuse of artists during the Cold War.

Sbardellati, John. *J. Edgar Hoover Goes to the Movies: The FBI and the Origins of Hollywood's Cold War*. Ithaca, NY: Cornell University Press, 2012. A scholarly work that is based extensively on FBI documents; perhaps the best work on this aspect of the Cold War in America.

Schlesinger, Arthur M. Jr. *Robert Kennedy and His Times*. New York: Mariner Books, 2002. Reprint. While very sympathetic, this remains an essential study on Robert Kennedy.

Schrecker, Ellen W. *Many Are the Crimes: McCarthyism in America*. New York: Little, Brown, 1998. A comprehensive study by a pre-eminent authority on McCarthyism.

Schwartz, Richard Alan. *Cold War Culture: Media and the Arts, 1945–1990*. New York: Facts on File, 1998. A useful and comprehensive reference work.

Schweizer, Peter. *The Fall of the Berlin Wall: Reassessing the Causes and Consequences of the End of the Cold War*. Stanford, CA: Hoover Institution Press, 2000. This collection of essays by American leaders in the Reagan administration is based on presentations and remarks made at a conference held in Washington, DC, in 1999.

Selverstone, Marc J. *Constructing the Monolith: The United States, Great Britain, and International Communism, 1945–1950*. Cambridge, MA: Harvard University Press, 2009. An important study on the emergence and impact of the image of monolithic communism.

Service, Robert. *Spies and Commissars: Bolshevik Russia and the West*. New York: Public Affairs, 2012. A new work by a noted expert on the Soviet Union and Russia that examines the early aggressive use of spies by the Bolsheviks and Western governments.

Shaw, Tony. *Hollywood's Cold War*. Culture, Politics, and the Cold War Series. Amherst: University of Massachusetts Press, 2007. An excellent study of the impact of the Cold War on the American film industry and its leadership.

Sherwin, Martin J. *A World Destroyed: The Atomic Bomb and the Grand Alliance*. New York: Random House, 1975. Emphasizes the impact of the atomic bomb on the origins of the Cold War.

Sibley, Katherine A. S. *Red Spies in America: Stolen Secrets and the Dawn of the Cold War*. Lawrence: University Press of Kansas, 2007. A well-researched and well-argued account of Soviet espionage in the United States during the 1930s and 1940s.

Skinner, Kiron K. (ed.). *Turning Points in Ending the Cold War*. Stanford, CA: Hoover Institution Press, 2008. A collection of scholarly essays by Soviet and Western experts such as Jack Matlock, Jr., Oleg Grinevsky, Anatoli Cherniaev, Robert L. Hutchings, and Michael McFaul.

Small, Melvin (ed.). *A Companion to Richard Nixon*. Blackwell Companions to American History. Malden, MA: Wiley-Blackwell, 2011. A useful collection of essays by scholars on a range of issues, including détente and Nixon's opening to China.

Smith, Jean Edward. *Eisenhower in War and Peace*. New York: Random House, 2012. A new and insightful study by the acclaimed biographer of Franklin D. Roosevelt.

Smith, Tony. *America's Mission: The United States and the Worldwide Struggle for Democracy*. Princeton, NJ: Princeton University Press, 1995. A seminal study that addresses the American view of its role in world affairs that emerged during the Cold War.

Smyser, W. R. *From Yalta to Berlin: The Cold War Struggle over Germany*. New York: St. Martin's Press, 2000. Considered by many the best book on Germany and the Cold War, with a foreword by Paul Nitze.

Smyser, W. R. *Kennedy and the Berlin Wall*. Reprint. Lanham, MD: Rowman and Littlefield, 2009. A highly acclaimed scholarly work that is also well written; should be valuable to all who are studying this topic.

Spalding, Elizabeth Edwards. *The First Cold War Warrior: Harry Truman, Containment, and the Remaking of Liberal Internationalism*. Lexington: University Press of Kentucky, 2006. An important reassessment of Truman as the central figure in American foreign policy in the mid-twentieth century.

Statler, Kathryn C., and Andres L. Johns (eds.). *The Eisenhower Administration, the Third World, and the Globalization of the Cold War*. Lanham, MD: Rowman and Littlefield, 2006. A useful collection of essays by scholars, including John Prados, Peter Hahn, and David Anderson.

Stern, Sheldon M. *The Week the World Stood Still: Inside the Secret Cuban Missile Crisis*. Stanford, CA: Stanford University Press, 2005. An important study based on transcriptions of ExComm meetings; relays the intensity and uncertainty within the American leadership.

Stern, Sheldon M. *The Cuban Missile Crisis in American Memory versus Reality*. Stanford Nuclear Age Series. Stanford, CA: Stanford University Press, 2012. An acclaimed study that examines and dismisses many of the erroneous notions that cloud the American national memory of the Cuban missile crisis.

Steven, Patrick Miller. *Billy Graham and the Rise of the Republican South.* Politics and Culture in Modern America Series. Philadelphia: University of Pennsylvania Press, 2009. An important scholarly study that focuses on Graham's impact on the transformation of Southern politics.

Stevens, Jason W. *God-Fearing and Free: A Spiritual History of America's Cold War.* Cambridge, MA: Harvard University Press, 2010. An important contribution to Cold War cultural history that assesses the impact of scholars such as Hannah Arendt and Richard Hofstadter, films, McCarthyism, and the religion and health movement on American life and thought.

Storrs, Landon R. Y. *The Second Red Scare and the Unmaking of the New Deal Left.* Politics and Society in Twentieth-Century America Series. Princeton, NJ: Princeton University Press, 2012. Storrs, using sources that have recently been made available, has provided a valuable study on the impact of the second Red Scare and the suppression of basic freedoms during the 1940s and 1950s.

Stuart, Douglas T. *Creating the National Security State: A History of the Law That Transformed America.* Princeton, NJ: Princeton University Press, 2012. A seminal study on the impact of the "national security state" on American life and culture.

Suri, Jeremy. *Henry Kissinger and the American Century.* Cambridge, MA: Belknap Press of Harvard University Press, 2007. A very good study of Kissinger's role in American history during the Cold War.

Szulc, Tad. *Fidel: A Critical Portrait.* New York: Harper Perennial, 2000. A valuable biography by a journalist who knew Castro personally.

Tanenhaus, Sam. *Whittaker Chambers: A Biography.* New York: Modern Library, 1998. The best study on Chambers; scholarly and well written.

Taubman, William. *Khrushchev: The Man and His Era.* New York: W. W. Norton, 2004. An excellent biography by a noted scholar.

Taylor, Frederick. *The Berlin Wall: A World Divided, 1961–1989.* New York: Harper Perennial, 2008. A solid history of the Wall and its place in Cold War history.

Taylor, Kiernan W., Robert W. Cherny, and William Issel (eds.). *American Labor and the Cold War.* New Brunswick, NJ: Rutgers University Press, 2004. This collection of essays addresses the experience of American organized labor from the close of World War II until the 1960s.

Thomas, Evan. *Robert Kennedy: His Life*. New York: Simon and Schuster, 2012. A sympathetic but reliable and useful biography.

Thompson, Nicholas. *The Hawk and the Dove: Paul Nitze, George Kennan, and the History of the Cold War*. New York: Henry Holt, 2009. An astute historical and biographical analysis of the opposing thoughts of Nitze and Kennan on the Cold War.

Trachtenberg, Marc. *The Cold War and After: History, Theory, and the Logic of International Politics*. Princeton Studies in International History and Politics. Princeton, NJ: Princeton University Press, 2012. An important new study on the impact of historical thinking on Cold War and its politics.

Trahair, Richard C. S., and Robert L. Miller. *Encyclopedia of Cold War Espionage, Spies and Secret Operations*. 2nd ed. New York: Enigma Books, 2012. An excellent reference tool that provides biographical information on hundreds of Soviet agents that worked during the Cold War.

Tucker, Spencer C. (ed.). *The Encyclopedia of the Cold War: A Political, Social, and Military History*. 5 vols. Santa Barbara, CA: ABC-CLIO, 2007. The most recent, comprehensive, and reliable reference work on the Cold War, including many documents and a very good bibliography.

Tudda, Chris. *A Cold War Turning Point: Nixon and China, 1969–1972*. Baton Rouge: Louisiana State University Press, 2012. A worthwhile study of Nixon's China policy and its impact as a defining event in the Cold War.

Ulam, Adam B. *Expansion and Coexistence: Soviet Foreign Policy, 1917–73*. New York: Praeger, 1974. Still an important study that needs to be consulted when focusing on the early decades of Soviet history.

Uldrich, Jack. *Soldier, Statesman, Peacemaker: Leadership Lessons from George C. Marshall*. New York: American Management Association (AMACOM), 2005. A valuable resource for developing an understanding of Marshall's strategic thinking on the Cold War.

Updegrove, Mark. *Indomitable Will: LBJ in the Presidency*. New York: Crown, 2012. A valuable biography that provides insights on Johnson's views and policies on the Cold War.

Villafaña, Frank R. *Cold War in the Congo, The Confrontation of Cuban Military Forces, 1960-1967*. Piscataway, NJ: Transaction Publishers, 2012.

A scholarly study of the crisis that gripped the Congo when Cuban forces were involved in the struggle.

Von Eschen, Penny M. *Satchmo Blows Up the World: Jazz Ambassadors Play the Cold War*. Cambridge, MA: Harvard University Press, 2004. A solid work on the early cultural exchanges between the West and the East.

Walker, William T. *McCarthyism and the Red Scare: A Reference Guide*. Santa Barbara, CA: ABC-CLIO, 2011. A useful resource and introduction that includes a narrative, chronology, primary documents, biographies of key participants, and an extensive annotated bibliography.

Watson, Robert P. *George McGovern: A Political Life, a Political Legacy*. Pierre: South Dakota State Historical Society Press, 2004. A sympathetic but still useful account of McGovern's impact on American politics.

Weinstein, Allen. *Perjury: The Hiss-Chambers Case*. Rev. ed. New York: Random House, 1997. Excellent scholarship; the standard work on the case.

Weinstein, Allen, and Alexander Vassiliev. *The Haunted Wood: Soviet Espionage in America; The Stalin Era*. New York: Modern Library, 1999. An excellent and intriguing study of the scope and depth of Soviet infiltration of the United States from the mid-1920s to Stalin's death in 1953.

Wells, Samuel F. (ed.). *The Helsinki Process and the Future of Europe*. Washington, DC: Woodrow Wilson Center Press, 1992. A collection of essays on the Helsinki accords and their potential legacy.

Wells, Samuel F., and Robert S. Litwak. *Superpower Competition and Security in the Third World*. Pensacola, FL: Ballinger, 1987. A useful analysis of scholarly sentiment on the issue prior to the end of the Cold War.

Wells, Samuel F., and Robert S. Litwak (eds.). *Strategic Defenses and Soviet-American Relations*. Pensacola, FL: Ballinger, 1987. Essays on the status of Soviet-American relations and defense capabilities.

Wengian, Gao. *Zhou Enlai: The Last Perfect Revolutionary*. New York: Public Affairs, 2007. The best biography of Zhou Enlai that is available, based on new primary materials.

Westad, Odd Arne (ed.). *Reviewing the Cold War: Approaches, Interpretations, Theory*. London and Portland, OR: Frank Cass, 2000. An excellent work that includes provocative and useful essays by many renowned scholars of the Cold War, including John Lewis Gaddis, Melvyn P. Leffler, Yale Ferguson, Geir Kundestad, Rey Koslowski, James G. Hershberg, Vladislav M. Zubok, Aaron L. Frindberg, Constantine Pleshkov, Wilfried Loth, Antonio

Varsori, Jussi M. Hanhimäki, Anders Stephanson, Richard Ned Lebow, William C Wohlforth, and Douglas J. Macdonald.

Westad, Odd Arne (ed.). *The Global Cold War: Third World Interventions and the Making of Our Times*. New York: Cambridge University Press, 2007. This important study demonstrates the Cold War origins of current international conflicts, including the war on terror.

Westad, Odd Arne (ed.). *Restless Empire: China and the World Since 1750*. New York: Basic Books, 2012. Includes valuable chapters on the emergence of China during the Cold War.

Wettig, Gerhard. *Stalin and the Cold War in Europe: The Emergence and Development of East-West Conflict, 1939–1953*. The Harvard Cold War Studies Book Series. Lanham, MD: Rowman and Littlefield, 2007. An acclaimed study largely based on Soviet and East German documents; provides valuable insights on Soviet society and its foreign policy.

White, Philip. *Our Supreme Task: How Winston Churchill's Iron Curtain Speech Defined the Cold War Alliance*. New York: Public Affairs, 2012. A detailed study of the origins, development, and consequences of Churchill's 1946 speech that was delivered at Westminster College in Fulton, Missouri.

Whitfield, Stephen. *The Culture of the Cold War*. Baltimore: The Johns Hopkins University Press, 1991. Still the best introduction to the impact of the Cold War on American culture.

Wiest, Andrew, Mary Kathryn Barbier, and Glenn Robins (eds.). *America and the Vietnam War: Re-Examining the Culture and History of a Generation*. London: Routledge, 2009. Essays that focus on the social and cultural aspects and impact of the war on American society.

Williams, William Appleman. *American-Soviet Relations, 1781–1947*. London: Octagon Press, 1971 (Originally published in 1952). An important revisionist critique of American foreign policy.

Williams, William Appleman. *The Tragedy of American Diplomacy*. New York: W. W. Norton, 2009 (Originally published in 1959). A study of American expansionism that led to Cold War ventures such as Vietnam.

Winks, Robin W. *The Cold War from Yalta to Cuba*. New York: Macmillan, 1964. A dated but important work by an acclaimed historian about the early years of the Cold War.

Wright, Jonathan, and Steven Casey (eds.). *Mental Maps in the Early Cold War Era, 1945–68*. New York and London: Palgrave Macmillan, 2011.

A collection of essays on the impact of the rapid transformation of geopolitics after World War II.

Zubek, Vladislav. *A Failed Empire: The Soviet Union in the Cold War from Stalin to Gorbachev*. Chapel Hill: University of North Carolina Press, 2008. A seminal study by a renowned scholar.

Articles

The topic of America and the Cold War continues to attract the interest of scholars who produce scores of important articles each year. For more than a decade the journal *Cold War History* has served as an essential resource for scholars and students of the Cold War. Published by Routledge and listed in the Thomas Arts and Humanities Citation Index, *Cold War History* is accessible through other databases that are frequently provided by libraries. This journal is based in the Cold War Studies Programme at the London School of Economics' Centre for International Affairs, Strategy, and Diplomacy. In 1999 Cold War Studies of the Davis Center for Russian and European Studies at Harvard University began publishing the acclaimed *Journal of Cold War Studies*. It publishes peer-reviewed articles based on primary/archival research. This journal is available in print and online; a selection of articles are available online at no cost at http://www.fas.harvard.edu/journal.htm

The list of articles provided here is not exhaustive. It includes standard works as well as notable recent scholarship.

Ahrari, Ehsan. "Why the Long War Can and Cannot be Compared to the Cold War." *Comparative Strategy*, 26, no. 4 (July–September 2007): 275–84. A comparative analysis of the strategies employed in the Cold War and the war on terror.

Barnhisel, Greg. "Cold Warriors of the Book: American Book Programs in the 1950s." *Book History*, 13 (2010): 185–217. A scholarly examination of the impact of the Cold War on U.S. book publication in the 1950s.

Bartley, Russell H. "The Piper Played to Us All: Orchestrating the Cultural Cold War in the USA, Europe, and Latin America." *International Journal of Politics, Culture, and Society*, 14, no. 3 (2001): 571–619. An important study of the significance and subtlety of cultural strategies during the Cold War.

Brzezinski, Zbigniew. "Communist Ideology and International Affairs." *Journal of Conflict Resolution*, 4 (September 1960): 266–90. A well-reasoned and well-documented essay by the author of the recent *Strategic Vision: America and the Crisis of Global Power* (2012).

Burr, William. "The Nixon Administration, the 'Horror Strategy,' and the Search for Limited Nuclear Options, 1969–1972." *Journal of Cold War Studies*, 7, no. 3 (Summer 2005): 34–78. Examines Nixon's pursuit of options to a full-scale nuclear exchange with the Soviet Union.

Cohn, Deborah. "Combatting Anti-Americanism during the Cold War: Faulkner, the State Department, and Latin America." *Mississippi Quarterly*, 59, no. 3/4 (Summer/Fall 2006): 395–413. A useful study of the application of arts and diplomacy in responding to anti-American sentiments and movements.

Coleman, David G. "Eisenhower and the Berlin Problem, 1953–1954." *Journal of Cold War Studies*, 2, no. 1 (Winter 2000): 3–34. An analysis of Eisenhower's response to the rebellion in the German Democratic Republic (East Germany) in the wake of Stalin's death and the uncertainty surrounding his succession.

Danielson, Leilah. " 'It is a Day of Judgment': The Peacemakers, Religion, and Radicalism in Cold War America." *Religion and American Culture*, 18, no. 2 (Summer 2008): 215–48. A worthwhile study of Protestant and Catholic reaction to Cold War protests and radicalism.

Dean, Robert. "Cultures of Secrecy in Postwar America." *Diplomatic History*, 35, no. 4 (September 2011): 611–13. A brief article on the rise and impact of the cults of secrecy since the end of the Second World War.

DeBenedetti, Charles L. "Educators and Armaments in Cold War America." *Peace and Change*, 34, no. 4 (October 2009): 425–40. A study of the impact of the arms race and McCarthyism on American education.

Dietrich, Christopher. "America's Cold War: The Politics of Insecurity." *Canadian Journal of History*, 46, no. 2 (Autumn 2011): 422–24. An important review of the book of the same title by Campbell Craig and Fredrik Logevall.

Ellis, Joseph. "Making Vietnam History." *Reviews in American History*, 28, no. 4 (2000): 625–29. A useful introduction to the historiography of American involvement in Vietnam.

Etheridge, Brian C. "The Desert Fox, Memory Diplomacy, and the German Question in Early Cold War America." *Diplomatic History*, 32, no. 2 (April 2008): 207–38. A provocative study of the impact of films in the early years of the Cold War.

Gibson, James L. "Political Intolerance and Political Repression during the McCarthy Red Scare." *American Political Science Review*, 82, no. 2 (June 1988): 511–29. A valuable article on the political and cultural impact of McCarthyism and its fundamental lack of tolerance.

Hendershot, Heather. "God's Angriest Man: Carl McIntire, Cold War Fundamentalism, and Right-Wing Broadcasting." *American Quarterly*, 59, no. 2 (June 2007): 373–96. An excellent scholarly analysis of McIntire's struggles with the American government and other Christians during the Cold War.

Jacobs, Bo. "Atomic Kids: 'Duck and Cover' and 'Atomic Alert' Teach Children How to Survive Atomic Attack." *Film and History: An Interdisciplinary Journal of Film and Television Studies*, 40, no. 1 (Spring 2010): 25–44. An analysis of the development and impact of two films that were developed by the Atomic Energy Commission.

Jo, Y. Hugh. "The Capitalist World System and U.S. Cold War Policies in the Core and the Periphery: A Comparative Analysis of Post–World War II American Nation-Building in Germany and Korea." *Journal of World-Systems Research*, 17, no. 2 (Spring 2011): 428–45. A useful article for the advanced student.

Karpovich, Michael M. "Russian Imperialism or Communist Aggression?" *New Leader*, 34 (June 4, 1951): 16–19. Argues that Soviet aggression was due to the "messianic" vision of the Soviet leadership.

Kennan, George F. "Sources of Soviet Conduct." *Foreign Affairs*, 25 (July 1947): 571–82. A classic article by one of the key participants and scholars of the Cold War.

Killmeier, Matthew. "America(n) abroad: The Third Man, International Audiences and the Cold War." *Radio Journal: International Studies in Broadcast and Audio Media*, 8, no. 2 (2010): 105–19. An analysis of the application of mass media with particular reference to the impact of the film *The Third Man*.

Knaus, John Kenneth. "Official Policies and Covert Programs: The U.S. State Department, the CIA, and the Tibetan Resistance." *Journal of Cold War Studies*, 5, no. 3 (Summer 2003): 54–79. An excellent article that examines the new American policy toward Tibet that was initiated in 1951.

Lynd, Staughton. "How the Cold War Began." *Commentary*, 30 (November 1960): 379–89. A standard work that is very critical of Secretary of State Cordell Hull and his policies.

Mathews, Jane de Hart. "Art and Politics in Cold War America." *American Historical Review*, 81, no. 4 (October 1976): 762–88. A useful discussion of leftist art and its reception in the United States.

May, Elaine Tyler. "Security against Democracy: The Legacy of the Cold War at Home." *Journal of American History*, 97, no. 4 (March 2011): 939–57. A recent article on the impact of the Cold War on American political values and politics.

Mosely, Philip E. "The Meaning of Coexistence." *Foreign Affairs*, 41 (October 1962): 36–46. Significant article that had impact on American political and diplomatic thought and practice during the 1960s.

Perucci, Tony. "The Red Mask of Sanity: Paul Robeson, HUAC, and the Sound of Cold War Performance." *Drama Review*, 53, no. 4 (Winter 2009): 18–48. An important article on the Robeson case and freedom of expression during the early Cold War.

Porter, Patrick. "Beyond the American Century: Walter Lippmann and American Grand Strategy, 1943–1950." *Diplomacy and Statecraft*, 22, no. 4 (December 2011): 557–77. A scholarly review of the thought and impact of Lippmann on American foreign policy during the last years of World War II to the outbreak of the Korean War.

Reston, James B. "Negotiating with the Russians." *Harper's*, 195 (August 1947): 97–106. By a *New York Times* journalist, a perceptive analysis of the inherent complexity of the Soviet Union and the inconsistencies of American diplomacy.

Tierney, Dominic. " 'Pearl Harbor in Reverse,' Moral Analogies in the Cuban Missile Crisis." *Journal of Cold War Studies*, 9, no. 3 (Summer 2007): 49–77. A provocative essay on moral issues related to decisions made during the Cuban missile crisis of 1962.

Tudda, Chris. " 'Reenacting the Story of Tantalus': Eisenhower, Dulles, and the Failed Rhetoric of Liberation." *Journal of Cold War Studies*, 7, no. 4 (Fall 2005): 3–35. An analysis of the contradictory elements that were pursued in Eisenhower/Dulles foreign policy.

Wells, Samuel F. "The Korean War: Miscalculation and Alliance Transformation." In *The Routledge Handbook of Transatlantic Security*, edited by Jussi Hanhimäki, Georges-Henri Soutou, and Basil Germond. New York: Routledge, 2010. A new interpretation of the Korean War that will be fully advanced in Wells's forthcoming work *The Korean War and U.S. Escalation of the Cold War*.

Winsboro, Irvin, and Michael Epple. "Religion, Culture, and the Cold War: Bishop Fulton J. Sheen and America's Anti-Communist Crusade of the 1950s." *Historian*, 71, no. 2 (Summer 2009): 209–33. An astute analysis of Sheen's influence on American society during the Eisenhower era.

Xia, Yafeng. "China's Elite Politics and Sino-American Rapprochement, January 1969–February 1972." *Journal of Cold War Studies*, 8, no. 4 (Fall 2006): 3–28. Argues that a consensus converged among Chinese leaders to enter and expand the dialogue with the United States during the Nixon era.

Yarrow, Andrew L. "Selling a New Vision of America to the World." *Journal of Cold War Studies*, 11, no. 4 (Fall 2009): 3–45. A review of the propaganda advanced by the United States during the Cold War, including the role of the U.S. Information Agency.

Other

Dobbs, Michael. "Why We Should Still Study the Cuban Missile Crisis." *Special Report 205*. Washington, DC: U.S. Institute of Peace, 2008: 1–12. Considers the application of aspects of the crisis, such as decision making, on current situations.

INDEX

About the Author

William T. Walker, Ph.D., is the former senior vice president and professor of history at Chestnut Hill College (Philadelphia, PA) where he continues to teach part-time. His published works include ABC-CLIO's *McCarthyism and the Red Scare: A Reference Guide*, and Greenwood's *Term Paper Resource Guide to Nineteenth-Century World History*. Walker holds a doctorate in history from the University of South Carolina.